# The Black Swan Problem

Founded in 1807, John Wiley & Sons is the oldest independent publishing company in the United States. With offices in North America, Europe, Asia, and Australia, Wiley is globally committed to developing and marketing print and electronic products and services for our customers' professional and personal knowledge and understanding.

The Wiley Corporate F&A series provides information, tools, and insights to corporate professionals responsible for issues affecting the profitability of their company, from accounting and finance to internal controls and performance management.

# The Black Swan Problem

*Risk Management Strategies for
a World of Wild Uncertainty*

HÅKAN JANKENSGÅRD

WILEY

*Library of Congress Cataloging-in-Publication Data:*

Names: Jankensgård, Håkan, author.
Title: The black swan problem : risk management strategies for a world of
 wild uncertainty / Håkan Jankensgård.
Description: First edition. | Chichester, United Kingdom : Wiley, 2022. |
 Includes index.
Identifiers: LCCN 2021062804 (print) | LCCN 2021062805 (ebook) | ISBN
 9781119868149 (cloth) | ISBN 9781119868156 (adobe pdf) | ISBN
 9781119868163 (epub)
Subjects: LCSH: Risk management. | Organizational effectiveness.
Classification: LCC HD61 .J355 2022 (print) | LCC HD61 (ebook) | DDC
 658.15/5—dc23/eng/20220112
LC record available at https://lccn.loc.gov/2021062804
LC ebook record available at https://lccn.loc.gov/2021062805

Cover Design and Image: Wiley
Illustration inspired by: © rainman_in_sun/Getty Images

SKYB8F32C55-1F19-4194-B59D-403BD18577DB_031622

*My dear children, Wilma and August, I wrote this book for you.*

# Contents

'Our world is dominated by the extreme, the unknown, and the very improbable . . . and all the while we spend our time engaged in small talk, focusing on the known and the repeated.'

Nicholas Nassim Taleb

# Prologue

M Y FIRST INTRODUCTION TO Black Swan thinking did not come from the famous book by Nicholas Nassim Taleb published in 2007.[1] It came well before that, courtesy of my instructor as I was training to get a driver's licence for motorcycles. We had stopped at an intersection, when the arrow turned green and I just rode off onto the highway in a nice left turn. The instructor immediately told me to pull over. Once we did, he started lambasting me for having made the turn without looking even once to my right. He was visibly upset, or at least played his part well. 'But the arrow was green,' I meekly responded, 'so the others must stop.' In my worldview, that was how it worked. My experience, while not exactly extensive, supported that notion. In fact, nothing had ever suggested otherwise. 'Do you think,' he yelled, 'that you can trust others to do what they are supposed to do? Never assume that!' The penny dropped. By operating on a very naïve assumption about how the world worked, based on a handful of observations, I had managed to make myself a sucker. I was setting myself up, unnecessarily, for a highly improbable major calamity.

The deeper meaning of the Black Swan idea is not to be paranoid and develop trust issues. Rather it is to resist the temptation to base our course of action on pristine ideas and models of how the world *ought* to be. Especially dangerous is our inclination to form expectations of a benign world based on recent observations that all seem to indicate stability. Taleb's choice of metaphor – the Black Swan – was meant to convey precisely this problem of induction. It had always been taken for granted that all swans are white, an assumption supported by millions of observations across centuries. Imagine the surprise when the black variety was sighted in Australia subsequent to the 'discovery' of that continent. All it took was one single observation to turn completely on its head what people had internalized as self-evident and

---

[1]Taleb, N. N., 2007. *The Black Swan: The impact of the highly probable*. Random House: New York.

true for hundreds of years. Likewise, a single rogue or inattentive driver can invalidate, in an instant, hundreds of observations of other drivers yielding when the arrow is green. A recurring theme in Taleb's Black Swan framework is that we fail to make provisions for such outliers because they are outside our mental models and decision-support tools.

So what is this famed and metaphorical creature more precisely? A Black Swan, according to Taleb, has three attributes. *Before* it occurs, it is considered extremely unlikely, to the extent we grant it for possible at all. *When* it occurs, its consequences are massive. *After* it has occurred, it makes perfect sense to us that something like that could happen. The last attribute is due to our brains being awesome 'explanation machines' that crave coherence. Dots will be ambitiously connected until coherence is established. The world inhabited by these Black Swans is characterized by uncertainty that is 'wild' rather than benign, meaning that there is always a potential for great dislocations and non-linearities. Even when we manage to bring our focus to the tail end of the distribution, we frequently find that it is in flux, with events greatly surpassing anything we have seen or heard before.

The impact of the Black Swan idea has been substantial. While it may not have trickled down into popular culture just yet, the educated public seems largely aware of it, whether or not they have actually read the book. Admittedly, Taleb has drawn a fair amount of criticism for his work. Often, the target has been his abrasive and self-aggrandizing style of writing and the use of fictional characters (the Tonys and the Valerias). Critics also claim to have found more than a few inconsistencies in his web of ideas. I do not wish to dwell on such trivial matters here. Instead, I would like to point to a habit among takers of the Black Swan concept to render it synonymous with low-probability high-impact events (usually disastrous ones). We certainly did not need a risk philosopher, somebody might go on to say, to point out the existence of that. In this view, Taleb just popularized what we already knew.

Reducing the Black Swan to be merely a shorthand for describing low-probability high-impact events is to do the construct significant injustice. It trivializes it and detracts from its core ideas. In this book, I will re-emphasize the importance of *expectations* in the formation of Black Swans. This is a crucial point because it means that we can turn at least some Black Swans into 'mere' tail risk of a more calculated sort by controlling and improving our expectations in various ways. I will also stress how differences in expectations have *strategic* implications. No doubt, a more realistic appreciation of the nature of randomness is valuable for its own sake, but it gets even more interesting when we realize that others may systematically get themselves into perilous positions because they operate on unrealistic assumptions about randomness. What is a Black Swan to others need not be to us, and we may stand to benefit from this in various ways.

The main ambition of this book, however, is to place the Black Swan framework in a corporate context and explore its ramifications for business strategy. Taleb, motivated as he is by the grand sweep of history and civilization, and the philosophical underpinnings of randomness, does not take more than a fleeting interest in the firm as an institution. Yet, if we accept the premises of the Black Swan framework, we should ask what the implications are for how businesses are to be run. Businesses, after all, are stewards of a large part of humanity's resources, and innumerable people depend on them for their livelihood as well as the hope of making it big. Extreme uncertainty may deliver great risk but also holds out the promise of great opportunity.

As it turns out, firms are peculiar entities in several ways. To begin with, they operate under a mandate to maximize value, which introduces a focus on cost minimization that hugely shapes the corporate attention span for extreme events. There are also interesting features like separation between ownership and control, limited liability and multiple layers of stakeholders with different viewpoints. All these features profoundly influence how we should process the fact that uncertainty is wild rather than benign, and this book is about exploring them. How are massive consequences to be understood when we take the vantage point of a firm? When is it justifiable to spend corporate resources in preparation for highly improbable catastrophes? When should we have a strategy for Black Swan events? When and how can we make wild uncertainty work for us rather than against?

We start out, however, by recapping some of the core themes in the Black Swan framework (Chapter 1, 'The Swans Revisited'). In this chapter, we take a fresh look at the question of what constitutes a Black Swan. We also revisit the issue of what kind of randomness we face as decision-makers in the real world, as well as the crucial role of expectations. We establish the relative nature of Swans: players in the same industry can have very diverging expectations and are therefore likely to display different levels of preparation and vulnerability.

In Chapter 2 ('Corporate Swans'), we begin our exploration of what the Black Swan framework means for corporate management. I argue that it is the expectations of the firm's Board of Directors that is the correct perspective for determining what counts as a Black Swan. This has the interesting effect of increasing the number of Swans because of the structural information disadvantage the directors find themselves in as compared to the executive team. Even more troubling, the rate also goes up because the executives are a potential source of Black Swans. We go on to explore several other Swans that are specific to the corporate domain, over and above the ones generated by the natural world and complex systems at the level of society.

In Chapter 3 ('The Black Swan Problem'), we dive deeper into the question of how risk, and tail risk more specifically, relates to firm value. The risk of wipeout and strategy disruption provide economic arguments in favour of managing tail risk. Ultimately, though, we want to be able to demonstrate that managing tail risk produces benefits that are larger than the costs. This proves somewhat harder than expected, because when the probability of something goes towards zero – as they do with Black Swans – the cost of risk also tends towards zero. The conundrum is that when the cost of risk is near-zero, there is little apparent justification for spending corporate resources on tail risk management. The second part of the Black Swan problem is the difficulty of mustering a proactive response to extreme events. A whole host of biases, both on the individual and organizational level, work against it.

In Chapter 4 ('Greeting the Swan'), we discuss the need to alter our attitude to randomness as a first basic step in developing a strategy for dealing with the Black Swan phenomenon. We also need to recognize that the resources and patience available for managing the risk associated with extreme events are very small. Running through this book is a persistent tension between tail risk management and economic efficiency. Another part of adapting our mindset to a world of wild uncertainty is to own up to the delicate matter that Black Swans are sometimes made closer to home by people we want to trust. The Board of Directors need to extend their Swan map to cover known company-wreckers like acquisitions, derivative portfolios and, yes, the executive team.

In Chapter 5 ('Taming the Swan'), we arrive at the issue of how to make ourselves robust to wild uncertainty, to continue to survive and thrive even in much-worse-than-expected scenarios. We dig deeply into the role of buffers and flexibility in achieving resilience, with particular emphasis on risk capital, a set of financial resources that absorbs shocks and ensures survival and strategy execution. Stress testing, I argue, is a particularly important, but currently under-used, tool in the corporate battle against Black Swans. In them, we push resilience to the limits to learn about breaking points that can inform risk management strategies. The chapter contains extensive discussions on the role of models in the process of developing resilience. On the one hand, they help us see by reducing complexity and clarifying important mechanisms. On the other hand, they can make us blind to whatever is outside the model, creating a potential source of vulnerability.

In Chapter 6 ('Catching the Swan'), we learn about the concept of anti-fragility, which goes beyond resilience to identify things that actually benefit from disorder. This is where we fully explore the strategic implications of differences in expectations and levels of preparedness. Black Swans have the potential to decimate corporate strategies, which may open up opportunities for stronger competitors. We move past the idea of designing our risk management strategy exclusively by looking at our own vulnerabilities – we now incorporate the vulnerabilities of our closest competitors.

In Chapter 7 ('Riding the Swan'), we switch into a risk-loving mode, searching for positive Black Swans. When our tinkering has yielded what is beginning to look like a beautiful, potentially world conquering strategy, the time has come to press the gas pedal to the floor. We go for maximum growth by pulling all the levers at our disposal, all the while tolerating huge amounts of risk. We reach the disconcerting conclusion that all the things that were undesirable in order to build resilience are now in high demand.

# Acknowledgements

THE AUTHOR WISHES TO express a heartfelt thanks to the following people for their feedback throughout the writing process:

Petter Kapstad
Stanley Myint
John Fraser
Vesa Hakanen
Ulrich Adamheit
Martin Stevens
Aswath Damodaran
Tomas Sörensson
Seth Bernström
Tom Aabo
Niclas Andrén
Jacob Pedersen
Carl Montalvo

# CHAPTER ONE

# The Swans Revisited

T HE BLACK SWAN OF the popular imagination is one that swoops down from a clear blue sky, creating massive disorder in a very short amount of time. We expect it to be sudden and dramatic. The archetypical Black Swan is perhaps the 9/11 attack on the twin towers in New York in 2001. Virtually nobody could have been able to imagine such a thing. It was simply not on the mental map that something like that should even exist. Yet it happened, and in a single stroke, the world was a different place. The path we were on changed. The attack led to a whole new security apparatus, the war on terror, and the war in Iraq, to mention but a few of its consequences.

Actually, the 'out of the blue' aspect is not part of the original framework. Some Swans cited by Taleb take years if not centuries to play out. According to Taleb, Black Swans have just three attributes, none of which refers to suddenness. First, they are highly improbable. Second, they are highly consequential. Third, they make perfect sense after the fact.[1] When people talk about Black Swans it is usually the first two aspects they focus on, as if the term were essentially shorthand for low probability high impact risks. Simplifying in this way is

---

[1] The Black Swan criterion where the 9/11 attack might falter is the ex-post explanation part. Black Swans are supposed to make total sense after the fact, once our brain gets to work connecting the dots, which ends up giving it an air of inevitability. At least I struggle to connect some of those dots. Of course, we now know there are Islamic warriors engaged in a cosmic war that ends either in their destruction or in that of their enemies. However, that they would choose that means of meting out their punishment, and that it could be pulled off, remains unfathomable to this day.

wholly consistent with the reason that the Black Swan problem exists in the first place, reflecting as it does our tendency to reduce the number of dimensions of the phenomenon before us down to something more tractable and convenient.

Equating Black Swans with 'mere' low probability high impact risk, however, is to do the concept significant injustice. In reality, the Black Swan framework is valuable because it represents an altogether different way of approaching the world. Taleb asks us to reconsider some of our core assumptions about the very nature of the randomness we face as decision-makers and the inferences we make based on what we can observe. Furthermore, he brings our attention to the crucial role of expectations and attitudes in dealing with uncertainty. The problem, Taleb explains, is one of not being humble enough with respect to the limitations of our knowledge. If we believe the world consists of a certain kind of randomness and that we can have mastery over it, we may be in for some pretty bad surprises if those beliefs do not conform with reality. We can try to impose crisp and stylized ideas that appeal to our aesthetic sensibilities as much as we want, but the chaotic world we live in refuses to bend. This insistence on abstract beauty is what Taleb has in mind when he labels something as 'Platonic', after the famed Greek philosopher who saw loveliness in order and maintained that it could be superimposed on the messy reality we can observe with our senses (Taleb, 2007, p.19).

##  THE NATURE OF RANDOMNESS

Randomness refers to unpredictability. It applies whenever the outcome for some variable, such as the number of visitors to the Louvre on a given weekday, cannot be known with certainty beforehand. It is a function of our inability to know and predict the future. Try as we might, we never seem able to build those perfect forecasting algorithms that get it right all the time. In fact, as Taleb is at pains to point out, our overall track record in forecasting is awful (more on this later).

Why is there a general failure to predict what the future will bring? To answer this question, first consider that one very basic source of randomness is the physical world itself, which is constantly changing through processes that we do not fully comprehend. Science marches on, chipping away at the ignorance that produces apparent randomness. But despite the many laws of nature that have been uncovered, we never know where the next lightning will strike or how ocean currents will respond to changes in melting ice sheets. In the end, there are too many variables and too many complicated feedback loops in these highly dynamic systems. On top of that there is human civilization itself. While once rudimentary and mostly local, over time society has become complex beyond imagination. Technical innovations have made possible advanced systems that increasingly connect people across different parts of the globe. It is *fundamentally unknowable* what outcomes these vast and interconnected systems of interacting people and technologies will produce. Human agency by itself ensures why the future keeps bringing so many surprises, as the 9/11 attack illustrates. It should be clear that we are up against a complexity that is beyond our ability to predict successfully.

The difficulties we face in predicting the future is related to the problem of induction, a classic problem in philosophy. While data can certainly teach us a great deal about the workings of the world, the philosopher and sceptic David Hume made us realize that we cannot arrive at *secure* knowledge on the basis of empirical observations. The problem of induction says that no matter how many observations you obtain, you cannot know for sure that the observed pattern is going to hold in the future. This inherent limitation is at the heart of the Black Swan concept. Any knowledge obtained through observation, Taleb says, is fragile. It is what the Black Swan metaphor itself is meant to convey. Recall that millions of observations on white swans had seemingly verified the notion that all swans are white, and it only took one observation of a black one to falsify it. Along the same lines, Peter Bernstein (1996) observed in his epic story about risk that: '. . . history repeats itself, *but only for the most part*'[2] (emphasis added). This sentence really sums it all up and explains why induction is treacherous ground for making assumptions about the future.

Once we capitulate to the fact that we cannot predict the future, the next best thing would be to be able to characterize randomness itself, i.e. describe it. In that way, we would have some idea about the scope for deviations from what we expect. A description of randomness would involve some degree of quantification of things like the range within which the values of a variable can be assumed to fall and how the outcomes are distributed within that range (frequencies). We might occasionally find such descriptions of random processes to be practically relevant insofar as they help us make informed decisions and our future wellbeing depends on the outcome of the variable in question. They are potentially helpful, for example, in coming up with a reasonable analysis of the trade-off between risk and return in different kinds of investment situations.

---

[2]Bernstein, P. L., 1996. *Against the Gods: The remarkable story of risk.* John Wiley & Sons: New York.

When characterizing randomness, a useful first distinction is between uncertainty and known odds.[3] Uncertainty simply means that the odds are not known, indeed cannot be known. When randomness is of this sort, there is no way of knowing with certainty the range of outcomes and their respective probabilities. Known odds, in contrast, means that we have fixed the range of outcomes and the associated probabilities. The go-to example is the roll of a dice, in which the six possible outcomes have equal probabilities. Drawing balls with different colours out of an urn is another favourite textbook example of controlled randomness.

Uncertainty, it turns out, is what the world has to offer. In fact, known odds hardly exist outside man-made games. This is the case for exactly the same reasons that forecasting is generally unsuccessful: there are some hard limits to our theoretical knowledge of the world.[4] There is ample data, for sure, which partly makes up for it. But the world generates only one observable outcome at a time, out of an infinite number of possibilities, through mechanisms and interactions that are beyond our grasp. There is nothing to say that we should be able to objectively pinpoint the odds of real-world phenomena. Whenever a bookie, for example, offers you odds on the outcome of the next presidential election, it is a highly subjective estimate (tweaked in favour of the bookie).

Whenever data exists, it is of course possible to try to use it to come up with descriptions of the randomness in a stochastic process. Chances are that we can 'fit' the data to one of the many options available in our library of theoretical probability distributions. Once we have, we have seemingly succeeded in our quest to describe randomness, or to turn it into something *resembling* known odds. This is the frequentist approach to statistical inference, in which observed frequencies in the data provide the basis for probability approximations. Failure rates for a certain kind of manufacturing process, for example, can serve as a reasonably reliable indication of the probability of failure in the future.

It is important to see, however, that even when we are able to work with large quantities of data, we are still in the realm of uncertainty. The data frequencies

---

[3]Frank Knight (1921) first made this distinction and referred to known odds as 'risk'. This epithet is unfortunate and will not be adhered to in order to avoid unnecessary confusion. In the present book, risk is construed of as the value of a random variable on which our well-being depends (such as corporate performance) falling below some aspirational or critical level (such as the level needed for debt servicing). Risk is thus a function of uncertainty, but has nothing to do with whether odds are known a priori or not. Knight, F. H., 1921. *Risk, uncertainty, and profit*. Hart, Schaffner & Marx: New York, NY.

[4]I leave out a consideration of particles at the subatomic level, which, according to important theories in physics, are governed by pure randomness. This randomness, say the same theories, can be described in precise, mathematical terms (i.e. the odds can be known).

typically only approximate one of the theoretical distributions. What is more, the way we collect, structure, and analyse these data points determines how we end up characterizing the random process and therefore the probabilities we assign to different outcomes. To the untrained eye, they might seem like objective and neutral probabilities because they are data-driven and obtained by 'scientists'. However, there is always some degree of subjectivity involved in the parameterization. The model used to describe the process could end up looking different depending on who designs it. Hand a large dataset over to ten scientists and ask them what the probability of a certain outcome is, and you may well get ten different answers. Because of the problem of induction, as discussed, there is always the possibility that the dataset, i.e. history, is a completely misleading guide to the future. Whenever we approximate probabilities using data, we *assume* that the data points we use are representative for describing the future.

##  THE MOVING TAIL

At this point, we are ready to conclude that the basic nature of randomness is uncertainty. Known odds, probabilities in the purest sense of the word, are an interesting man-made exception to that rule. If we accept that uncertainty is what we are dealing with, a natural follow-up question is: What is uncertainty *like?* A distinction we will make in this regard is between 'benign' and 'wild' uncertainty.[5] Benign uncertainty means that we do not have perfect knowledge of the underlying process that generates the outcomes we observe, but the observations nonetheless behave *as if* they conform to some statistical process that we are able to recognize. Classic examples of this are the distribution of things like height and IQ in a population, which the normal distribution seems to approximate quite well.

While the normal distribution is often highlighted in discussions about 'well-behaved' stochastic processes, many other theoretical distributions appear to describe real-world phenomena with some accuracy. There is nothing, therefore, in the concept of benign uncertainty that rules out deviations from the normal distribution, such as fat tails or skews. It merely means that the data largely fits the assumptions of *some* theoretical distribution and appears to do so consistently over time. It is as if we have a grip on randomness.

[5]In Taleb's terminology, wild uncertainty is found in a place called Extremistan, whereas benign uncertainty harbours in Mediocristan (Taleb, 2007, p. 35).

Wild uncertainty, in contrast, means that there is scope for a more dramatic type of sea change. Now we are dealing with outcomes that represent a clear break with the past and a violation of our expectations as to what was even supposed to be possible. Imagine long stretches of calm and repetition punctured by some extreme event. In these cases, what happened did not resemble the past in the least. Key words to look out for when identifying wild uncertainty is 'unprecedented', 'unheard of', and 'inconceivable', because they (while overused) signal that we might be dealing with a new situation, something that sends us off on a new path.

The crucial aspect of wild uncertainty is precisely that the tails of the distributions are in flux. In other words, the historically observed minimum and maximum outcomes can be surpassed at any given time. I will refer to the idea of an ever-changing tail of a distribution as *The Moving Tail*. With wild uncertainty, an observation may come along that is outside the established range – *by a lot*. Such an event means that the tail of the distribution just assumed a very different shape. Put another way, there was a qualitative shift in the tail. Everything we thought we knew about the variable in question turned out to be not even in the ballpark.

An illustration of wild uncertainty and of a tail in flux is provided by 'the Texas freeze', which refers to a series of severe blizzards that took place in February 2021, spanning a 10-day period. The blizzards and the accompanying low temperatures badly damaged physical structures, and among those afflicted were wellheads and generators related to the production and distribution of electricity. As the freeze set in, demand soared as people scrambled to get hold of whatever electricity they could to stay warm and keep their businesses going. In an attempt to bring more capacity to the market, the operator of the Texas power grid, Ercot, hiked the price of electricity to the legally mandated price ceiling of 9,000 $/MWh. The price had touched that ceiling on prior occasions – but only for a combined total of three hours. The extremeness of this event lay in the fact that Ercot kept it at this level for almost 90 consecutive hours.[6] A normal trading range leading up to this point had been somewhere between 20–40 $/MWh.

Any analysis of this market prior to February 2021 would have construed tail risk as being about short-lived spikes, which, when averaged out over several trading days, implied no serious market distress. The Texas freeze shifted the tail. It was a Black Swan. The consequences for market participants were

---

[6]www.griddy.com, accessed 10 July 2021.

massive,[7] and there was nothing in the historical experience that convincingly pointed to the possibility that the price could or would remain at its maximum for 90 hours. After the fact, it looked obvious that something like that could happen. Prolonged winter freezes in Texas are very rare, but with the climate getting more extreme by the day, why not?

The 'by a lot' is actually an important qualifier of wild uncertainty. To see why, consider that whenever we have a dataset, some of the observations will represent the tail of the distribution. They are large but rare deviations from some more normal state. Let us say that we have, in a given dataset, a handful of observations that can be said to constitute the tail. There will be, by construction, a minimum and a maximum value, which are the most extreme values that history has had to offer so far.

Unless we are talking about a truly truncated distribution, like income having zero as the lower limit, it is a potential mistake to think that the 'true' underlying data-generating process is somehow capped by the observed minimum and maximum values. If we feed all the observations we have into a statistical software, we can ask it to analyse which random process that most plausibly generated the patterns in the data. Now, if we immediately take the process identified by the programme and draw random values based on it in a simulation, it will come up with a distribution that contains outcomes that *go beyond* the lowest/highest observed values in the dataset without the probability of that dropping to virtually zero. This will always happen as long as the approach is to assume that there is some underlying random process generating the data and use real data to approximate it. It is as if the software doing the fitting 'gets it' that if we have observed certain extreme values, even more extreme observations cannot be ruled out. If we have observed a drop in the S&P 500 of minus 58% over a certain period of time, who would say that a drop of minus 60% is outside the realm of possibilities? The simulated extremes will lie somewhere to the left (right) of the minimum (maximum) observed in the data. The tail we model in this way will encompass the observed tail *and then some*.

The upshot of this discussion is that experiencing an outlier that is only *somewhat* more extreme than the hitherto observed minimum/maximum should fall within the realm of benign uncertainty. We should not be surprised or taken aback by it. There is an implied probability of that, meaningfully

---

[7] Some retail customers had opted out of the standard fixed-rate utility plans and instead bought their electricity from businesses that passed wholesale prices on to them directly. Some of these customers racked up electricity bills in the range of $8,000–10,000 in a matter of days (Winter storm fallout sends Texas power firm Griddy into Bankruptcy. *Financial Times*, 15 March 2021).

separate from zero, being handed to us by the fitted distribution. We have to add 'by a lot' for it to count as wild uncertainty, because then the tail has shifted dramatically and in a way that was by no means implied by the historical track record. It is an outlier so extreme that it has a probability of effectively zero, even when the underlying random process we use to form a view of the future has been fitted to all the tail events in the historical track record.

Under conditions of wild uncertainty, it is clear that the concept of probability starts looking increasingly subjective and unverifiable. Indeed, Taleb calls probability 'the mother of all abstract concepts' (Taleb, 2007, p. 133) and maintains that we cannot calculate probabilities of shocks (Taleb, 2012, p. 8).[8] It is important to see, though, that his scorn is reserved mostly for those who insist on using the symmetric normal distributions and its close relatives. The properties of the normal are seductive because we can derive, with relative ease, all sorts of interesting results, but it is, Taleb maintains, positively dangerous as a guide to decision-making in a world of wild uncertainty. Why? Primarily because of how it rules out extreme outliers and blinds us to them. A key feature of the normal distribution is that its tails quickly get thinner the further removed from the mean you move, which implies that their likelihood of happening gets lower and lower. In fact, as we move away from the mean, the assigned probabilities drop very fast – much too fast, in Taleb's view (Taleb, 2007, p. 234). The stock market crash in October 1987, for example, saw a return of minus 20.5%. The odds of a drop of at least that magnitude would have been roughly *one in a trillion* according to the normal. In other words, anyone going by that distribution would have considered it, for practical purposes, an impossible event.

The first priority, therefore, is to avoid the normal distribution like the plague. In its place, if we still feel compelled to work with probabilities, Taleb offers the idea of fractals. Fractals refer to a geometrical pattern in which the structure and shape of an object remains similar across different scales. The practical implication is that the likelihood of extreme events decreases at a much slower rate. If one subscribes to this view, the probability of finding an exceptionally large oil field is not materially lower than a large or medium-sized one because the geological processes that generate them are scale-independent. This relation between frequency and size is associated with the so-called power law distributions, which we will relate to socio-economic processes in Chapter 7. According to Taleb, the idea of fractals should be our

---

[8]Taleb, N. N., 2012. *Antifragile: Things that gain from disorder.* Random House: New York.

default, the baseline mental model for how probabilities change as we move further out on the tail (Taleb, 2007, p. 262).

In many cases, we lack data that we can explore for mapping out the tail of a random process. In this kind of setting, uncertainty tends to be wildly out of the gate. Technological innovation fits right into this picture, because it brings novelty and injects it into the existing, already volatile, world order. New dynamics are set in motion, triggering unintended consequences and side effects that ripple through the system in an unpredictable fashion. Because we keep innovating, we also keep changing the rules of the game, forever adding to the complexity. Two Black Swans that have sprung from the onward march of technology are the emergence of the internet and the more recent invasion of social media and mobile phones into our lives. There was no existing dataset that we could have studied prior to them that might have suggested that such transformations of our reality were about to happen. Or, more importantly, that they were even possibilities at all. To appreciate how technologies that we are completely immersed in today and take for granted are actually Black Swans, cases of wild uncertainty, consider the words of Professor Adam Alter of New York University:

> 'Just go back twenty years [to 2000] . . . imagine you could speak to people and say, hey, you are going to go to the restaurant and everyone's going to be sitting isolated and looking at a small device, and then they're going to go back home and spend four hours looking at that device, and then you're going to wake up in the morning and look at that device . . . and people are going to be willing to have body parts broken to preserve the integrity of that device . . . people would say that is crazy'[9]

Alter's thought experiment of going back 20 years in time and imagining talking to people about something highly consequential that later happened is a useful one for deciding whether something is to be considered a Black Swan. If you imagine their reaction to what you describe would be that it is ridiculous or inconceivable, chances are that you have found one.

 ## THE ROLE OF EXPECTATIONS

To continue our story, it becomes clear that any characterizations of random processes will be increasingly subjective as we move away from data-driven

---

[9]Episode #1564 of the Joe Rogan Experience. Alter is referring to the claim made by some, mostly the young, that they would rather have a finger broken than their phone smashed.

approaches. We leave the world of inference from data and enter the realm of the imagination. Our faculties for reasoning and logic can partly make up for a lack of data – we can figure certain stuff out. When the imagination fails us, we have those truest of Black Swans, the inconceivable ones, the 'unknown unknowns'. We have already mentioned the 9/11 attack as being in this category. In a similar way, the collapse of the Soviet Union was utterly unthinkable to the Western intelligentsia and political establishment at the time. George Kennan, an American diplomat and historian, commented as follows, based on a review of the history of international affairs in the modern era:

> '[It is] hard to think of any event more strange and startling, and at first glance inexplicable, than the sudden and total disintegration and disappearance . . . of the great power known successively as the Russian Empire and then the Soviet Union.'[10]

That is, nobody expected the Soviet Union to crumble at this point in time. One of the most crucial aspects of Black Swans is that they are always measured against expectations and prior knowledge. This is an underappreciated point. As noted, most people use the term loosely, largely equating it with high-impact outcomes that were somehow shocking to us. With the considerable difference, perhaps, that calling it a Black Swan provides an air of complete unpredictability and that, therefore, one is not to be blamed for what just happened. Getting tail risk wrong may be an indictable offense. But Black Swans? They seem to absolve everyone of any responsibility for what went down, because nobody could have seen it coming.

The habit mentioned earlier of equating Black Swans with 'mere' tail risk misses out on what is perhaps its most important dimension, namely the expectations we had going into the situation. Because of the role of expectations, what is a Swan to you may not be one to me. It is, in Taleb's preferred terminology, a 'sucker's problem'. Naïve and ignorant individuals are more prone to experience Black Swans simply because they fail to form realistic expectations. To illustrate this idea, Taleb uses the example of a turkey somewhere in the US as Thanksgiving approaches. Having walked about generously fed for its entire life, the turkey is unsuspecting of the calamity that is about to befall it. The butcher, however, is obviously not unsuspecting, and he is therefore not in for a Black Swan – exactly the same event, but wildly diverging expectations.

---

[10]For this quote, and other useful perspectives, read the article *"Everything You Think You Know About the Collapse of the Soviet Union Is Wrong"* on foreignpolicy.com. Everything you think you know about the collapse of the Soviet Union is wrong, *Foreign Policy*.

The relativity of Black Swans has wide implications. Whenever a high impact event occurs, this may or may not be shocking. The more interesting discussion to be had is about who was attuned to this possibility and who was caught out? A Black Swan always requires a vantage point. To the suckers, it appears as if the tail just moved, but not necessarily to someone who sees the world a bit differently. Whenever we hear the term Black Swan mentioned, therefore, what should immediately spring to mind is the follow-up question 'Well, a Black Swan to whom?'

The Covid-19 pandemic is a case in point. Was this a Black Swan? It certainly meets the criterion of being a highly consequential event. Interestingly, Taleb himself has gone on record saying that C-19 was *not* a Black Swan. His argument is that there is a history of pandemics, based on which popular films were made well before C-19. A basic analysis of the connectivity of the modern world (i.e. means of travel) would also have pointed to the obvious plausibility of a global pandemic. Respected institutions issued reports warning of global pandemics already in the early 2000s. Bill Gates gave a thoughtful talk on the subject in 2015, also issuing words of warning for those willing to listen.[11] These considerations may well have sensitized students of history who also had the wisdom to internalize the possibility that this could happen in their own lifetime.

However, casual observation suggests that most of us have not reached such a state of immaculate wisdom. Many do not read books and have never heard of connectivity. All of our egocentric biases make going into denial about pandemics the easiest thing in the world, something which Albert Camus, the French philosopher, understood well:

> 'Everybody knows that pestilences have a way of recurring in the world; yet somehow we find it hard to believe in ones that crash down on our heads from a blue sky.'[12]

For most of us, watching a film about something makes it seem even more unreal. It puts it in the same category as Bruce Willis drilling holes in meteorites about to smash into Earth – pure entertainment.[13] If so, consuming films

---

[11]The next outbreak? We're not ready, Bill Gates – YouTube.

[12]Camus, A., 1947. *The Plague*. Librairie Gallimard.

[13]I should be careful here. The Earth is under threat from rocks in space. While earthlings' primary tactic, if detected in time, is likely to be to try to nudge such an object on to another course using force. Perhaps, however, the response will also involve some attempt at sending people up there to deal with the problem on site. Let us leave all options on the table.

may turn us into even bigger suckers because they warp our expectations. Since we are now discounting zombies heavily as just movie entertainment, woe on us the day they show up on the doorstep, because we have not prepared one bit for that eventuality!

At any rate, even if we had read about pandemics and realized that the probability of another one is clearly not zero, there is something about the magnitude of the consequences. Just like the 'business-as-usual' risk, Black Swans have two dimensions: possibility and consequence. Granting the possibility of something is a binary situation: a recognition that such a thing could happen (as opposed to saying there is no way it ever could). Even if we are willing to entertain the possibility of something, we could still be suckers with respect to the consequences once the event is unleashed. This is why C-19, for most people, was a genuine Black Swan. Pandemics, sure, I think I heard about that in school. But who could have imagined entire countries shutting down? Spending months on end in lockdowns? Tourism coming to a near stand-still? Mad dashes – knife fights even – for toilet rolls? It would take a pretty serious student of history, and one with a very fertile imagination at that, to envision the severity of the consequences along so many paths. Therefore, for a substantial majority of the planet's inhabitants, C-19 was a Black Swan. Along the same lines, it would be questionable not to label the French Revolution with its decidedly wild consequences a Black Swan just because there had been revolutions prior to that.

When it comes to the possibility of something happening, history by now offers a pretty impressive palette of different types of events. We might think of these as 'known unknowns', as it is clearly within our reach to form an understanding of them. What even the most creative and superbly educated mind cannot envision, however, is the magnitude of the consequences of those events as they would play out in the present day. The dynamics are truly impossible to imagine, and hence the consequences. History only repeats itself for the most part. With respect to the consequences, most of us are suckers, especially when it comes to our own lives and times. Whenever something impactful but entirely conceivable hits our vicinity, we are stunned no matter what.

##  WHAT MAKES US SUCKERS?

The previous section referred briefly to the 'not in our lifetime' perspective. Let us linger on this point for a bit, as it is one of the keys to understanding Black Swans and why we are essentially born suckers. Most of us will freely admit that humanity is in for one disaster or other. Sooner or later, that asteroid will knock us out of our pants, for sure, but it is always later, somewhere out in the distant future. It is not going to happen in my lifetime. Why? Because I am somehow special. Stuff only happens to other people, whereas I am destined to lead a glorious and comfortable existence. Based on such egocentric beliefs, we might coolly concede that in the larger scheme of things, something is sure to happen, yet almost completely discount the possibility as far as our lifetime and corner of the world is concerned. Not that we always say so publicly or even think in those terms outright, it is more of a tacit assumption.

This 'because I'm special' protective mechanism goes a long way in setting the stage for Black Swans. However, it is only one of the many ways in which our outlook is warped, which brings us to the long catalogue of biases that have been identified and described by scholars. A bias can be said to be a predisposition to make a mistake in a decision-making situation, because it leads us away from the decision that would be taken by a rational and well-informed person who diligently weighs pros and cons. What biases tend to have in common is that they make us more of a sucker than we need to be. They are a staple of business books nowadays (those on risk management in particular) and may bore the educated reader. Since they are so fundamental to the concept of Black Swans, we must briefly review them nonetheless. What follows is a non-exhaustive list of certain well-documented biases that in various ways contribute to the Black Swan phenomenon. As is commonly pointed out, these biases have been mostly to our advantage over the long evolutionary haul, but are often liabilities in the unnatural and complex environment we find ourselves in today.

▪ **The narrative fallacy**

In explaining why we are so poorly equipped to deal with randomness, Taleb focuses on what he refers to as 'the narrative fallacy', which he defines as 'our need to fit a story or pattern to a series of connected or disconnected facts' (Taleb, 2007, p. 309). We invent causes for things that we observe in order to satisfy our need for coherent explanations. It turns out that we do not suffer dissonance gladly, so our brain will supply any number of rationalizations to connect the dots. By reducing the number of dimensions of the problem at hand and creating a neat narrative, things become more orderly. Everything starts to hang together and make sense, and that is how the dissonance is resolved. Since we are lazy as well, we often converge on the rationalization that satisfies our craving with the least amount of resistance. However, when we force causal interpretations on our reality, and invent stories that satisfy our need for explanations, we make ourselves blind to powerful mechanisms that lie outside these simple narratives.

▦ **Confirmation bias**

This is one of the leading causes of Swan-blindness discussed in The Black Swan, where Taleb refers to confirmation as 'a dangerous error' (Taleb, 2007, p. 51). It has to do with the general tendency to adopt a theory or idea and then start to look for evidence that corroborates it. When we suffer from this bias, all the incoming data seems, as if by magic, to confirm that the belief we hold is correct; that the theory we are so fond of is indeed true. Whatever instances contradict the theory are brushed aside or ignored, or re-interpreted (tweaked) in a way that supports our pre-existing beliefs. Out the window goes Karl Popper's idea of falsification, the true marker of science and open inquiry. Using falsification as a criterion, a theory is *discarded* if evidence contradicting it becomes undeniable. In the specific context of managing risks, the confirmation bias is a problem because we will be too prone to interpret incoming observations of stability to suggest that the future will be similarly benign.

▦ **The optimistic bias**

Research has shown that humans tend to view the world as more benign than it really is. Consequently, in a decision-making situation, people tend to produce plans and forecasts that are unrealistically close to a best-case scenario.[14] The evidence shows that this is a bias with major consequences for risk taking. In the words of Professor Daniel Kahneman (2011): 'The evidence suggests that an optimistic bias plays a role – sometimes the dominant role – whenever individuals or institutions voluntarily take on significant risks. More often than not, risk takers underestimate the odds they face, and do not invest sufficient effort to find out what they are.'[15] Pondering on extreme and possibly calamitous outcomes will clearly not be a priority for an individual with an optimistic bent. Taking a consistently rosy view distorts expectations and therefore invites the Black Swan.

---

[14]This bias co-exists with a negativity bias that has us putting undue focus on negative aspects and overreacting to them. For example, if you receive 100 great reviews for something you did, but only one negative, you are quite likely to spend the rest of the week ruminating over that negative review.

[15]Kahneman, D., 2011. *Thinking fast and slow*. Farrar, Straus and Giroux: New York.

### ▦  The myopia bias

Myopia, in the literature on the psychology of judgement, refers to the tendency to focus more on short-term consequences than long-term implications. Because of our desire for instant gratification, we tend to place much less weight on future gains and losses relative to those in the near-term. Professors Meyer and Kunreuther call this the most 'crippling' of all biases, resulting in gross underpreparedness for disasters that could have been mitigated with relatively simple measures.[16] This was the case, for example, with the tsunami in the Indian Ocean in 2004. Only a few years prior, in Thailand, relatively inexpensive mitigation measures had been discussed – and dismissed. The reason? There were many reasons, but among other things, there was a worry that it might cause unnecessary alarm among tourists. Such miniscule short-term benefits got the upper hand in preparing for events with colossal consequences.

### ▦  The overconfidence bias

Humans are prone to overrate their own abilities and the level of control they have over a situation. The typical way of exemplifying this tendency is to point to the fact that nearly everyone considers himself an above-average driver. Taleb prefers the more humorous example of how most French people rate themselves well above the rest in terms of the art of love-making (Taleb, 2007, p. 153). As for the effect of overconfidence on decision-making, it is profound – and not in a favourable way. Professor Scott Plous (1993) argues that a large number of catastrophic events, such as the Chernobyl nuclear accident and the Space Shuttle Challenger explosion, can be traced to overconfidence. He offers the following summary: 'No problem [. . .] in decision-making is more prevalent and more potentially catastrophic than overconfidence.'[17] Overconfidence has been used to explain a wide range of observed phenomena, such as entrepreneurial market entry and trading in financial markets, despite available data suggesting high failure rates.

Considering the above, one is inclined to agree with Taleb when he remarks that '. . . it is as if we have the wrong user's manual' (Taleb, 2007, prologue xxii) for navigating successfully in a world of wild uncertainty. We crave simple but coherent narratives. We value elegant theories and become committed to them.

---

[16]Meyer, R. and H. Kunreuther, 2017. *The Ostricht Paradox: Why we underprepare for disaster.* Wharton School Press.

[17]Plous, S., 1993. *The psychology of judgment and decision making.* McGraw-Hill: New York.

We think we are special and that the world around us is benign. We are equipped with a mind that was created for an existence with much fewer variables and more direct cause-and-effect mechanisms. Reflecting deeply about interconnected systems was not key to survival in our evolutionary past. In a somewhat shocking passage, Taleb says that 'our minds do not seem made to think and introspect' because, historically speaking, it has been 'a great waste of energy' (ibid.).

In fact, information, which potentially helps us rise above sucker-status, is costly to acquire and process. Imagine that I bring up the possibility of nuclear terror affecting a major US city. Such a scenario involves hundreds of thousands of dead and an upheaval of life as we knew it, before even considering what the countermeasures might be. Any firm with operations in the US is likely to be greatly affected by this calamity. Now what is your gut reaction to this proposed topic of conversation? In all likelihood, your kneejerk reaction is to immediately try to shut it down. The sheer unpleasantness of the topic makes us not want to go there, even for a brief moment of time. It is too much to take in, and frankly too boring, so, to save us the mental energy, we are perfectly willing to resort to the handy tactic of denial.

As problems, extreme and abstract possibilities, remote from everyday practicalities, are not inspiring enough to energize us. They are out of sight and therefore out of mind. We are unable to maintain a focus on them for long enough. Our thoughts will gravitate towards something more tangible, some action that yields a more gratifying sense of accomplishment here and now. It often takes a herculean effort to process remote possibilities and we are rarely in the mood for it. They are therefore not necessarily 'unknown unknowns', rather they can be thought of as 'unknown knowables'. Unknown knowables is meant to convey that it is within our reach to form an understanding of the possibility and most of its consequence, but we fail to do so because of our laziness or disinterest. That makes it, for practical purposes, a Black Swan, at par with the unknown unknowns. At least to some, that is, because others might be prepared to take up the challenge.

## THE RELATIVITY OF BLACK SWANS

Earlier in this chapter, we noted that the popular view of Black Swans is that they strike quickly and unexpectedly. Except that there is nothing in the Black Swan framework that says it has to be sudden or even happen within a reasonably short time-period, like a few months. In fact, many of the examples discussed in Taleb's book are episodes that may seem like distinct and well-delineated events in a history book, but were prolonged affairs with a long lead-up. World Wars I and II are both in this category. The rise of Christianity is mentioned as another Black Swan event. A dominant Christianity would no doubt have appeared like an absurd proposition to someone living around the time of the birth of Jesus. Its consequences were certainly immense, so it meets this criterion too. It also took *centuries* to gain a foothold and start making its impact felt. The rise of the internet and social media were mentioned earlier as examples of technology-driven Black Swans. They too emerged gradually over many years, infiltrating our lives one small step after the other. Therefore, from the viewpoint of a decision-maker in the real world (which is the perspective that Taleb urges us to take) they were not instantaneous.

The fact that monumental changes can take a long time in gestation adds to the relativity of Black Swans. Those that are less wedded to specific ideas and more open to rewriting the story they tell themselves come around quicker to change. This introduces a strategic dimension to Black Swans, massive agents of change as they are. The observation to make is that when others refuse or are unable to see a changing reality, the value of being a non-conformist increases. The sucker status of those that you interact with competitively is a variable of interest, a theme we will come back to many times in this book.

Apart from the biases that shape our thinking, the relativity of Black Swans is also a matter of information and knowledge in the more traditional sense. The more we invest in high-quality information and capabilities for processing it, the wider our frame of reference will be, and the fewer Black Swans we will experience. Take Donald Trump's ascendancy to president as an example, which was a Black Swan to those who kept discounting him heavily. As his candidacy was first announced, many took it as a joke, and went on to seriously underestimate him throughout the race. The general assumption was that America would somehow come to its senses and see him for what he was, which, in their view, included being wholly unfit for office. However, those who had had their ears on the tracks and picked up on the dark undercurrents of American society knew better. In their eyes, the arrival of Trump was the culmination of a process that had been long in coming. They had realized that a substantial number of people had come to resent the system and thought it was rigged against them, feeling that nobody stood up for them except Trump. Out of spite, they were prepared to vote for someone who promised to shake the system up. This undercurrent unleashed the mindboggling Trump presidency, which culminated in the Capitol Hill insurrection. What a Black Swan, to all those who had not noticed the sentiment that had developed among broad layers of the US population.

For students of Swanology, the #1222 episode of the Joe Rogan Experience podcast is a gem. It illuminates several of the mechanisms involved in turning some (most) of us into suckers, and highlights the enormous differences in expectations that can arise *even when we are looking at the same set of facts*. The topic of conversation is about the mother of all Black Swans, the wiping away of the existing world order by way of an asteroid impact. According to Rogan's guests, Graham Hancock and Randall Carlson, there is compelling evidence to suggest that there have been repeated cosmic impacts during the 180,000 years or so that anatomically modern humans have existed. Besides transforming the geography of the Earth, these events may have erased civilizations existing at the time so thoroughly that no archaeological evidence of them can be found today. Hancock and Carlson, labelled 'catastrophists' by some, argue that human civilization did not begin to stir around 12,000 years ago, which is the conventional view, but that it was *rebooted* following a near-complete destruction caused by an asteroid that smashed into Earth a number of centuries before. The asteroid impact they refer to was followed by extreme shifts in the global climate. One consequence was a near-instantaneous melting of the ice sheets and the flooding that resulted completely overwhelmed humans living at the time. (Fascinatingly, if true, this could explain the enduring myths handed down to us from deep history regarding an epic flooding.)

Mainstream science, however, adheres to a view referred to as 'gradualism', which holds that we can extrapolate backward in time from processes we are able to observe today. In this view, everything we see in the landscapes today are the result of gradual processes that have been going on for eons. As a result of the vested interest in this narrative by academics who have built a career on it, they have put up quite a resistance to the ideas put forth by Hancock and Carlson. This resistance takes us into Black Swan territory with respect to the civilization-destroying potential of cosmic impact. Below are some excerpts from their conversation. We do not have to take any sides with respect to the facts being discussed to enjoy the insights it brings about the Black Swan formation process.

> GH:  Whenever you propose a cataclysm and present evidence for it . . . you can be sure that you will be descended upon by a crowd of furious critics.
>
> JR:  As a species, we have amnesia.
>
> JR:  Why would they try to ignore something like that?
>
> GH:  When new information emerges that contradicts established theories . . . when you get very committed to a model or idea . . . you start to connect your personality to it, and any attack on it becomes an existential attack on you.

GH: Again and again, what we see is new facts being dismissed because they don't fit into the existing theory . . . this is a problem in the whole history of science. I've come to view archeology and history as more ideology, really, than science.

GH: There is an ideological view of how civilization developed, that there is this long, slow, gradual, politically correct rise . . . and here we are, the apex and pinnacle of this story, and gosh, we are so proud of ourselves and our achievements.

GH: They are in a state of denial and just don't want to recognize it.

JR: It is so sad. You count on these people to distribute the information but their ego gets involved in things . . . if you have an absolutely established narrative that you teach and you are unwilling to look at any possible deviation from that, you are saying, almost from an authority position, 'we know what happened and we know where we are going'.

RC: We're kind of in this mode now where there's a very large and growing political agenda around the idea that humans are the sole cause of global change . . . now we come along and say, no, there's actually been forces unleashed on this planet that utterly dwarfs anything we've done yet. What does that do to that paradigm?

GH: . . . south of Minnesota you [had] a heavily vegetated area covered with primal forest and that is what goes on fire and the reason it goes on fire is because when these impacts come in they generate huge amounts of heat . . . and it [sets] the world on fire.

JR: Oh that gives me goosebumps . . . a single afternoon all over the world and everything changes forever and it's [ruined] for a thousand years.

GH: We all need to know about this . . . this is our background, this is where we come from, the present order of the world has descended from that moment.

The conversation points to several biases at work that lull us into a state of ignorant bliss highly conducive to Black Swans. There is scientific dogma, which is a kind of confirmation bias in which incoming evidence is fitted to the received models of explanation. Any dissenters presenting alternative interpretations of the evidence are (according to Rogan's guests) ruthlessly clamped down on and stripped of their sources of funding. There is also the issue of political agendas, where the ruling ideology will only accept facts that support the preferred narrative (currently, man as solely responsible for global warming). Finally, there is the sheer existential discomfort that results from having to ponder the fact that asteroid impacts are a regularly occurring phenomenon in deep history. Many of us just do not like being told that the Earth is essentially a sitting duck in space just waiting for the next swarm of asteroids to come our way. Others, in contrast, remain open to consider what the facts are trying to tell us no matter what conclusions they lead us to. A wide gap in expectations has opened up, and this matters, not least in the kind of competitive interaction we will take an interest in later.

##  MEET THE PREPPERS

Few would be more open to alternative interpretations of the facts than the so-called 'preppers'. These are the folks who take the issue of cataclysms very seriously, and who prepare for them with passion. In fact, you could accuse them of having an overactive imagination, of buying into conspiracy theories left and right. There is indeed a fringe element in this movement, with a clear anti-government stance and a penchant for organizing into paramilitary units, the so-called 'survivalists'. But Professor Bradley Garrett, who has carried out in-depth investigations of the phenomenon, argues that prepping is actually going mainstream, and has developed into a prospering multibillion dollar industry.[18] Interestingly, and perhaps worryingly, the elites have taken a keen interest in preparing for doomsday scenarios. There is now an active market in bunkers offering luxury and comfort, enabling you to sit out the end times in some style. Apparently, well-to-do tech-entrepreneurs are very active in the market because they foresee a breakdown of the social contract as technology continues to remove the need for millions of workers.

If preppers can be accused of having overactive imaginations, perhaps that makes up for the deficiency that the rest of us consistently display in this area. In fact, preppers could be rated the finest Black Swan spotters out there. There are levels to this, and they have explored remote and disastrous possibilities to a degree that the average person is not even close to. Given their orientation, they are not constrained by the need to conform or any stigma that may come from expressing unorthodox views. Instead, they revel in it. Consequently, they have taken the process of turning 'unknown unknowns' into 'known unknowns' as far as you reasonably could. If they have turned every

---

[18]Garrett, B., 2020. *Bunker: Building for the End Times*. Scribner: New York.

stone in search of what could trigger an upheaval, why not see what they have come up with? In Table 1.1 I have listed, for future reference, all the extreme events brought up by the preppers interviewed in Garrett's book.

A recurring theme in the prepper world-view is that many of the events in Table 1.1 will play out in an interlinked sequence. In the parlance, there will be 'ripple effects' where various parts of the system fall apart like domino bricks. I have organized the list loosely from meta-events that trigger a shock to the system, down to some of the societal consequences that could follow. There is no particular ordering implied here. Things further down the list could of course happen for reasons unrelated to those higher up, and the top entry

**TABLE 1.1**   The prepper's list

Nuclear war

Nuclear terror

Pandemics

Synthetic biotech (engineered pandemic by rogue nation/scientist)

Asteroid impact

Electro-magnetic pulse from sun (will 'fry' all electronics)

Man-made electro-magnetic impulse (ditto)

Mega volcano eruptions

Run-away technology (a bit vaguely)

Artificial intelligence turning hostile

Hurricanes and floodings and wildfires

Sea-levels rising (by 2040 Florida will be sea-floor according to one prepper)

Desertification (by 2040 Europe will be Saharan, same source)

Blackout of electric grids

Collapsing eco-systems

Crop failures

Cessation of global trade networks

Hyperinflation

Collapse of paper currency

Financial collapse

Government collapse

World without rule of law

could take us directly to the last, and so on (and government collapse could easily be the precipitating factor for nuclear havoc!). The permutations are endless. The point to be made is simply that misfortune rarely comes alone. When it hits the fan, as preppers like to say, things could quickly be going wrong on multiple fronts. It has long been known that risks are not independent of each other, and that we have to take these tendencies to co-vary this into account when designing risk management strategies. As per the preppers, the same appears to be true in the tail of things.

# CHAPTER TWO

# Corporate Swans

A T THIS POINT IN the book, we change gears and take the perspective of a company. What does it mean to the managers of a firm that we live in a world of wild uncertainty? What is it that they can do that will increase the odds that they survive and thrive in such a Black Swan infested place? And what is there to say that they should care about tail risk in the first place?

As we take the corporate perspective, several interesting things happen. Firms are strange creatures in more than one way. They have several unique features that all profoundly affect how we should think about Black Swans. We will explore them all in this book. One central aspect about firms is that they operate under a specific mandate, which is to generate profits, or, as it were, to 'create value' for those who have invested in them. More often than not, the owners are not the ones managing the firm. Instead, they delegate the daily running of the firm to the executive team, which creates a separation between ownership and control that has far-reaching implications. Firms are also peculiar because of something called limited liability, a feature of corporation law that implies that shareholders cannot lose money beyond the size of their original investment. Yet another aspect that makes firms fascinating entities to study is the complex nature of their decision-making processes. A firm has many stakeholders who try to influence policy for their maximum benefit and a variety of checks and balances to keep any group from becoming too influential. In this chapter, and the following ones, we will explore the meaning of wild uncertainty for firms given these peculiar features.

**THE BOARD'S PERSPECTIVE**

Just talking about 'the firm' as if it were a unified and rational entity with a mind of its own can be misleading. It downplays the potential for interests to diverge on many issues, including tail risk and its possible management. There are the directors of the board, the executive team, business unit leaders, corporate functions and so on, all with different world-views and priorities. As discussed, Black Swans require a specific vantage point and we have to make a choice. I hereby submit that the most relevant and useful perspective is that of the Board of Directors ('BoD'). The reason for taking this view is that they represent the firm's owners and are supposed to look after their best interest. The board ultimately 'owns', i.e. is responsible for, the firm's risk profile, contrary to a common misperception that risk management is exclusively an 'operational' issue. Their task includes finding ways to ensure that any risks taken are proportionate to the upside potential in the firm's business pursuits rather than reckless.

Shifting the view to that of the directors of a company has the interesting consequence that the number of Black Swans will go up. How do we magically bring more Swans into existence by a simple waving of the wand? Taking management's perspective, which is customary in business books, misses the crucial point that managers can be a *source* of Black Swans. You may not believe this, but part of the function of a BoD is actually to watch out for misbehaviour by the executives. Companies, with all their resources, are loot. If a group of people is left in control of such assets unsupervised, they are bound to become more and more inventive in finding ways to channel some of that loot into their own pockets. This is the classic agency problem, which has been analysed at length in the corporate finance literature. It may sound cynical, but the evidence on this point is beyond dispute. Problems related to the separation between ownership and control is one of the main reasons a board exists in the first place. In fact, the board can be viewed as a line of defence in the struggle shareholders face in holding management accountable. It is essentially a mechanism for stopping things from getting out of hand.

Also, recall from our earlier discussions that Black Swans are functions of expectations, which are heavily shaped by information and knowledge. Directors are at a serious disadvantage in both of these respects compared to the executive team. They convene only a few times per year, and often the board consists of people from outside the industry the company operates in. The make-up of the board also changes frequently, preventing the accumulation of firm-specific knowledge. Management has a great deal of control over the flow of information and may choose not to make the Board privy to all of it.

So taking the Board's perspective lowers the bar for what counts as a Black Swan, for the simple reason that *to them* whatever happened came as a great surprise. Managers, in contrast, may have seen it coming, but suppressed the information. Even worse, perhaps they were in on it. If they were, it certainly was no Black Swan as far as they were concerned. As for risk managers, they may be supremely educated and skilful individuals, and they may figure out lots of things about Black Swans that represent real threats to the company. However, what good is that if those insights do not reach the BoD to the point where they can grasp them and mount some kind of response? Pockets of enlightenment in a company do not count for much if they do not translate into action.

Our working definition of a Corporate Swan will be an event that is highly consequential (massive impact) for a firm, yet that arrives as a complete surprise for an unsuspecting Board of Directors (the independent directors, that is). Taking a corporate view on Black Swans, from the vantage point of the BoD, means that several new types of Swans can be sighted, some of which are unique to the corporate domain. We will, as part of this sighting trip, look deeper into the unnerving theme already hinted at, that some Swans are made closer to home and that they, rather than swooping down from the outside, emerge from the depths within. Before we get to that, however, let us first have a look at the Corporate Swans generated by forces outside the firm's control.

##  SWANS ATTACK

One of the basic sources of randomness, we have concluded, is the opaqueness of the natural world. Since nature operates on a grand scale, the consequences are often terrifying. Every day we are confronted with news about wildfires, hurricanes and flooding of the extreme – and 'unprecedented' – sort. It is self-evident that the people and physical structures on which firms rely are affected by the unleashing of such forces.

Then there are the various man-made structures that make up civilization. These technical, economical and political systems introduce another layer of randomness and are capable of generating failure and violence on a terrible scale. It should be said, though, that the purpose of these systems is normally to make our existence more enjoyable *and* safe. Were it not for things like the power grid, central heating and treatment plants, we would be an awfully lot more exposed to the vagaries of nature. Any centralization of power has, as long as that power is reasonably benign, a risk-dampening function. Centralization of decision-making authority reduces the risk in the system because it pools resources and allows for the coordination of actions. When a natural disaster happens, we should consider ourselves lucky if there is a national guard and other centrally run departments there to watch out for us. Many countries operate elaborate systems of social security that provide a measure of support when we suffer a loss of health or income. These safety nets clearly soften the blow whenever unexpected problems arise. We can conclude, therefore, that, most days of the week, these systems make existence less risky.

Occasionally, however, the systems we organize start to malfunction and can turn on us. This is when the system itself, from the firm's point of view, becomes a generator of Black Swans. Political coups or regime collapses, for example, can have devastating consequences for firms' ability to do business. If you were a contractor in the Soviet system, for example, its falling apart might have been the end of that business model. As for failures of technical systems, consider the power outages in California in the early 2000s. For multiple underlying reasons, the grid repeatedly shut down, a situation that turned into a nightmare for many businesses who were unable to keep operations going. Often, the technical systems are brought into disarray by events in the natural world, pointing to the ripple effects that the preppers talk about.

Recessions are a prime example of a risk generated internally by the system that drops down on firms' heads. The lows of the business cycle are episodes when people stop believing that their future is a good one, and animal spirits go into reverse on a broad scale. One of the consequences of such a deflated mood is, of course, that people spend less money, which, if you are a business, is bad news. While recessions are reasonably well understood, we should remain open to their Black Swan potential. As noted, we may accept that a certain phenomenon is bound to happen every once in a while, but still be taken in completely by the ferocity and strangeness of its consequences. The Great Recession of the late 2000s was just such a destructive force. In his highly readable book, *Swimming with Sharks: My Journey into the World of Bankers*, Joris Luyendijk explains the impression it made on financial market participants who witnessed it first hand:

> 'Some talked about the hours, days, and weeks after the Lehman Brothers' collapse . . . as the most harrowing period in their careers, if not lives. They spoke of colleagues sitting frozen before their screens, paralysed, unable to act [. . .] some got on the phone to their families: "Get as much money from the ATM as you can." "Rush to the supermarket to hoard food [. . .] Even alpha-Sid spoke in a grim tone: "That was scary, mate. I mean, not film scary. Really scary."'[1]

---

[1]Luyendijk, J., 2015. *Swimming with sharks: My journey into the world of bankers.* Guardian Faber: London.

Whether you want to call the Great Recession mere tail risk or a Black Swan proper is up to you, but sharp recessions are rare events with vicious consequences and they all have their unique features. They are imposed on firms from the outside and can inflict significant harm on even well-run establishments that have done nothing imprudent that could be said to have contributed to the unfolding events. Dramatic upheavals imposed from the outside are an important category for sure, and we will have them in mind on our journey. For firms it is not the end of it, though. There are more types of Swans to consider. We need to adjust the focus on our binoculars and keep looking.

 ## STRATEGY SWANS

Some Black Swans prefer to sneak up on firms and pull the rug from under their feet. What I am referring to is the possibility that, perfectly outside a recession, a firm's strategy can be completely derailed and left largely useless *by a competitive move*. In order to arrive at some understanding of what can undermine a strategy, it would be helpful to have a definition of it. A strategy can be a surprisingly elusive thing to define, however. To make a long discussion short, we will simply understand it as an approach or formula for generating profits and creating value (which is understood as the sum of discounted future profits, the maximization of which requires long-term viability). It involves things like coming up with an attractive product offering, cost-efficient production, setting up a supply chain to ensure timely delivery and a host of other components that, considered as a whole, add value. That is, the strategy delivers some kind of net benefit to its customers and lets the firm monetize some of the value created. While we struggle to define a strategy, it is clear when it is not working because a fledgling strategy will deliver neither healthy profits nor growth that promises profits in the future.

As the ever-changing environment provides feedback, a firm adjusts and fine-tunes its strategy over time. When a competitor launches a new product or a successful marketing campaign, the firm may be able to retaliate and recover some of what has been lost. If a certain design or offering proves moderately popular with its customers, it can learn its lesson and come up with something that is more in favour. This can carry on in a continuous reconfiguration of the firm's resources and capabilities in light of emerging realities.

There may also be changes in the environment that are more fundamental and from which the firm finds it hard to recover. This is the domain of the Strategy Swan, which constitutes a threat to the very viability of the strategy.

It is not the usual back-and-forth in the battle for market share that we are talking about. Rather, these Swans bring consequences that are massive, bordering on the existential. They are often caused by the emergence of a new technological innovation or a societal trend that renders the firm's strategy a shadow of its former self. A Strategy Swan may also refer to the unexpected appearance of a competitor that outcompetes the firm so thoroughly that a large chunk, perhaps all, of the value of the strategy simply melts away. The essence of this variety of Swan is that we can become, in a single blow, outcompeted. They are undoubtedly rare things. All it takes for them to qualify as a Swan, then, is a certain naiveté, or blindness, with respect to its possibility on the part of those who are about to be swept away.

A nice example of a Strategy Swan is a stellar competitive move that took place in the year of 1892, when the likes of Standard Oil and the Rothschild family were striding the Earth. In that year, a London-based merchant named Marcus Samuel devised a veritable coup. The move toppled even the mighty Standard Oil, who had made a habit of crushing everything that dared to cross its path (this was prior to the anti-trust laws). The prize Samuels was after was the lucrative markets for kerosene in East Asia, which would provide an ideal outlet for the voluminous production his company had set up in Baku, Azerbaijan. As told by Professor Daniel Yergin in his grand story about the history of oil,[2] Samuels concocted an ingenious move to achieve his desired outcome. He planned and executed this strategy in secrecy, through a series of co-ordinated actions that were to unfold simultaneously, so as not to give Standard a chance to pre-empt. Working with trading houses in Asia, and ensuring the collaboration of a branch of the Rothschild family, he moved swiftly to grab a large swathe of the markets he was after. Entering all these Asian markets at once meant that the gushing wells Samuels had access to found outlets. The resulting economies of scale made it impossible for Standard to deploy its favourite strategy of lowering prices by enough to force any competitor that stood up to it out of the market.

The move into East Asia meant overcoming daunting logistical challenges. It was critical that the tankers met the safety requirements necessary to pass through the Suez Canal, because it would radically reduce shipping costs (ships would no longer have to round the Cape of Good Hope). At the time, the canal was closed to ships carrying fuel on safety grounds. Samuels overcame this obstacle through technological innovations, such as refitting bulk ships to carry the kind of light fuel oil he wanted to bring to the market.

---

[2]Yergin, D., 1990. *The prize: The epic quest for oil, money, and power*. Simon & Schuster: New York.

He also deftly navigated the political intrigues and business connections that paved the way for the decision to allow his tankers to pass. At the time, *The Economist* commented that 'the new move is one of singular boldness and great magnitude' and that the 'Eastern case-oil trade must needs become obsolete'. The shell-shocked executives of Standard, waking up to a new reality, realized they had been taken in. The East Asian markets were now effectively lost to them. Samuels had achieved a feat with massive consequences that was not on the mental map of the BoD of Standard Oil. Hence, it was a Strategy Swan.

A Strategy Swan has certain hallmarks. They generally revolve around doing things in a completely new, and superior, way. Nobody had used the Suez Canal for shipping flammable light fuel before. It took a visionary to see that bulk ships could be used to carry vast quantities of such liquid, and to see that they could be built according to standards that made them safe enough to travel through a crucial bottleneck. Pulling off what most people casually think of as impossible or out of the question is almost certain to spell the demise for some of the incumbents. A common theme in Strategy Swans is therefore technological innovation. Game-changing innovations have a tendency to render existing products obsolete by redefining the customer experience. Alternatively, the innovation makes the cost of production so low that industry peers have no realistic chance of striking back, such as when Henry Ford introduced mass production of the T-Ford on assembly lines.

Technology, as noted earlier, is inherently a generator of Black Swans because it virtually guarantees unpredictability (and exponential effects) over the longer term. Corporates very much live that reality. They are in the business of supplying the products and services we all use, nearly all of which depend on technology in some form. When the dominant technology changes, those that continue to identify with the old one are in for some trouble. Consider the photo labs that processed and printed film. They were never to recover from the emergence of a major Black Swan, the digital revolution. These labs were pretty big business at a certain point in time, but crumbled when the benefits of going digital became undeniable.

In certain sectors, supplying the technology itself is the business. This is where Schumpeter's process of 'creative destruction' is at its most ferocious. The ground is always crumbling under the feet of established companies, as new entrepreneurs and innovators are forever looking to take their place with a new and improved technology. The literature on corporate strategy is in fact largely about giving advice on how to play this game successfully by constantly innovating and reconfiguring one's activities for maximum advantage. There is a certain paranoia with respect to Strategy Swans, and the overall message is one of never standing still, of being the disruptor rather than the disrupted. You would rather be the butcher than the turkey.

Strategy Swans are different to other Swans from the outside in that our response to them could actually be something along the lines of 'well, fair enough. We just got outcompeted, and congratulations on them for pulling off something we had a shot at doing but failed to think of.' Dynamic competition is the very nature of business and it is something anyone who enters into it must accept. Once digitalisation arrived, there was not much that the photo shops could have done. In some cases, though, some of the damage might have been preventable. Kodak's inability to wake up to the consequences of digitalisation counts as a classic case of strategy failure. Unlike the photo labs, Kodak had enough resources to invest in the newly emerged technology. Defying belief, the digital camera was actually invented by a Kodak engineer. It was just that the company's managers did not see that digitalisation was a disruptive technology that offered untold opportunities, treating it instead as a cute distraction.[3]

What happened to Kodak is probably best explained as a version of the endowment effect: our tendency to develop emotional bonds to things that we possess. Sometimes we just do not want to let go. Translated into strategy, it means that managers are overly attached to a formula for making profits that has served the company well historically. The effect will be even stronger if this formula is closely intertwined with the identity of the firm, a big part of how the firm defines itself. Because Kodak's film-based business was so dear to them, its managers went into collective denial about digital technology. It was probably inconceivable to them that there could be a world where film-based cameras were utterly marginalised and hence the revolution that subsequently took place was a Swan to them and their directors.

As an aside, consider that the world's ever-growing addiction to tech is setting in motion developments on the level of society whose logical end consequences are still unfathomable to most of us (i.e. paving the way for a slow-moving Black Swan experience). A major concern in some quarters is that the world is tilting heavily in favour of a tech-savvy minority, which appropriates an ever-larger portion of the world's wealth. All the while, more and more traditional businesses and lines of work become obsolete. As wealth is increasingly extracted by a high caste of tech-entrepreneurs and their associates in the world of finance and politics, instability and social unrest

---

[3]According to a Forbes article from 2012, the response of Kodak's managers to the engineer who came up with the first digital camera was along the lines of: 'that's cute – but don't tell anyone about it.' How Kodak Failed (forbes.com).

may ultimately follow. This thesis is pursued by Andrew Yang (2018) in the context of the US, whose big-fish-eat-little-fish ethos has led to a situation where a small group of people lead a charmed existence in coastal cities whereas the rest of the country sinks into poverty and gloom.[4] Yang argues that there is a growing mass of the permanently displaced and that automation is accelerating to a point where it soon threatens the social fabric.

Yang's storyline could be construed as another Black Swan in the making. If he is right, a great many of us may be suckers with respect to what automation is about to do for our prospects of earning a living. If a breakdown of the social contract in the US strikes you as an inconceivable event, you might take a cue from the fact noted earlier that wealthy tech entrepreneurs are among the most active in the market for bunkers.

##  THE SWAN WITHIN

The next Corporate Swan we are going to discuss is found even closer to home. In fact, its mastermind is someone within our own ranks. For anyone who cares to look, there is no shortage of corporate disasters stemming directly from the actions of the people within the organization. In addition to bringing out the binoculars to try to spot bricks falling from the sky, we need to take a long look in the mirror and ask, is there a Swan within? It is time to ask in what ways a firm can be tripped up, massively, by its own people. As per our definition, all it takes to be considered a Corporate Swan is for these machinations to be hidden from view from the BoD long enough.

One category of Swans within that frequently gets a mention is the rogue trader. Jerome Kerviel of Société Générale offers a useful example. In 2008, Mr. Kerviel caused an enormous trading loss by taking positions that allegedly far exceeded his authority. The lawsuit that ensued accused Kerviel of 'breach of trust and forgery', for which he was eventually convicted. The autonomous actions of a single trader caused financial and reputational damage beyond the imagination of the bank's directors.

A more relevant Swan within for our purposes is the rogue executive. Enron, once a proud Houston-based energy company, provides one of the finest case studies on this phenomenon. Enron emerged as a much-feared competitor in the late 1990s and intimidated everyone with their ability to innovate. So good were

---

[4]Yang, A., 2018. *The war on normal people: The truth about America's disappearing jobs and why Universal Basic Income is our future.* Hachette Books: New York.

they at managing this perception that Forbes, six years in a row, named them the most innovative company in the US. Star academics wrote books hailing Enron's accomplishments, and they were supported in their endeavours by no less of a thinker than McKinsey & Co. When they filed for bankruptcy, it was like a bomb had detonated, with massive consequences to go around (for instance, its auditor, Arthur Andersen, went under, as did Enron itself). Enron at the time of its collapse was listed as the seventh largest company in the US. The following statement by the Permanent Subcommittee on Investigations (on behalf of the US senate) makes clear the Black Swan nature of the collapse, i.e. its inconceivability:

> 'One of the striking features of the Enron collapse is the company's abrupt and dramatic transformation from a well-respected and award-winning company to a disgraced and bankrupt enterprise in less than three months.'[5]

Enron's executives were, as it turned out, bestowed with not only great ingenuity, but also a criminal mind. Court records revealed an impressive array of accounting and business shenanigans meant to keep an appearance of growing profits.[6] It turned out that the bedazzled stock market, and many other stakeholders, had simply taken the company's managers at their word. This kind of blind faith is, of course, perfectly consistent with the confirmation bias and sure-fire way to generate Black Swans. We want to believe, so we keep finding excuses and explain away facts to the contrary. In fact, Enron showcases the narrative and confirmation biases in perfect harmony. We invent a grossly simplified story that we find convenient and interesting ('Enron is a marvellous and innovative company that can do no wrong. They will come to wholly dominate US energy markets, nay the world') and then start to look for evidence that confirms this, whilst ignoring suggestions to the contrary. ('Enron uses creative accounting and nobody can understand their financial statements, but hey, these guys speak with great confidence and seem to know what they are doing.')

Dieselgate, the scandal that badly rocked German carmaker Volkswagen, offers another good case study of rogue executives.[7] The background for

---

[5]https://www.hsgac.senate.gov/imo/media/doc/REPORT – Role of Board of Directors in Enron's Collapse (July 2002). pdf.

[6]Someone may remark that this example is not well chosen because Enron's Board of Directors seems to have capitulated completely and signed off on what seems afterwards like comically aggressive practices, like booking fair value gains upon the initiation of almost any kind of deal or activity. The true Swans were perhaps inflicted on the directors of the poor companies that were trusting counterparties to Enron at the time they collapsed.

[7]This section draws on Professor Amy C. Edmondson's book, 2019. *The fearless organization: Creating psychological safety in the workplace for Learning, Innovation and Growth.* Wiley & Sons.

Dieselgate was the desire of Volkswagens' executives to reach the omission standards necessary for the lucrative US market. Presented to the world as 'clean diesel cars' and a cornerstone of the firm's strategy for growth, their diesel vehicles were in fact not able to meet the omission standards set by US regulators. Finding the task of reaching the standards ultimately impossible, its engineers took to tinkering with the software code that regulated emission levels as measured in the tests. Quite deviously, the solution they came up with contained an instruction to turn off two of the wheels during the testing, which drastically lowered emission levels compared to driving on the road. Volkswagen had built a cheating device! The modified software was deployed on a grand scale, affecting about 11 million cars between the years 2007 and 2015. Caught, Volkswagen tried to first deny the scheme and then to cover it up. Facing overwhelming evidence, the company finally pleaded guilty to criminal charges in 2017. In the days following the revelations, its share price was down by more than a third. Several executives were arrested and a seemingly endless string of lawsuits followed. The accumulated fines were estimated, as of June 2020, to be in the order of $33 billion. Fines of this magnitude, along with the trashing of the company's reputation, easily qualifies Dieselgate as a Corporate Swan. To outsiders, the company's long-standing reputation for engineering prowess and its association with German 'reliability' amplified the shock. Those markers created an energy-saving narrative about Volkswagen that activates the confirmation mechanism. We happily take them as shorthand for future stability.

Importantly, in both Enron and Volkswagen there was intent. The executives were deliberately cheating to achieve what they wanted, and did not let the possible consequences for the company or other stakeholders get in their way. It may not amount to outright treachery, which is what Cicero had in mind when he commented on enemies within, but at the very least personal ambition drove the whole enterprise towards the brink. In the next couple of sections, we explore the role of personal ambition further. We need to drill deeper and look for root causes.

##  THE GROWTH FETISH

It is an inconvenient truth that the executives are sometimes part of the problem rather than the solution. Those who are supposed to steer the firm with capable hands, and keep it safe from harm, stop doing that. Instead they behave in ways that generate risk or, occasionally, even Black Swans. We need to keep things in perspective, though. It is appropriate to think of rogue executives as tail risk because they are very rare events. Most managers are decent and hard-working people who care deeply about the organization and I do not mean to cast them as the villains of the story. However, when these things do happen, the consequences can be calamitous and usually involve a violation of trust and fiduciary duties (i.e. expectations), which takes us into Black Swan territory.

Given that there have been such a large number of Swans emanating from within, what has history taught us about their underlying causes? What drives executives to go rogue? There are of course multiple explanations, and it is beyond the scope of this book to map out all of them. We will settle for a few common denominators. The first is that management teams are under a lot of pressure to create growth for their firms. By growth, we generally mean increasing revenue or earnings from one year or quarter to the next. To see why this desire is so heartfelt, it is useful to consider that stock markets, firms, and managers collectively appear ensnared in what might be best described as a 'growth fetish'. For publicly listed firms, the pressure to generate growth can be tremendous, as it is one of the two main value drivers in the formula for firm value.[8] If the market is disappointed by the growth the firm has achieved and writes down its forecasts for the future, it can instantly wipe off a large portion of the firm's stock market capitalization. If managers own stocks in the firm, which most of them do these days, there is a very directly felt impact on their wealth from growth disappointments. No wonder they obsess about it.

Valuation effects from disappointing growth aside, there is something in the managerial ethos that makes growth a highly desirable item. It comes across as a very compelling objective in its own right, something deeply ingrained in their psyche. A manager, quoted in Yang (2018, cited earlier), puts it in the following way:

> 'The way management teams work is that we generally try to grow and take advantage of opportunities. We try to operate efficiently, but it is not our number one priority all of the time.'

What is going on here? Why do managers want growth so dearly? Over and above the pure wealth effects discussed above, we must consider that growth numbers coming in below expectations is a signal, plain for everyone to see, that the management team was not able to deliver. It is therefore something of an ego thing. One may speculate in an even deeper fear: that mediocre growth signals that the best is behind us. That from now on, there is only

---

[8]Profitability is the other. The firm's tax rate and cost of capital are also value drivers in the theoretical formula for value, but they are to a lesser extent under management control and thus largely off the minds of managers.

stagnation, and all that befalls us is to administer this entity and keep an eye on whatever profits it is still able to generate. Perhaps we need expansion to keep things interesting, to feel good about our ourselves. Growth below expectations is bad enough; non-growth is a horror.

It is when the pressure to grow gets too intense that managers may start to ponder more aggressive tactics to accomplish their aspiration level. This will increase the likelihood of somebody crossing a line that should not be crossed. The Enron example illustrates this principle well. Their executives were highly aware of the expectations that the hype had built up, and clearly felt stressed about delivering on them. Anyone who still doubts the role of growth-induced stress is invited to read Luyendijk's (2015, cited earlier) account of the experiences of people in the financial sector and what it is like to work there. For the bankers, visible reminders in the form of people, former colleagues, who are being led out the building by security, compound the stress.[9] The message is stark: it could be you next. The only way to keep the sharks at bay is to keep growing. In one passage, one of the investment bankers puts it in the following way:

'Everybody – and I mean everybody – is focused on business, on revenue responsibility . . . claiming deals is an endless preoccupation.'

If we want to fully understand the consequences of the growth fetish, we have to pay attention to the fact that not all forms of growth are equivalent. There are three basic ways to grow, which are different in terms of their contribution to both value and risk. Sector growth is generally regarded as the best and most benign sort, as it represents a windfall for all the firms in that sector. Demand is improving overall and everyone in the industry is benefitting from it. It is a matter of responding to this new demand and enjoying the tailwind. No overstretch is implied. Market share growth, based on getting ahead of one's peers, is more risky. It takes more investment and competitors may well retaliate. After some low-hanging fruit, less attractive and more expensive outlets will be considered for expansion, which means we are climbing up the risk scale.

Finally, we have the most expensive and risky form of growth of them all: acquisitions. In this case, the revenue and earnings of the target company are added to the consolidated numbers. Growth is therefore guaranteed, which is

---

[9]Security is advised in these situations because there is a risk that the former employee attempts to do damage out of a desire for revenge.

one of the main attractions of buying other companies. The main problem is that acquisitions are super-expensive. The acquisition premium can easily be in the 30–40% range, which is, if you stop and think about it, an incredible amount that has to be recovered through synergies. On top of that, there are all the usual post-merger risk factors: cultures not integrating well, key personnel leaving, and so on. The extensive academic evidence on acquisitions is pretty clear. On average, they destroy value for the buying company. Whatever synergies are realized, for the most part they do not match the hefty premium paid. Professor Aswath Damodaran, a leading valuation expert, has summarized the evidence on corporate acquisitions as follows:

> 'If you look at the collective evidence across acquisitions, this is the most value destructive action a company can take . . . I firmly believe that acquisitions are an addiction, that once companies start growing through acquisitions, they cannot stop . . . Targets win. You wake up the next morning and say thank God for capitalism.'[10]

Mostly, acquisitions just destroy value, but occasionally they turn into Corporate Swans because of the sheer size of the value destruction. Microsoft's $7 billion acquisition of Nokia in 2015, for example, was decidedly a flop as no commercial products coming out of that venture managed to achieve anything useful. Two years later, the acquisition was written down in its entirety. HP's purchase of Compaq in 2001 also holds legendary status in the annals of merger disasters. ABB, for their part, paid top dollars in 1999 for Combustion Engineering, a US-based power generation firm. While questionable based on the price paid alone, the true nightmare was the hidden liabilities related to asbestos claims that ABB inherited. When the last settlement was finalized, the ordeal had cost ABB $1.4 billion, almost as much as ABB had originally paid for the acquisition. Managers, however, tend to be immune to facts like these about acquisitions. Acquiring other companies, to them, is a sure-fire way of generating revenue growth and increases in that most abused metric of them all, Earnings-per-Share.

Channelling our ambitions into growth *targets* adds another dimension. In a strange way, risk is transformed when targets (or objectives) are introduced. Whatever risk was before, it now becomes the possibility that the target is not met. Falling short of the aspiration level is the risk that is likely to loom large over many decision-makers. There is a sense in which you, by deciding on a

---

[10]Aswath Damodaran on Acquisitions: Just Say No, CFA Institute Enterprising Investor.

target or aspiration level (which people now strive for), simultaneously decide on how people view risk (as deviations from that target).

Chasing a target has a powerful effect because it means that we are, psychologically speaking, in the domain of losses. It is a well-known result in studies on decision-making under uncertainty that people become more risk seeking when they have lost money. Our impulse is to win back whatever we have lost, and quickly at that. If we have to gamble in order to do so, we are going for it. Managers who are behind on targets are under the same spell, which explains why they become more reckless. As the saying has it, desperate times require desperate actions. We can use these perspectives to make sense of Volkswagen's fall from grace. Martin Winterkorn, the newly installed CEO, had announced in 2007 that the company's goal was to triple its US sales within 10 years, thereby becoming the world's largest carmaker. As Professor Amy C. Edmondson's account of the episode makes clear, these incredibly demanding goals had an instrumental role in shaping the behaviours that led to the firm's undoing (Edmondson, 2019, cited earlier).

Wells Fargo, a US bank, provides another fine illustration of how callous behaviours can become normalised under the influence of hard-charging growth targets. The NY Times described the company's sales targets as 'stratospheric' and stretched to the point of being mathematically impossible.[11] The employees came under heavy pressure to meet their targets and to squeeze more profits out of each customer. Unsurprisingly, the company engaged in a host of deceitful practices, such as creating phantom accounts for customers and tricking them into paying for products they had not asked for. According to estimates, some 3.5 million fraudulent accounts were created. The scandal erupted in 2016 when the firm's dubious practices broke the news. The company paid a heavy price in the form of the loss of a previously pristine reputation, and the Federal Reserve forbade the bank from expanding its assets until it had improved its culture and its internal control, a cap it still had not escaped from by early 2021.[12]

We have focused on growth in this section, but the point generalizes to other kinds of performance targets as well. Take profitability for example. Managers who are under pressure to reach a profitability target may be tempted to cut corners and compromise not only company policy but broader ethical

---

[11]Wells Fargo says its culture has changed. Some employees disagree. *The New York Times* (nytimes.com).
[12]Adding to the injury, penalties and lawsuits came in at over $2 billion. This may sound like a lot but is a paltry sum next to Wells Fargo's annual earnings, typically in the $80–100 billion range.

standards as well. Such breaches of norms and protocols can, in much the same way, lead to Swans arising from within. On-time targets, i.e. cases in which the bonus is conditional on a project or task being delivered within the specified time limit, put a similar pressure on managers. The oil spill in the Mexican Gulf caused by BP and its subcontractors in 2010 caused tragic deaths and an environmental disaster of enormous proportions. The accident had complex technological explanations, but it is clear enough from the subsequent investigations that the managers on site were under stress to meet profitability and on-time targets. The conclusion is the same as earlier: falling behind aspirations can induce stress of a kind that breeds desperation, and by extension behaviours that put the firm and its reputation on the line.

##  THE FEAR FACTOR

The previous section established that a disproportionate number of Corporate Swans can be traced back to aggressive targets and a never-mind-the-consequences pursuit of their achievement. A survey of company-made disasters reveals another pattern that recurs in an outsize number of cases: a culture of fear. In certain organizations, dissenting views are just not that welcome. Instead, a conformist culture of yes-people emerges. To use modern terminology, it is not psychologically safe to speak up. In extreme cases, the tone from the top is one of direct hostility to people who question the line taken. Edmondson (2019, cited earlier) provides several examples of firms in which a state of fear prevailed. The spirit of this approach is nicely captured in a quote by Volkswagen strongman Ferdinand Piech, who at the time was addressing a group of engineers:

> 'I am tired of all these lousy body fits. You have six weeks to achieve world-class body fits. I have all of your names. If we do not have good body suits in six weeks, I will replace all of you. Thank you for your time today.'

Fear would have been one of the dominant moods in Enron as well. It was company policy that every year, in what became known as 'the cull', 10% of the workforce was asked to look for another position in the firm, or otherwise be removed. The way to end up in that unfortunate group was to rank in the lowest tier in peer evaluations, a harshly Darwinian practice known as 'rank and yank'. That is, your colleagues (who you might normally think of as friends) might well be plotting behind your back to arrange your departure. That way, they could ensure that they could hang on for another year and have a greater chance of advancing in the system. It is not hard to imagine the detrimental effects on morale from having that threat constantly over one's head.[13]

A culture of fear provides another tail risk mechanism. This happens in two ways. First, people do not dare to speak up, so necessary discussions about critical exposures to risk are never had. There is silence where there should be a free exchange of ideas. According to Edmondson, this problem is widespread in the corporate sector:

> 'In one study . . . 85% of respondents reported at least one occasion in which they felt unable to raise a concern with their bosses, even though they believed the issue was important . . . the fear of speaking up can lead to accidents that were in fact avoidable . . . the free exchange of ideas, concerns, and questions, is routinely hindered by interpersonal fear more often than most managers realize.'

The second way that fear cultures create tail risk is that they foster unacceptable behaviours that are allowed to go on until some breaking point is reached. A desire to avoid the ire of a temperamental superior can drive people to consider actions they would normally think of as against their moral convictions. In this regard, we should be mindful of just how powerful the impact of culture really is. As Professor Zimbardo has demonstrated in his research, bad systems win out over good people – almost every time.[14] 'Evil', to use a word, is much more situational than most of us think, and much less about people being intrinsically good or bad. This was the conclusion Zimbardo drew from his infamous Stanford Prison experiment in 1971. In it, normal young men were randomly assigned into two groups, the prisoners and their guards. It did not take much more than a day for them to fall into their roles and completely internalize it. The guards took to humiliating and bullying, causing psychological suffering to the point where some of the 'inmates' broke down. It turns out that, when confronted with norms, authority and expectations from peers, we capitulate – just like that. Importantly, we do so even when it goes against our sense of morality. We like to think that we would be that hero with complete integrity, but we should stop flattering ourselves.

---

[13] In fairness to Enron, 'rank-and-yank' is considered a standard business practice by some and was championed by, among others, Jack Welsh, the legendary leader of General Electric.

[14] Zimbardo, P., 2007. *The Lucifer Effect: Understanding how good people turn evil.* Random House: New York.

No wonder then, given our eminent corruptibility, that corporate cultures are so powerful and can normalize behaviours that in retrospect look horrendous. This is fertile breeding ground for Corporate Swans.

 ## THE CHIEF EXECUTIVE SWAN

Interestingly, fear cultures and aggressive targets do not seem to be independent of each other. Where one is found, chances are that you will encounter the other as well. How can this be? The Wells Fargo case is instructive: when targets are stretched, this induces a keenly felt desire to reach them. Managers operating under these targets feel stressed and therefore more impatient with anything that seems to stand in the way. It is imperative to move forward, and quickly so. Therefore, at any sign of resistance these managers resort to a form of bullying. Anyone who vents a dissenting view or does not measure up will feel the heat, with the logical consequence that fear is instilled not only in the individual on the receiving end, but also in anyone who hears of this treatment. Word of such things quickly gets around and people adapt to it. A culture of fear now rules, spurred on by the overstretched targets. In this account, stretch the targets enough and a culture of fear is likely to follow.

An alternative interpretation is that none of them is causing the other. Instead, something else drives both. I will posit that this something is managerial power and desire for glory, in splendid combination. Let us first reflect for a second on the idolization of modern-day CEOs. CEOs, who tend to be of a forceful nature already, can wield a considerable influence on their organization in their capacity as top dog. In the age of the 'celebrity CEO', some CEOs capitalize on this sentiment and set themselves up as a kind of royalty. Corporate jets, for example, fall right into this category. Hardly justified on any economic or efficiency grounds, they serve another purpose: bolstering the mystique and star power of the executives.

According to the line of interpretation that I am proposing, forceful CEOs, bent on maximizing their personal wealth and prestige, hustle the BoD into giving them high-powered incentive schemes. The focus, nay obsession, of the CEO now becomes meeting these targets successfully, so equally powerful incentives are pushed down through the organization. The same CEO, being of a forceful nature and used to getting his or her way, takes poorly to criticism and negative feedback, so a culture of fear arises that discourages open debate and risk assessments. We have therefore been able to marshal a potential explanation of the association between aggressive targets and cultures of fear in terms of CEO personality.

A handy term for this personality, by the way, is narcissism. Narcissism refers to a personality trait characterized by certain core features that are stable over time and situations (as opposed to more situational moods like overconfidence). To begin with, narcissists are driven by a strongly felt desire to obtain the admiration of others and to stand at the centre of attention. They want to win, quite simply, and to bask in the glory of their achievements. Their sense of self-importance is highly exaggerated. The narcissistic individual, in turns out, engages in elaborate strategies in order to maintain a positive perception of himself or herself. Getting those accolades is at the very top of their list of priorities. Another core feature of this condition is that the narcissist is known to feel little remorse. They are therefore quite willing to pursue the goal of social praise even when it comes at the expense of others. Further underscoring the dark side of narcissism, such individuals have been shown to be more susceptible to mood swings and to react more strongly to negative feedback than others.[15]

The reason I go to such length to describe the narcissistic condition is that it is all over the place in the business community. CEOs with the kind of personality just described are more common than you might think, which makes it of interest to understand their role as we explore corporate tail risk. A corporate career offers all the visible markers of success narcissists so crave, and is lucrative enough to let them acquire all the shiny things that informs the world that they have made it. It has even been said that narcissism is 'at the heart of leadership'. In the words of Professors Rosenthal and Pittinsky (2006):[16]

'It is clear that a significant number of world leaders have grandiose belief systems and leadership styles [. . .] whose aspirations, judgments, and decisions, both good and bad, are driven by unyielding arrogance and self-absorption.'

Rising to the top of an organization is actually facilitated by a dose of narcissism. It takes a certain ruthlessness to make it in this world, so that, career-wise, the lack of remorse found in narcissists becomes an asset. Narcissism among corporate executives, furthermore, seems to be rising over time, perhaps

---

[15]The interested reader is referred to a recently published paper by yours truly, Emanuele Bajo, and Nicoletta Marinelli, Me, myself and I: CEO narcissism and selective hedging – Bajo, European Financial Management, Wiley Online Library. The references supporting the claims about narcissism made in this section are provided there.

[16]Rosenthal, S. A., and T. L. Pittinsky, 2006. Narcissistic leadership. *The Leadership Quarterly*, 176, 617–633.

fed by the power of social media. Which is potentially worrying, because wherever we find cultures gone wrong, there is a fair chance that it can be traced back to behavioural issues starting at the top.

Academic research has confirmed that firms with CEOs classified as narcissists behave differently than other firms.[17] For one thing, they do more acquisitions, presumably for the attention from analysts, bankers, and the business press that it generates, and for the thrill of the deal. They have also been shown to use derivatives in a more speculative fashion. Excessive usage of acquisitions and derivatives are generally not positives from a shareholder point of view. If that was not bad enough, they are also overrepresented in the context of transgressions of ethical norms, for example in the sense of being willing to tamper with financial accounts and engage in fraudulent behaviour (all in the name of reaching goals or presenting an image of success). Moreover, narcissism implies a much higher acceptance of risk and willingness to push limits than in the average person. The 'pushing the limits' part is key as far as the tail-risk mechanism is concerned, as is the way CEO narcissism can effectively shut down a climate of open debate. According to a study by Professors O'Reilly III, Doerr, Caldwell, and Chatman:

> '. . . narcissistic leaders have been shown to be more likely to violate integrity standards [. . .] have unhappy employees and create destructive workplaces [. . .] and inhibit the exchange of information within organizations . . . .'[18]

On the back of the empirical evidence, it seems safe to conclude that the narcissistic condition is having an impact on the way companies are run. We face the sobering thought that CEOs managing trillions of dollars of assets may be motivated primarily by a desire to win praise and extract compensation from their companies as a way to mitigate their insecurities. This is something quite different from the intrinsic motivation of building a fine business and may even be detrimental to it. Load such a person up with stock options, and other ambitious targets, and what happens? You have dynamite, because sharp incentives align with a deeply felt need to win praise and a chronic disregard for the

---

[17]The reader should know that researchers do not have access to medical records showing a formal diagnosis of narcissism made by actual physicians. They are instead classified based on publicly available information. The most common approach is to take, say, earnings calls, and count the number of times they use words like 'I', 'Me' and 'Myself' versus the frequency of 'We', 'Us' and 'Ourselves'. An example of this method is provided in Chapter 7. CEOs who constantly refer to themselves are assumed to be more egocentric and narcissistic.

[18]Narcissistic CEOs and executive compensation (escholarship.org).

emotions of others. With this explosive mix of narcissistic personalities and powerful incentives at the top, we should not be surprised that companies get themselves into trouble! To unsuspecting and underinformed directors this will show up in dramatic fashion, i.e. as a Corporate Swan, when it is all too late.

##  SWANS ON THE RISE

We have discussed at length some of the cultural aspects that are conducive to Swans from within. We will come back to these themes later in the book. However, taking the corporate perspective on Black Swans enables a completely different approach. This time, we bypass the mechanisms that create them, and instead look directly at some important corporate performance measure. The observation we are going to make is that any shock afflicting a corporation must ultimately pass through the filter of financial performance, which we can measure. Thanks to extensive reporting requirements, we have a great deal of data on how firms are doing. The main accounting standards, US GAAP and IFRS, establish a set of principles for how firms are to report on their income, cash flow, and balance sheets. While certainly firms have leeway in interpreting these standards, the basic framework is set. In fact, the standards came about as a way for creditors and other stakeholders to assess a firm's financial standing, and comparability across firms is a key objective. For many decades, much of this data has been systematically collected and organized into huge databases, which are the foundation for academic studies of the corporate sector. The Compustat database, for example, provides complete accounts for publicly listed US companies beginning in 1955.

Here is the thing: events that most of us think of as Black Swans in the sense of path-changing shocks on the level of civilization filter down to firms through a myriad of channels. Civilizational Swans may or may not affect the firm a great deal. It all depends on what the shock is about and what the firm's business model looks like. It takes some exposure to the practical consequences of the Black Swan for it to trickle through to performance. The fall of communism was undoubtedly an unexpected event of epic proportions that surely had an existential impact on firms in the vicinity of the former Soviet Union. But what was the impact material for a trucking company operating out of Des Moines? Probably none. The Great Recession in the late 2000s most likely did, however, because there was a sharp contraction in aggregate demand that spelled lower demand for most operating firms. For Corporate Swans, there have to be specific mechanisms that transmit broader shocks and connect them with performance. More concretely, a higher-level Black Swan has to affect either the firm's revenue-generating ability or its cost structure, because those two determine the profits the firm ultimately lives off (the shock may also affect expectations about *future* revenues and costs, in which case the value of its assets and liabilities registers a change).

Over the course of the decades for which financial statements data has been available, there have been a fair number of events that could be characterized as Black Swans. Likewise, competitive dynamics over the same period has produced a great number of company-specific disruptions. Did these events, we wonder, end up having a measurable impact on the corporate sector? Since we have the data, we just need a working empirical definition of Corporate Swans to be able to shed some light on the tail risk question. If a shock to performance is large enough, it meets the Black Swan criterion of having a massive consequence. What we need to add to that is that whatever caused it was largely unexpected, at least relative to the naive expectations of a director of the board, and we have what effectively amounts to a Swan. The ex-post rationalization is rarely a problem given how our brains excel at this chore, so we safely assume that this criterion is met.

To draw some insights about this kind of shock to corporate performance, I undertook a research project together with Nick Christie of Lund University and Nicoletta Marinelli of Universita di Macerata.[19] Any such investigation has to frame Corporate Swans in terms of a very specific, and arbitrarily chosen, aspect of corporate performance. There are many different ways to measure performance, such as gross, operating or net profit. Which of them makes most sense depends on your angle. The approach we took in this study was to look at large shocks to revenue. This is the 'top line' as far as performance is concerned, and not just in the accounting sense. Revenue is existential for a business. It is, at the end of the day, what a firm lives off. If you do not generate revenue in sufficient amounts, you have no business to speak of. The position taken throughout this book is therefore that the analysis of enterprise risk starts with the corporate top line.

In our study, we define a Corporate Swan as a year-on-year drop in revenue between 30% and 90%.[20] That is, it qualifies as such if the firm loses at least a

---

[19]*The Black Swan Problem: The role of capital, liquidity and operating flexibility* by Nick Christie, Nicoletta Marinelli, and Håkan Jankensgård, SSRN.

[20]The 90% cut-off is implemented to filter out observations that arise due to issues with the data. There is a certain over-representation in the extreme part of the distribution, which are unlikely to correspond to some kind of economic reality. In any case, drops in revenue that big may not be of much interest because there is not much of a business left anyway if over 90% of the business is gone.

third of its sales compared to the previous year. For most firms, losing such a large fraction of the business in the space of one year is indeed a serious issue. Therefore, the economic relevance of such a drop is not in doubt. But how can we make sure that the decline in revenue was really unexpected? After all, a firm could be in visible decline and corporate restructurings can create sudden breaks from the historical pattern. To ensure a high probability that the event was indeed unexpected, we excluded firm years in which there was a disposal of assets larger than 5% in the year we measure revenue or the year prior to it. In parts of our analysis, we also required that there be two consecutive years of positive revenue growth prior to the shock. When this stricter definition is used, our practical definition of a Corporate Swan is *a decline in revenue of at least 30% that comes on the back of two years of growth and is not driven by asset sales*. Again, this is not to suggest that serious spikes in costs and liabilities cannot constitute Swans. A similar analysis could be conducted targeting unexpected increases in costs.

Our reason for undertaking this project was a curiosity about performance tail risk and firms' resilience to it. There were a number of questions we felt deserved looking into. First, what is the lay of the land? What kind of tail risk are companies dealing with? Part of the project was therefore to map out and describe stylized facts about revenue shocks. Second, is the claim true that risk is on the rise, as is commonly argued? The way we define a Corporate Swan offers a possibility to look into this question. The rate at which large revenue shocks occurs (i.e. the fraction of firms experiencing one in any given year), when followed over a long time span, holds important clues as to whether the performance risk of the corporate sector is on the rise or not.

Taleb himself actually does not speak a great deal about whether Black Swans are increasing in frequency or severity over time. Instead, he appears to take it for granted, stating that 'sources of Black Swans have multiplied beyond measurability', noting that 'clearly, [natural disasters] have not changed much over the past millennium, but what have changed are the socio-economic consequences of such occurrences' (Taleb, 2007, p. 61). An earthquake today, Taleb goes on to note, wreaks much more economic havoc than in more primitive eras because of 'network effects', i.e. the interlocking relationships between economic entities. We also note that a story about risk on the rise is a convenient way of getting people to fret about something, and then selling them a solution to this scary problem. Consulting firm PwC, for example, matter-of-factly states that the world is getting riskier and that 'organisations are increasingly vulnerable as business becomes more complex, virtual and interdependent'.[21] It should come as no surprise that such a statement appears adjacent to an offer to provide services that mitigate such risk.

Contradicting such narratives about increasing risk, there is also evidence to support a different conclusion. In the broader scheme of things, war and violence, undoubtedly two of the biggest disruptors out there, have been in steady decline. This is the thesis of Steven Pinker, backed up by considerable amounts of data and investigations (Pinker, 2011).[22] Life appears to be, broadly speaking, more comfortable and less at risk of violence in the twenty-first century than ever before. Poverty and homicide rates, for example, are decidedly down when considered over the long haul, and in a material sense most of us are better off.

We could perhaps reconcile the two views by noting that they refer to different time scales. Pinker's perspective is the long haul, the entirety of human existence. Present-day people who argue that the world is getting riskier probably have the early phases of modernity as their reference point. World War II was a cataclysmic event, a big reset, from which the world emerged a different place. The decades that followed were about creating peace and prosperity for broad classes of people, and, at least as portrayed in US popular culture, an era of stability, family values, and optimism about the future. Compared with the tranquillity of the quaint-looking 1950s, the world might indeed seem more of a mess today, with several mega-trends breaking down the traditional and the familiar.

To address the claim that the world is getting riskier, therefore, we first have to agree which historical era we are comparing with. In our study, we decided to settle for 1955 as a reference point in order to give the 'risk-is-on-the-increase' crowd a fair deal (and because data before that was unavailable to us). To this end, we collected data on all firms in the US, outside the finance and utility sectors, between 1955 and 2020, and looked at the frequency of large revenue shocks over time. To understand this analysis, it is important to see that the variable of analysis is a binary indicator that takes the value 1 if the firm experiences a large revenue shock, zero otherwise. What we do is to compute the yearly average of this variable across all firms. This indicates the fraction of firms that experience a Corporate Swan in each year, or the 'Swan rate'. This series is plotted over time in Figure 2.1. In addition to the baseline

[21]*Enterprise Resilience: Boosting your company's immune system*, PwC. Retrieved at: gc-enterprise-resilience.pdf (pwc.com).

[22]Pinker, S., 2011. *The Better Angels of Our Nature: Why violence has declined.* Viking: New York, NY.

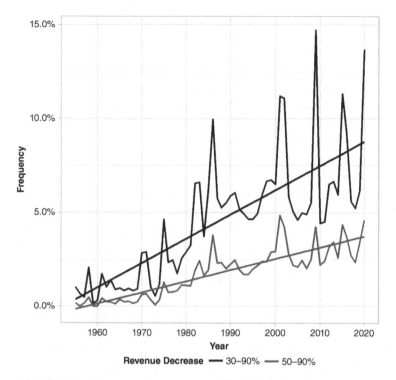

**FIGURE 2.1** Corporate Swan rates 1955–2020

30–90% definition, we also use a definition that targets an even more extreme part of the tail (50–90%, i.e. losing more than half or more of revenue over the course of a year.)

Figure 2.1 has a clear message: performance tail risk in the corporate sector is on the increase. The rate of Corporate Swans up until 1975 is about 1.2%. That is, out of 100 firms, in any given year, fewer than two of them, on average, experience a revenue shock of 30% or more. Therefore, we are definitely talking tail risk here. (We should not be misled by the seemingly wide range we use for defining a Swan, which is revenue falling between 30 and 90%. Losing a third or more of sales is an exceedingly rare event.) In the 2000s, in contrast, the same rate is 6.3%. For contemporary firms, that number can be seen as the unconditional likelihood of experiencing a Corporate Swan.

An important take-away from Figure 2.1 is that there are several cyclical peaks, coinciding with known recessions in the economy. This is entirely to be expected, as one of the key characteristics of recessions is a slump in aggregate demand, which shows up in our data as rapidly contracting revenue streams in the corporate sector. What is more, the incidence of cyclical peaks in the Swan rate seems to be increasing over time.[23] In fact, four out of the five years with the highest spikes are found in the 2000s.

In conclusion, Corporate Swans, measured in this particular way, are increasing over time, and the severity of cyclical peaks seem to be on the increase as well. To these findings one may object that the upward trend really only reflects a change in the sample composition towards smaller and riskier firms, such as those in the IT and biotech industries. This is certainly a valid argument. The industry that has seen the largest upswing in the Swan rate is the biotech industry, which barely existed in the first third of the sample period. However, we find an increase in the Swan rate in all the 10 industries investigated, including more traditional sectors like manufacturing. As for size, the median size in the sample is actually increasing over time (presumably reflecting ongoing consolidation through acquisitions), so the Swan rate is going up *despite* firms being larger.

We can also analyse Figure 2.1 from the perspective of the Moving Tail. Let us say we are a young analyst of the corporate sector in the late 1950s, too young to have experienced the deprivations of World War II and too clueless to look at any data that might have been available from the time before the war. For whatever reason, we decide to follow the Swan rate as an indicator of risk in the corporate sector. Starting out very low at around 1% or even below, in 1957 it jumps to over 3%. After that, it is back to around 1% for several years. We might think, in our youthful innocence, that 3% is how bad it really gets in an awful year. This goes on all the way to 1970, when again the rate shoots up to about 3%, confirming our understanding that this is where the tail is at. Then we are back to low levels until 1975, when there is another jump, this time to close to 5%. This is an eye-opener. The new observation is worse than anything we have experienced so far. In response, we calibrate our view of what tail risk is and move on. The new incoming data seems to validate our view all the way until 1983, when the rate exceeds 6%. Once more, we must conclude that it got worse than previously thought, but the increment was not shockingly large this time either, so perhaps we did not think of this as outside the realm of possibilities.

---

[23]More pronounced spikes are also implied by Taleb's connectivity argument about interlocking economic entities.

Just a few years after, however, the tail moves again, to almost 10%. This is actually quite shocking. It is almost twice our previous estimate of the tail. However, we collect ourselves and carry on. We gradually realize that the level of risk has shifted as it hovers at around 5% throughout the 1990s. This is apparently the new normal. Then, in 2001, it again shoots up to 10%, suggesting that this is indeed what tail risk is like these days. We have this thing figured out, yes. Then, in 2009, the tail moves again as the Great Recession shows its teeth. A whopping 15% of firms lose more than a third of their revenue in that year, representing a 50% increase in the worst outcome on record. Our appreciation of what tail risk is like again has to shift. At this point, our no-longer-so-youthful analyst is getting rather wise. The tail is actually in a flux, he realizes. Who knows what the future might hold. We had better, he is becoming convinced, keep an open mind and assume the tail can move again – even by a lot.

# CHAPTER THREE

# The Black Swan Problem

I N THE PREVIOUS CHAPTER, we developed some ideas about how Black Swans can be interpreted from the vantage point of firms that are in the business of creating value. In this chapter, we will deepen our understanding of what makes firms special. Central to a firm's existence is its strategy. A firm invests resources to get a strategy in place, which hopefully is executed well and generates profits over time. Any strategy comes with risk – sales may not materialize to the extent hoped for and costs could end up much higher than expected. In fact, any number of disasters can befall the business plan and lead to wildly different outcomes from those anticipated. If we grant that firms have the means to reduce that risk and protect their strategy, would they be right to do so? Can we assume that managing risk is a good, value-creating activity?

In thinking about these questions, a fallacy is often at work. People take it as a given that risk management is desirable because risk is perceived as inherently bad. We cheer at any proposal to do away with it, almost reflexively. However, managing risk means that resources have to be diverted from other uses. Risk management is rarely for free. This makes *over*-management of risk a clear possibility: investing more resources in risk mitigation than what would be justified by the fundamentals of the situation. It would therefore be helpful to have a framework for knowing when spending money on risk management is motivated. We need to find a way to assess whether the pros outweigh the cons. Risk management has a business case, as some like to put it, only if the pros are clearly larger.

##  TAIL RISK AND FIRM VALUE

By taking a little bit of time to understand the relation between risk and firm value, we will come to see the trade-offs involved when deciding on whether or not to commit resources to risk management. In the case of Black Swans, a curious paradox emerges as we ponder this issue. The paradox suggests that we might not be able to justify spending any resources at all, despite the massive and transformative consequences they might bring. So let us have a look at how we are supposed to determine firm value and see how the Black Swans might fit in.

In theory, the value of a firm is given by the surplus cash flows that we expect the firm to generate in the future, its free cash flows. What makes cash flows 'free' in this context is that all good investment opportunities have been fully funded. Free cash flow is thus operating cash flow less capital expenditure. We need to invest to ensure that the firm's competitive position is not undermined. Once investment needs have been addressed, any remaining surplus is free to distribute to investors. The chance of receiving such future surpluses (in the form of dividends) is why holding shares in a firm is valuable.

Once we have made a forecast of the future free cash flows from the business, we discount them back to present value using the relevant discount rate. Let us call this PV(Strategy), as in the present value of all the free cash flows that the strategy is expected to yield. A simple way to obtain PV(Strategy) is to use the formula $FCF_{t+1}/(k - g)$, where $FCF_{t+1}$ is our forecast of free cash flows, $k$ is the discount rate, and $g$ is the rate at which the free cash flows are expected to grow (in perpetuity). These are the three inputs required to value a business in the most bare-bones version of a discounted cash flow valuation.

Now, PV(Strategy) strictly speaking only captures the value of the business operations, i.e. the firm's commercial activities. In case the firm holds any financial assets, those are added to obtain *firm* value, i.e. the value of all assets that the firm controls.[1] For a firm whose only financial asset is cash, we can thus establish the following formula for firm value:[2]

$$\text{Firm value} = \text{Cash} + \text{PV}(\text{Strategy}) \tag{3.1}$$

---

[1] What I label 'firm value' here is called 'enterprise value' in valuation textbooks.
[2] Firm value is not the same thing as equity value. To complete the valuation of equity, we would subtract the value of any non-equity claims, such as debt, from Equation (3.1). We do not need to add that here to make the points we are about to make. In nearly all cases, maximizing firm value and equity value amounts to the same thing. A rare possible exception will be investigated in Chapter 7.

It is not immediately clear from the above reasoning how Black Swans, or any risk for that matter, affects firm value. Well, the thing is, we have to see that $FCF_{t+1}$ is not really supposed to be a single point estimate. It is the *expectation* of free cash flow, written as $E(FCF_{t+1})$. Taking the expectation means that we weigh many different scenarios, or possible outcomes, for future free cash flows *according to their probability of happening*. The procedure is to identify a set of scenarios we deem plausible, ask how the strategy would perform in those scenarios, derive a value of the free cash flows in that scenario and finally attach a weight to each scenario considered.

This is the point in the valuation process where we acknowledge that more than one thing can happen and that a firm with a significant downside risk is not going to command the same price as one without. If something major goes south, the stream of future free cash flows will not be the same as in the 'business-as-usual' scenario. When Netflix launched into its strategy of developing content in-house, for example, the success it eventually achieved was by no means a given. Any long-term investor pondering a purchase of the Netflix shares at the time would have to envision what a best-case scenario might look like and attach some weight to that. Likewise, he or she would have to attach a weight to a scenario in which the strategy flops.

Now we begin to see where risk might fit into this framework: it is a specific *scenario*, to which we have to attach a certain weight. One can entertain as many scenarios as one wants in such a valuation, but let us keep it at one and call it the risk scenario. When we introduce a risk scenario, uncertainty about future performance is formally acknowledged in the valuation process. With the two scenarios, the formula for firm value is now as follows:

$$\text{Firm value} = \text{Cash} + (1 - P_R) \times \text{PV}(\text{Strategy}) - P_R \times \text{PV}(\text{Risk}) \qquad (3.2)$$

In Equation (3.2), $P_R$ is the probability of the risk scenario happening. The difference compared to Equation (3.1) is that there is now a term called PV(Risk), indicating that there is a reduction in value relative to the base case. We assume that the risk that materializes with probability $P_R$ either decreases revenue or increases costs, therefore reducing free cash flow and by extension firm value. PV(Risk) captures the present value of all the lost revenue and additional costs that are associated with the risk scenario. As per the formula, the higher the probability we attach to the risk scenario, the lower the firm value will be. An important assumption in Equation (3.2) is that the strategy itself is unharmed by the risk event. Once the loss is incurred, the strategy goes on according to the original forecast. It is just that a certain amount of value is 'knocked off' as the firm deals with the consequences of the undesirable event.

To fix ideas, let us say we are looking at the prospect of a flooding that might occur at one of the firm's production sites, taking out productive capacity and increasing the cost of transportation under the new and more challenging conditions. There would be extensive repairs adding to costs for years to come. Since this would lower output and push up costs, free cash flows are reduced in this scenario relative to the baseline scenario. The term PV(Risk) captures the sum total of all the discounted free cash flows that we stand to lose out on if the flooding materializes. When coming up with a price we are willing to pay for this company, we have to consider how likely such an event is and the kind of damage it could inflict. If we want to turn this into a classic tail risk problem, all we have to do is increase the severity of the consequence and lower the probability of its happening. For example, what if the production site is crucial to the firm's entire operations and that the impact of the flooding would be extremely severe? According to the data, on the other hand, that kind of event only happens once every 100 years or so, so if we go by that data we would attach a low probability to it.

We now introduce a concept that will be useful to our story, namely *the cost of risk*. The observation we are going to make is that focusing exclusively on either probability or impact leads to errors in decision-making. We cannot just stare at the cost something would entail: we have to factor in how likely it is. Likewise, going only by probability would lead to the wrong prioritization. If a risk factor has a slightly lower probability compared to another one but much graver consequences, we would not be well advised to base our risk management prioritizations solely on the probability aspect.

The cost of risk is obtained by multiplying probability and impact. It is a summary measure of how much the presence of risk, here in the sense of uncertainty that would affect us negatively, reduces firm value. In our simple example, the cost of risk is given by $P_R \times$ PV(Risk). As we consider tail risk, the impact, given by PV(Risk), tends to go up, but the probability normally decreases (though not, mind you, as fast as the normal distribution would suggest). This means that tail risk has an ambiguous impact on firm value compared to business-as-usual risks. In fact, the same cost of risk can result from very different combinations of the two inputs (probability and impact). For example, a loss of \$1,000,000 with a 1% probability ('tail risk') has the same expected value as a loss of \$100,000 with a 10% probability. The cost of risk is \$10,000 in both cases. From a purely economic standpoint, this would suggest that we should be equally concerned about these two configurations.

The conclusion that we should treat tail risk identically just because the cost of risk is the same, however, would almost certainly be wrong.

The reason is that we may struggle to recover from the larger loss, but may escape relatively unscathed from the lesser one. The conceptual step we are taking at this point is to recognize that losses can trigger consequences and that those consequences can get disproportionally worse the larger the size of the loss. That is to say, there can be *collateral damage* from losses. Collateral damage, as the term will be used in this book, means that the firm's strategy *is* affected by the loss incurred in the risk scenario (contrary to our assumption in the stylized example above). If the loss is grave enough, it could spell trouble for the firm's ability to undertake actions that would be beneficial for long-term value creation. That is, there is a negative feedback loop from the short-term losses caused by the risk and long-term value as captured by PV (Strategy). It may not be a matter of simply paying some extra bills and then carry on as usual. Losses, if large enough, could be *disruptive*.

In fact, the case for corporate risk management in the academic literature rests on an assessment of such collateral damage. Very briefly put, the argument is that reducing variability per se is not enough to build a case. Risk management reduces downside risk, yes, which is good, but it simultaneously reduces upside potential, which is negative. A risk management tactic like hedging an exposure to market risk would therefore tend to reduce variability, but not the expected mean, since lower upside potential cancels out the benefit of less downside risk. Because of this symmetry, nothing is really gained in present value terms. In fact, you actually destroy value insofar as the hedge is costly (the bank will collect some fee or margin for providing the service). Unless, that is, you introduce the notion of collateral damage, in which case the effect of risk management is no longer symmetrical. By reducing variability on the downside, you now reduce the size of the loss *and* the collateral damage, which is enough to tip the scale in favour of risk management.

This is a crucial point, because it creates the asymmetry we needed to claim that risk management is valuable. Eliminating collateral damage is what places a premium on risk management. For practical purposes, it means that a firm must identify the scope for such collateral damage and design its risk management strategy to deal effectively with it. This, not reducing variability for its own sake, is the logic that should underpin an effort at managing corporate risk.[3]

---

[3]For an extended discussion of this logic, the reader is referred to *The handbook of corporate financial risk management* by Stanley Myint and Fabrice Famery (Risk Books, 2019).

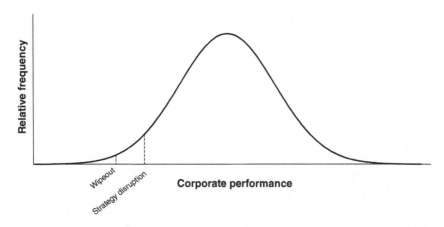

**FIGURE 3.1** Collateral damage

Because of the havoc it can bring to the firm's strategy, to the point of shutting it down for good, tail risk is qualitatively different from medium or small-impact risks. In the pages that follow, we will consider two types of collateral damage that are at the core of the academic literature on the topic and explore their meaning. The first is when the loss wipes out shareholders entirely and the second is when it disrupts the firm's strategy. In both cases a great deal of value stands to be lost, so they present good arguments why tail risk should be given more than a fleeting thought. The idea of collateral damage is illustrated in Figure 3.1, which depicts variability in corporate performance and connects it with harmful consequences that occur in the tail of the distribution.[4]

##  UNDERSTANDING WIPEOUTS

A wipeout in its purest form is dangerous and undesirable because it is game over. It is when shareholders either nail the boutique shut or hand over the keys to the creditors and say goodbye. Whatever happens next, they are not going to be part of it. It is the ultimate in the way of collateral damage if short-term variability in performance triggers this outcome. As we shall see, the firm itself can be wiped out and cease to exist (in a liquidation), but a shareholder wipeout can occur even in cases when it continues to operate as a going concern.

---

[4]I apologize to all risk philosophers for using a bell curve.

When the possibility of complete ruin is on the table, it very much ought to inform our risk management strategy. A primary goal of risk management is to make sure that the probability of ruin is zero or very close. The maxim 'First do not get wiped out' is a good one to live by for most of us. It is an argument that resonates with most people and may hardly seem to beg for an explanation. However, we should actually stop and think for a minute what ruin actually means and in what sense it is costly. For shareholders, I will argue, the main economic cost of a wipeout is that all possibilities of future success vanish.[5] The prospect of a rebound goes up in smoke. This is a significant point because in a world of wild uncertainty, there could be some chance of hitting it off in a different set of circumstances. The fact that our venture is not thriving under the current set of circumstances does not necessarily mean that it never could. The breakthrough may be around the corner, or at least there may be a shot at achieving decent profitability and make a living off something we enjoy. This possibility means that we want to live to fight another day. As long as we do not legally cease to be the owners of the equity, there is some hope.

The ultimate form of wipeout is a liquidation. That is when you know it is really over. At this point, the firm's assets are divided up among its various investors and creditors, all of who try to recover as much as they can. While differences exist between countries, the process usually follows some version of what is known as the absolute priority rule. According to this principle, the assets are distributed to investors according to the seniority (legal status) of their claim. The group of investors with the most senior claim get first dibs, typically secured lenders. If any value remains after that, those assets go towards the second-highest ranking group in terms of legal protection (senior unsecured lenders). Then junior unsecured debtholders. Any debts to derivative counterparties, suppliers, and so on, must also be settled. Shareholders are last in this queue. Virtually all other claims on the firm have a higher legal status in a liquidation, so the former owners of the company should consider themselves very lucky if they get anything. In the unlikely event that they do receive something, it is a one-off handout. Any value that came from the possibility of a rebound is gone.

---

[5]Firms have multiple stakeholders, and risk carries very different meanings depending on whose perspective you take. For employees, the demise of a firm can be nothing short of a tragedy: the loss of a steady income, camaraderie and identities. For communities and entire towns, it is the same. While the fates of various stakeholders should matter to decision-making, there also has to be an economic analysis of wipeouts from the owner's point of view, which is what we are focusing on in this book.

Bankruptcy is not the same thing as liquidation. A bankruptcy sometimes leads to a liquidation, but it does not have to be the case. A bankruptcy tends to happen in a situation where the burden of debt has become unsustainable, which is to say the operating cash flows are not sufficient to service debt obligations. This is the point where a mismatch between the size of the firm's liabilities and its ability to deal with them has arisen and become impossible to ignore. The firm's management may opt to file for bankruptcy, the purpose of which is to seek 'protection' from creditors, who otherwise might move in to start salvaging what they can by forcing a liquidation. Declaring bankruptcy is the preferred course of action if managers suspect creditors would do that rather than agree to renegotiate the terms and allow the firm to continue operating. Debtholders with claims backed by collateral of reasonable quality may believe that it is in their own interest to grab the assets they are entitled to as soon as possible, at least if they can recuperate most if not all the money owed them that way.

When a firm files for bankruptcy, it does not mean that the firm's business is worthless. It only means it is too burdened by debt to continue to operate and that it cannot, in the present set of circumstances, honour the terms in the loan agreement. There may still be value in the business, and with a restructuring of its liabilities, there is a chance it could carry on indefinitely. This is what the bankruptcy process is for: seeking opportunities for reconstruction that are beneficial, or at least acceptable, to all parties involved. This may involve selling a fraction of the firm's assets to repay debtholders; turning a debtholder's claim into equity (a debt-for-equity swap); deferring some of the payments on the loans; and so on. When a bankruptcy is filed, therefore, there is a window of opportunity in which solutions can be found such that liquidation is averted.

Interestingly, the value of equity often does not go to zero when a bankruptcy has been initiated, despite being the least prioritized claim in the liquidation that looms in the not-so-distant future. There are many examples of shares in bankrupt firms trading at a positive value after the firm has declared formal bankruptcy. This happens precisely because of the chance of a rebound, the notion that the future might turn out to be brighter than the present. The bankruptcy offers some breathing space and therefore a limited hope that some kind of favourable turn of events will materialize. One of the best things that can happen in this situation is that an interested buyer shows up, willing to bid for the business. Alternatively, even better, there may be more than one suitor and a bidding war ensues. In these cases, many claimants have a good chance of recovering most of their value. Perhaps even shareholders are able to get some piece of the business that emerges. There are many factors that together end up shaping the outcome in this unpredictable process where negotiations and deal-making go into overdrive.

When do firms go bankrupt then? One common way of thinking about bankruptcy is in terms of insolvency, i.e. when the value of the firm's assets fall below the value of its liabilities. When that happens, the value of equity is negative, suggesting that any claim on it is now worthless (such a firm is said to be "balance-sheet insolvent"). This might indeed appear like an unsustainable situation and grounds for starting a bankruptcy process. However, as long as we are talking about book values, this is not necessarily a very concerning situation at all. Book equity is quite an arbitrary thing, heavily affected by various accounting conventions. It can be completely detached from the cash flow-generating ability of the firm, which is what really supports the value of equity.

Often, negative equity has no clear-cut meaning and can go on for years. In fact, it has been observed in perfectly viable firms. Even a stellar performer like McDonalds has experienced negative equity, hardly what you would think of as a defunct entity. In their case, the situation arose due to large share buybacks and grossly understated book values of assets (the assets cannot be written up because of an accounting principle that favours conservatism). Even when negative equity occurs because of accumulated losses, it may bear little relevance for the firm's overall long-term prospects. We therefore tend to observe a deviation between the book value of equity and its market value equivalent, the 'market cap'. The market cap indicates what the market thinks the equity is worth; the book value of equity is what the accountant thinks it should be in the light of existing accounting standards.

Insolvency in a deeper sense is when the economic value of the firm's business is below the value of its liabilities. It is now 'under water' and, in a way, no longer viable as a business as it is not able to turn a profit on the current trajectory. It may well be tempting, then, to think that, for shareholders, it is time to call it a day and go home. It turns out, though, that the value of equity can be hard to kill off. Again, it is due to the option value that comes from the possibility of a rebound. If the best of all worlds comes true, the firm might spring back to profitability and create a surplus that is captured by its shareholders. As long as it has not been liquidated, that option is alive and will confer some value upon equity. As the probability of such a best-case scenario shrinks towards 5, 2, 1% or even lower, the value of equity quickly recedes towards zero. Somebody might be willing, however, to pay a penny for the equity just to see if some unexpected news arrives at the last minute. It only becomes nil when the probability is effectively zero, which is when there is no credible pathway to save the business in any scenario.

The above reasoning has the powerful implication that a wipeout can be a nightmare for equity holders. They could see their option value slip out of their hands in such a process. As long as the firm continues to operate, the option is alive. If the firm is operating at a loss, it means that resources are flowing out of the company. It is perhaps burning through cash on a daily basis. However, this tab is being picked up by debtholders. Every day that more cash is spent means that they will recover less once a liquidation is initiated. For shareholders, this is an attractive proposition in the sense that their option value, derived from the possibility of a rebound, is kept alive at the expense of somebody else.

As noted, a particularly dreaded combination is when the long-term value is considerable, but the bankruptcy process is started by some short-term disarray. What we are talking about here is a liquidity shock that makes the firm incapable of servicing its upcoming debt payments, which is a clear violation of the terms of the loan agreement. Then we have what is referred to as a default: not honouring the terms one has agreed to as part of the deal. Key among the promises made in any loan agreement is of course making the required payments on schedule. The legal powers of debtholders increase significantly when there is a failure to do so, and they may be about to look at liquidation as a possible way forward. Defaulting on a debt payment effectively puts the lender's finger on the trigger. They can negotiate and play nice – or pull the trigger. The managers and owners are no longer masters of their own fate and a bankruptcy and even liquidation may await. This is bad news if there is a significant option value that makes it interesting for owners to keep the business going.

A lesson in the meaning of wipeout and the whole bankruptcy process comes from Hertz, the car rental company, in 2020/21. When the C-19 pandemic erupted, the car rental business was among those most badly hurt. As travel slowed to a trickle, few people had any interest in renting a car. The operators of such fleets were left with the cost of maintaining them while the revenue stopped coming in. Hertz was a clear victim of the C-19 Swan. As so often, what went down was partly of the managers' own making. Debt-financed acquisitions had played a role in the lead-up, such that its debt was standing at $19 billion when the pandemic hit. As Hertz's revenue melted away, it found itself unable to make payments that were coming due on its loan facility. Strapped for liquidity, its managers saw no recourse but to file for bankruptcy, which they did in May 2020. Importantly, this did not mean that the value of its shares went to zero. Instead, some traders figured that the firm could emerge from bankruptcy with some value intact for shareholders. It was by no means an implausible idea that Hertz could make a comeback, since the bankruptcy took place at the depth of the pandemic, which, it was widely hoped, was going to pass. If the world emerged from the ordeal resembling its pre-pandemic self ever so slightly, it could be presumed that there would be travel again. The pandemic did not change the long-term attractiveness of the industry by nearly as much as its short-term performance.

What these traders may not have been fully aware of, however, are the hard facts about bankruptcy: that there is no guarantee that shareholders get anything. That they are completely at the mercy of other players when the bankruptcy dice is rolled. Luckily, however, as restructuring options were considered, various investor groups began taking an interest in taking over Hertz's operations. In what became known as the Centerbridge plan, so named after the firm that co-ordinated the bid, existing shareholders were initially left with nothing. If their bid went through, shareholders stood to be wiped off the map. Unsecured creditors, in contrast, were to receive equity in return for agreeing to cancel the debt – so any rebound potential would end up in their hands! Shareholders were petitioning to get what they felt was a fair share of the value that was inherent in the assets. As 2021 progressed and vaccination programmes were rolled out, there were indeed increasing signs of an economic recovery and a return of travel. However, such is the lot of shareholders in bankruptcy that their pleas that asset values had risen sufficiently to give them a share of the spoils did not necessarily count for much. In the end, shareholders did manage to prevail. Thanks to the prospect of a sharp economic recovery, the situation improved to the point where they were considered entitled to a stake in the post-bankruptcy firm. They were offered what amounted to a $8 per share bid, well over the price of about $2 at which the stock had traded throughout bankruptcy.

Despite the glimmer of hope afforded by the bankruptcy process and the unlikely reversal of fortunes in Hertz's case, the sad truth is that bankruptcy is very hard on shareholders. One study reported that in nearly 82% of bankruptcy cases, the existing shareholders were wiped out and received nothing.[6] The authors of the study summarized their findings:

'We find pervasive creditor control . . . in contrast to traditional views of Chapter 11, equity holders and managers exercise little or no leverage during the reorganization process. 70% of CEOs are replaced within . . . two years, and few reorganization plans (at most 12%) deviate from the absolute priority rule to distribute value to equity holders.'

---

[6]Ayotte, K. M. and E. R. Morrison, 2009. Creditor control and conflict in Chapter 11. *Journal of Legal Analysis*, 511.

At least in the US, the trend is that the position of senior lenders has strengthened over time, which has served to make bankruptcy a riskier proposition for shareholders. Consistent with this, the study further reports that there has been a substantial increase in the proportion of Chapter 11 cases that result in piecemeal liquidation or a going-concern sale. As noted, since senior lenders have the best hand in a liquidation, they may not fear it as much. Their priority is getting paid in full and liquidation may well accomplish that objective. In fact, the more 'over-secured' the senior lenders are, in the sense of collateral exceeding the notional value of their claim, the more likely it is, as per the study's findings, that liquidation is initiated.

What do we take away from these discussions? First, bankruptcy processes are heavily skewed towards wipeout and should thus be considered dangerous rather than a safe haven for reorganization. Second, a particularly spiteful outcome is a bankruptcy triggered by short-term liquidity problems. Equity is bound to have an option value if the shock is caused by temporary and external factors, rather than a failing business model per se, but this value could be lost in the process that unfolds when bankruptcy is initiated. Liquidity-driven bankruptcies caused by transient shocks is a recipe for maximum loss and regret. These are lessons that we will revisit later in the book.

 ## STRATEGY DISRUPTION

Surviving, most of the time, is a first-order goal of risk management. We do not just want to survive, though. We also want to thrive. To have a thriving business means that the strategy is implemented optimally, the way we intended, rather than some compromised, scaled-down version of it. This must hold true not just in the expected scenario, but in *all* scenarios, including the worst-case one. This is one of the key perspectives of this book – the idea of being able to do well, at least in relative terms, even if a tail risk scenario were to play out. What we mean by a strategy disruption is that a firm performs below potential so that the value that was within reach is not realized.

Now, a strategy can fail for many reasons. If a firm does not deliver the right mix of product, price and service in the eyes of its potential customers, that is a failure of strategy, not risk management. What is more interesting for our purposes is when the strategy is disrupted because some kind of shock unexpectedly occurs that hampers strategy execution. That is, the company is fundamentally viable but derailed by a tail risk event. This falls under the purview of risk management insofar as we define it in terms of making the necessary provisions for tail risk events. Crucially, then, a failing strategy *can* be a result of a failure to manage risk, as opposed to being based on a flawed business logic.

The point we are about to make is that a fully performing strategy is conditional on having the appropriate financial muscle. Put another way, a strategy disruption can occur for lack of financial resources. Corporate strategy books nearly always talk about strategy as if the financing of it is a non-issue and can be taken for granted. The money is just magically there and managers can manoeuvre for maximum advantage unbothered by such lowly issues. The reality is that carrying out a strategy translates into growing and innovating, which are things that require investment. If funds are lacking, something has to be scaled back and a lesser alternative chosen, which amounts to suboptimal execution.

What are the mechanisms through which a firm's strategy can be disrupted? One direct consequence of being financially weak is that otherwise good and profitable projects are left unfunded – and thus fail to materialize. Growth that would have been in the best interests of the firm never takes off the ground. Good projects are those for which we believe that the benefits, in the form of future surplus cash flows, would be larger than the cost of implementation. When we underinvest, future competitiveness is undermined and there is value left on the table.

One of the classic arguments in the corporate finance literature is indeed that risk management can be used to safeguard a firm's growth opportunities by making sure it has, at all times, the means necessary to invest. The theory, developed by Professors Froot, Scharfstein, and Stein in an article from 1993, views the firm's internal cash flow as a crucial source of financing.[7] For various reasons, outside financing is not always available on attractive terms, so our ability to invest may hinge on cash flow from operations.[8] Managing risk means to reduce the variability of these cash flows to make sure that they are sufficiently high to cover investment needs in as many scenarios as possible.

Pay attention to an important shift in perspective that has taken place here. The underinvestment theory posits that the risk management strategy be designed to minimize this collateral damage, not variability (gains and losses) in performance per se. An instructive practical application of this logic is described in a case study based on the currency hedging strategy of Merck,

---

[7]Froot, K. A., D. S. Scharfstein and J. C. Stein, 1993. Risk management: Coordinating corporate investment and financing policies. *Journal of Finance*, 485, pp. 1629–1658.
[8]Writing financial contracts can be a complicated process because of the risks involved. Information generally is unevenly distributed (in the firm's favour) and financiers suspect that the firm's managers do not always have their best interests at heart.

a US-based pharmaceutical company.[9] The company's managers argued that the source of its value-creation is its research and development (R&D), without which innovation would stagnate and performance decline. To them, therefore, a crucial component of thriving was being able to keep up the R&D programme. At the same time, a considerable part of the company's sales was generated from exports in foreign currency, which exposed it to exchange rate risk. The managers at Merck realized that if one or more of its key currencies would weaken against the US dollar, the shortfall in revenue might become severe enough to leave the company unable to fund its R&D. The value from managing currency risk would partly come from reducing the likelihood and size of disruptions to their R&D-based strategy. In the early 1980s, they had observed that a weaker dollar caused a reduction in R&D spending, which later translated into lower revenue growth. Risk management, the thinking went, could be used to reduce such collateral damage.

The underinvestment argument has been very influential in the risk management literature. A less acknowledged argument, but probably just as important, is that risk management can be used to protect against excessive cost cutting. A predictable response to a distressed situation is that a company starts looking for ways to trim costs. Some of these cuts may well be economically defensible on the grounds that, given the new and worsened outlook, it is not rational to keep them. It can go too far, however, if a firm cut costs in panic, in which case it is liable to create permanent damage to the business's long-term prospects. What is dismantled cannot always be pieced together and be as good as it was. When growth picks up, as it is statistically likely to do, a firm that has cut capacity too much is at risk of experiencing bottlenecks or shortages in production and distribution. First scaling down and then trying to rebuild is also associated with so-called 'adjustment costs', by which is meant the costs related to, for example, training new employees or paying severance to those fired.

In other words, adjusting the workforce to accommodate to varying degrees of business activity is costly and it may well be optimal to retain some costs in the face of a downturn. Risk expert Gary S. Lynch discusses a bottleneck in the supply of bolts resulting from harsh cuts a few years earlier:

> 'After the 9/11 attacks, the airline industry cancelled hundreds of orders and Boeing laid off 35,000 workers. As a result, Alcoa laid off

---

[9]Lewent, J. C. and A. J. Kearney, 1990. Identifying, measuring, and hedging currency risk at Merck. *Journal of Applied Corporate Finance*, vol. 2.4 (Winter).

41 percent of employees at its fastener division. More than five years later, the resulting bolt shortage was a direct result of these events.'[10]

Consistent with the notion that making adjustments to the labour force is costly, empirical studies show that firms engage in what is known as 'sticky cost behaviour'.[11] What is meant by this term is an asymmetry between how much companies reduce costs in response to a fall in revenue compared to how much costs are scaled up when revenue increases. When revenue grows, firms willingly commit resources to support the expansion. When revenue contracts, in contrast, there is less of an adjustment downward as companies prefer to maintain the cost structure relatively unchanged (in anticipation of future increases in business activity). This means that the model of cost behaviour in traditional textbooks – fixed versus variable costs – is not empirically well supported. Firms do not just mechanically scale costs up and down in direct proportion to the volume of business. Sticky costs can be thought of as a form of optimized cost behaviour given that there are adjustment costs and a general tendency for revenue to revert back to growth.

Importantly for our argument about thriving, in an article co-authored with Nick Cristie,[12] we find evidence suggesting that financial weakness matters to cost behaviour. According to our analysis, the most financially unconstrained group of firms engage in optimizing behaviour. Their response to a decrease in revenue is generally to maintain a large portion of their costs, whereas they are quick to commit more costs to support growth, i.e. sticky cost behaviour. Firms that lack financial resources, in contrast, have less sticky costs or even do not exhibit such behaviour at all. These firms apparently cannot afford to engage in labour hoarding and other efforts at maintaining operating costs at levels that would be optimal in the long term. They immediately start cutting.

To see what is going on, you can view cost cutting as a way to reduce bankruptcy risk. When you are weak and suffer a negative shock to your performance, you cannot accept the risk of running with higher operating costs because at this point bankruptcy is a real threat. In weak firms, there is *out of necessity* more scaling up and down of costs as business activity

---

[10]Lynch, G. S, 2009. *Single point of failure: The ten essential laws of supply chain risk management.* John Wiley & Sons: Hoboken, New Jersey.

[11]See, for example, Anderson, M. C., R. D. Banker and S. N. Janakiraman, 2003. Are selling, general, and administrative costs 'Sticky'? *Journal of Accounting Research*, 41, pp. 47–63.

[12]'Do financial resources determine cost behavior?' by Håkan Jankensgård and Nick Christie, 2020, SSRN.

fluctuates. What is more, we find evidence that firms that scale down costs more in response to revenue decreases have lower levels of cost efficiency. The interpretation is that, over time, adjustment costs accumulate and push up their cost level above those of peers.

The conclusion we draw in the study is that overly aggressive (forced) cost reductions indeed appear to be a real cost associated with financial weakness. Compared to underinvestment as a motivation for risk management, 'over-cutting of costs' has received too little attention. Cutting deep into the cost structure disrupts the strategy and prevents future thriving, because it means that the firm, due to capacity constraints, is bound to fall behind once growth resumes. Managers like to talk about how employees are their most valuable asset. However, when there is a shock to revenue, that asset can be badly bruised if there is a lack of financial resources.

There are more subtle mechanisms at work as well when we consider how financial weakness plays into strategy disruptions. Generally speaking, weak firms will find that the cost of doing business goes up. Various stakeholders will start having doubts about the firm's future viability and think twice about whether it is a good idea to do business with it. This idea can be summarized in the term 'stakeholder risk premium'. When faced with a higher risk, the normal thing is for people to want compensation for that. Firms that look weak and start to come across as 'high risk' are no exception to that rule. Stakeholders, looking after their best interests, will want to make sure that they are compensated for accepting the risk of dealing with you. This translates into terms and conditions that are more unfavourable than they would have been had you been in a more pristine condition. In summary, a too-high-for-comfort risk profile pushes up the cost of doing business.

Consider customers. It is a big deal if they start to shy away from a company because they do not like the way its long-term prospects look. A classic example of this is airlines. If it has become obvious that a carrier is on the ropes, many travellers will hesitate to buy tickets from it if an alternative is available. After all, the company may go bankrupt in the meantime and getting the money back is fraught with difficulties. Alternatively, would-be customers may fear that they might be stranded in the location they are headed to. There is thus a clear risk scenario involved and the rational response is to either book with someone else or demand terms that are good enough such that it is worth it to take the gamble. Either way, it translates into less revenue for the airline, because offering terms that are more generous translates into lowering the price and/or increasing the perks.

Another manifestation of the stakeholder risk premium is when key employees choose to quit. Especially in small and technology-intense firms, it is hard to create success without top talent to drive your innovation. Sensing that risk is going up because money is becoming scarce, talented individuals might decide to manage their personal risk by walking out and switch to a more promising environment. According to serial entrepreneur and presidential candidate Andrew Yang (2018, cited earlier), it is a truism in venture capital that when things start to go badly, it is the best people who leave first. Such departures send the firm down a death spiral: without its most precious talent, selling the firm's prospects to financiers will become even harder and the decline accelerates.

##  ALL YOU ZOMBIES

The bottom line is that when financial resources wear thin, things are no longer done on the company's own terms and it starts to weigh down on strategy execution. Actions become geared towards putting out fires in the short term rather than building value for the long term. In this respect, firms are no different from people, who, studies show, do not thrive when money is an issue. Thin economic margins generate a mindset of scarcity (as opposed to abundance) and we simply do not perform at our best if we are under chronic stress, fearing what tomorrow might bring. Our minds are focussed on scraping by rather than the realization of long-held dreams or general self-improvement. According to Yang, who surveys the evidence on the relation between economic resources and human flourishing:

> 'Scarcity has a profound impact on one's worldview . . . A culture of scarcity is one of negativity. People think about what can go wrong . . . . Tribalism and divisiveness go way up. Reason starts to lose ground. *Decision-making gets systematically worse.*' (Emphasis added. Yang, 2018, cited earlier.)

The truth seems to be that when financial resources are chronically low, we operate below potential. When the buffers are increased, the situation improves on all these dimensions. With sufficient margins, we take steps towards what might be called thriving. There is nothing to suggest that the same would not be true for firms.

In fact, there is a whole category of firms that seem stuck in this low-margin, unproductive mode. They are the so-called 'Zombie' firms. They too are just scraping by. The predicament of Zombies is that, because they lack resources, they cannot invest for the future. Capital expenditure is crowded out by the need to meet debt payments, so there is little or no money left for growth. This is another kind of self-fulfilling downward spiral: due to a persistent lack of investment, the firm ends up being less and less competitive. Instead of being finished off, however, they go on existing in a Zombified state (as in neither dead nor alive). As long as the firm does not default on its interest payments, the bank will be content to refinance the loans (again, they have less interest in pursuing upside potential through capital expenditure than shareholders).

There is actually an even deeper level of Zombiehood. A true Zombie does not even manage to cover its debt obligations on a cash flow basis. To survive, they need to be continually shored up by their banks, who postpone instalments and accommodate in different ways. Why would a creditor do this rather than go for liquidation? One reason is to avoid having to write off the loan from their books, which would deplete their equity and endanger their capital ratios. This dynamic has been a chronic problem in Japan, where large amounts of bad debt have been propped up. Ultimately, these unproductive assets become a drag on the economy as the normal competitive outcome of bankruptcy and market share loss does not happen. Stronger competitors therefore earn less than they would have in fully competitive markets and accordingly invest less, which holds back economic growth.

There may not be much in the current business plan to suggest that our firm would be engaging in harsh cuts to investment and operating costs, or face increasing costs of doing business from being perceived as too risky. We may feel we are at some distance from all that. However, this is what tail risk can change. Set loose a Black Swan and some of these prospects could suddenly start to look very real.[13] An article by Bloomberg expressed precisely this concern in relation to the fall-out from the C-19 pandemic, noting that a large number of public firms in the US, including many household names, were unable to generate enough cash flow to cover their interest payments during 2020. While noting that many were likely to bounce back once a recovery got underway, there was a worry that the borrowing spree they resorted to in order to stay alive would doom some of them to Zombiehood:

'More than 200 corporations have joined the ranks of so-called Zombie firms since the onset of the pandemic. . . . Not only are firms staying in a zombie state for longer than in years past, but of the roughly 60% of firms that do manage to ultimately exit zombie status, many nonetheless experience prolonged weakness in productivity, profitability and growth, leading to long-term underperformance.'[14]

---

[13]Black Swans unleashing Zombies is a nice double metaphor.
[14]'America's Zombie Companies rack up $2 trillion of debt', Bloomberg.

##  THE AFFORDABILITY ISSUE

In our formula for firm value we assumed that the firm has some cash and we are now going to assume that it can use some of that cash for risk management purposes. We use the term risk management generically in the sense of anything that has the effect of reducing the variability of performance (and any associated collateral damage). In our earlier example, this might mean investing in protective gear that makes the impact of a flooding less severe or coming up with a business continuity plan that helps us deal better with its consequences. The effect of risk management, if well executed, is to lower the probability and/ or consequence of the risk scenario, and any collateral damage implied by it. By way of our formula, this increases firm value.

A reduction in the cost of risk is of course welcome. What is not so welcome is the fact that we have to spend money to achieve it. This expenditure on risk management shows up as a reduction in the cash balance, which produces an off-setting negative effect on firm value. It is rarely presented as such, but risk management is actually an investment decision. We accept costs and efforts now in the hope of experiencing fewer bad outcomes in the future. Oddly enough, the most widely used risk management frameworks often depict risk management as something that we can just decide to do at practically zero cost. Identify a risk, assess it, and then go right on to mitigate it. This is job done – on to the next. This representation of risk management is clearly not realistic in many cases. True, low-cost alternatives may be available that we simply had not thought of before, but solutions that are effective in reducing risk are usually the more expensive ones. If it were not so, one might presume that we would have chosen to implement it already.

The investment aspect makes risk management problematic because money flows out of our pockets here and now. When we use some of our cash to engage in risk management, we record an expense that shows up in our income statement in this period, weighing down on the profitability margins that corporates obsess about.[15] The basic problem we encounter is that the benefits of risk management lie somewhere in a possibly distant future and they may not materialize at all. Implementing risk mitigation actions, in contrast, generally pushes the cost of doing business up *in the short term* in a very tangible way.

---

[15]In some cases, the firm may be able to capitalize and amortize the expense, in which case its effect in the income statement is spread out over a number of future periods.

The aversion to pay upfront for risk management is plain to see in the oil and gas industry. The strategy of cash-financing put options is, despite its theoretical attractiveness (manage downside risk, keep upside potential), a rarity. In fact, according to a study of derivative users I undertook, this strategy is utilized by less than 10% of firms that engage in hedging.[16] Imagine a company that regularly buys put options to protect against tail risk, just in case. This will generate a cash outflow every quarter as the position is rolled over. Soon enough this outflow will start to grate on some of the managers: 'We keep paying this money but never seem to get anything in return.' At some point, a drive to save costs will be initiated and one of the first and easiest actions to implement will be to halt the option programme. The company is back to living with tail risk exposure.

In this sense, the problem of under-management of tail risk faced by corporates is similar to the predicament of contrarian investors. They have to put up with relatively small but continuous losses for a possibly very long time. It becomes, in the end, psychologically heavy. One has to keep defending the strategy, quarter in and quarter out, in the face of accumulating losses. All the while, the stock market may be soaring, further testing the patience of the investors who stick to the contrarian strategy. More than a few have simply given up, as the pressure gets too hard to sustain. Likewise, insurance programmes and business continuity plans are tempting early targets in cost reduction initiatives.

One of the key themes of this book is that there is a persistent tension between tail risk management and (short-term) efficiency. Managing risk pushes up costs and therefore lowers profitability. Not managing risk, on the other hand, means that we may occasionally suffer heavy losses and disruptions. One way or the other, risk costs money. We look for cheaper alternatives and ways to save costs, but this may simultaneously increase the risk of a serious disruption in the future because we become less robust.

Global supply chains provide us with a useful setting for exemplifying the balancing act between efficiency and vulnerability. There is a distinct drive towards minimizing costs in these networks of interacting firms and intermediaries. The Just-in-Time philosophy that has guided supply chains over the last decades can be seen largely as an attempt to do away with inventories. Rather than stocking up on materials and goods, various modes of transportation

---

[16]Croci, E., A. del Guidice and H. Jankensgård, 2017. CEO age, risk incentives, and hedging strategy. *Financial Management*, 46, pp. 687–716.

become moving inventories. This approach has helped drive the cost of the end product down, as some of the savings from reduced inventories can be passed on to the customer. So has a certain callousness with respect to people and the environment. Many shipping companies are somewhat shady outfits, some of whom duck their responsibilities as best they can by searching out the least restrictive regulatory regimes and the cheapest labour. 'Flags of convenience' imply that safety regulations and environmental concerns are rock bottom. If it were not so, things would be more expensive!

This is the affordability issue. There is a reason why you can buy plastic toys from the other side of the world for next to nothing in your local shopping mall. However, the ferocious drive to reduce costs has the inevitable effect of making supply chains more fragile and therefore increasing risk. Risk can be suppressed for a while, but is bound to pop up somewhere – eventually.

The car industry got a taste of such fragility when it ran into a severe shortage of semiconductor chips during 2021, partly by its own making. The carmakers, anticipating a rapid drop in demand when the C-19 pandemic hit in 2020, cut orders in order to slow down production and minimize the inventory of unsold cars. These cancelled orders, done in the name of saving on inventory costs, left the chip producers to deal with the consequences of uncertainty. When demand recovered faster than anticipated, a severe bottleneck in the supply of chips had developed, not least because consumer electronics experienced a significant boost in demand due to the pandemic. This chip shortage led to economically very significant production cuts among car companies, with some of the larger ones announcing negative effects on earnings for 2021 running into billions of dollars.

Note that there is a legitimate concern about profitability here. A firm that goes for maximum risk management effort at any turn will push its costs up to a level where it is no longer able to be competitive. It has risk managed itself out of business! The problem is when it is taken too far in the other direction. Pushing costs lower will, if pursued far enough, make it more vulnerable and ultimately invite disaster.

We would like firms to approach the efficiency-vulnerability question with an open mind and genuine concern about long-term viability. However, there is a heavy skew in corporate incentive systems that produces a temptation to skip on costs for the sake of short-term margins. Because of these incentives, profitability targets in the near term can easily take precedence over any concern about long-term sustainability. This goes a long way towards explaining the general problem of undermanagement of risk or why firms underprepare for business interruptions. Risk expert Gary S. Lynch succinctly summarizes this phenomenon:

'Many managers adopt the attitude that risk management is complicated, impacts the bottom line, and they are prepared to take the risk that disaster will not take place on their watch.'[17]

Due to the affordability issue, paying too little attention to tail risk is a built-in problem in the corporate sector. It amounts to a form of myopia, the ongoing prioritization of short-term objectives, with the result that we underinvest in risk management that would support long-term goal achievement. When we ignore tail risk, i.e. do not even stop to consider it, we get the trade-off wrong. It is as if we optimize under an assumption, or hope, of 'fair weather' variability rather than the wild uncertainty of the real world. When we systematically underinvest in risk management, we should expect an increase in the cost of doing business over time, as risk eventually makes itself felt. Unattended vulnerabilities will gradually erode the firm's competitiveness because peers with a more balanced approach to risk management are less prone to disturbances. Time is the enemy of firms that ignore risk in pursuit of short-term margin improvements.

The undermanagement problem gets worse the lower the perceived probability of the events, precisely because the supposed benefits become more vague and easy to dismiss. Sometimes the tail risks recede out of view altogether and the myopia spills over into outright blindness. All the biases reviewed in Chapter 1, such as the optimism, overconfidence, storytelling, ego-centrism, and so on, also put up a wall of resistance to tail risk management. It is important to recognize that for corporates, the affordability issue by itself creates a significant bias to the same effect, this time on the organizational level rather than the individual level. The cost issue is what makes firms vulnerable to Black Swans. Cost, to a fair extent, explains vulnerability.

Many factors – incentives and biases – thus work against any effort at proactive risk management of tail risk. This is a pity, because that is the only kind of risk management there is. While the term 'proactive' might suggest that there is such a thing as 'reactive risk management', that conclusion would not be wholly accurate. The opposite of proactive risk management is putting

---

[17]Lynch, G., 2008. *At your own risk: How the risk-conscious culture meets the challenge of business change.* John Wiley & Sons: Hoboken, New Jersey.

out fires, or 'crisis management', i.e. a situation in which we are no longer masters of our own fate. In panic mode, nothing comes cheap, bargaining power is weak and execution is often rushed and inferior.

In fact, a peculiar paradox of risk management is that it gets costlier the deeper in trouble you are. A series of academic studies have neatly conveyed this point in the context of the corporate hedging decision (which is the proxy for risk management in these studies). Their starting point is that a hedging position has to be financed somehow, either through existing cash (when you buy options) or by using collateral that placates the counterparty's fears about credit risk (when you sell options or enter forward contracts). For a weak firm, capital markets will be increasingly closed and its internal resources (cash and collateral) will be increasingly scarce. When this is the case, risk management comes with not only transaction costs, but an opportunity cost as well. Taking scarce internal resources and using them for risk management means that there is less available for other uses. What if, for example, the firm still has some good investment projects it would like to pursue? Then, if you use some of your remaining internal resources for risk management, you are going to have less money to invest. The conclusion in these studies is that we should actually expect to see more risk management in healthier firms with more abundant cash and collateral – not in the ones that seemingly need it the most!

This paradox is illustrated in Figure 3.2. As the financial condition worsens, the cost of executing risk management goes up. While a firm that is doing supremely well and has abundant resources may not feel very compelled to worry extensively about risk, there is a 'sweet spot' where the firm has clear incentives to engage in proactive risk management, yet can still do so on good terms because its prospects are not in doubt. A bit to the right of the sweet spot, there is a point of no return, where the cost of risk management is already starting to bite as it crowds out other activities.

 ## THE CONUNDRUM

In this book, while my usage of the terms overlaps, I try to maintain a distinction between tail risk and Black Swans. Tail risk concerns a situation where the risk is thought to be of the low-probability high-impact sort. The term also implies that the risk is known, in the sense of being identifiable with relative ease. Most people in the organization would agree that there is a possibility that something like that could happen, but also that it is very unlikely. The tail risk problem is that we have a tendency to neglect to take actions to address it even

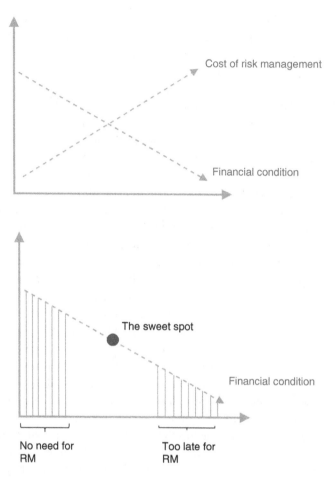

**FIGURE 3.2** The risk management paradox

when doing so has, objectively speaking, a business case. To see what I mean by business case, imagine a well-informed decision-maker who is free of biases and whose view is not distorted by incentive systems. Having a business case means that such a person, after carefully weighing pros and cons, would conclude that mitigation makes sense even after considering what that mitigation would cost to implement.

Black Swans are qualitatively different from tail risk in three main respects. The first refers to the purest form of Black Swans, the ones that are truly inconceivable to just about any person alive. If nothing in our collective experience points convincingly to such a phenomenon being possible, it is generally not part of our mental processes. In this category, we may also include phenomena that we formally acknowledge as such, but rate as impossible. (The phenomenon is either truly inconceivable or we can conceive it but do not grant it as possible.) The second way in which Black Swans are different is when we have identified and assessed a risk and believe ourselves to have a grip on it, only to wake up and realize that the tail shifted – in a big way. This is the Moving Tail: while we may acknowledge the existence of a phenomenon and that it could affect us, we get the magnitude of the consequences wildly wrong. (We can conceive the phenomenon as such but not the full extent of its consequences.) The third point of differentiation is that our ignorance, naiveté and laziness may convert what could have been tail risk into a Black Swan, adding surprise and consternation to an already bad situation. (The phenomenon is not inconceivable, we just did not conceive it.) These are the 'unknown knowables'. Recall the point that Black Swans occur relative to expectations, which depend on information and knowledge. The lower a firm sets the bar in those respects, the more Swan-filled its existence will be. If we do our homework, it is tail risk, but if not, it will take us in like a Black Swan.

The difficulty of conceiving extreme events is one stumbling block in our quest to survive and thrive in a world of wild uncertainty. Another is that we cannot easily buy products suitable for tail risk management even if we do the homework, at least not in the sense of using derivative or insurance markets for risk transfer. There is no market for the transfer of risks related to inconceivable events with massive consequences, and, unfortunately, nor is it possible to write contracts that transfer general performance risk to an insurer. It would have been helpful if we could have insured against the risk of, say, a very large and destructive decrease in cash flow, but insurance tends to be available only for well-defined contingencies that are reasonably beyond the influence of the party buying it.

Of course, there are other ways to manage risk other than transferring it. Going back to our formula for firm value, we still have the cash position. Even if we cannot use it to implement risk mitigation, the cash balance is itself a form of risk management device. Firms with plenty of cash can afford to self-insure, which means that the cash we have at hand covers any loss that might occur (as opposed to risk transfer, where it is the cash-at-hand of the counterparty that takes care of it). This seems to offer a way forward that solves the problem of having to *act* here and now. There is no need to shell out expenses on an ongoing basis, just pile up some cash and do not give it any further thought. From this perspective, it seems like the ideal way of managing tail risk.

A big pile of cash is indeed a nice way to achieve a care-free existence. Except, of course, that this strategy also comes at a price. It would have been surprising if it was that easy, right? The problem is that most of the time the cash just sits there. In the terminology favoured by market participants, the cash is not 'working', in the sense of it being unproductive. If the money instead were returned to investors, it could be put to better uses by investing in promising projects elsewhere. Comparisons of returns are tricky because of the need to adjust for differences in risk profiles. Cash generates a very low income, but it is steady. Commercial projects may promise much higher returns, but they are also riskier. Difficulties in making fair comparisons notwithstanding, let us assume that cash earns 2% whereas the typical return available out there at a not-too-high-a-risk is 8%. The spread of 6% represents an opportunity cost. Keeping cash will also manifest itself in the corporate accounts as a lower return on assets (ROA), one of the most widely used metrics for assessing performance. From a shareholder point of view, a large cash balance comes with additional dangers. The firm's managers may use it to make acquisitions! This is rarely good news, and when acquisitions happen merely because cash is bountiful then we have a real problem.

To escape some of the consequences of Black Swans, a firm can also avoid debt financing. In fact, if the firm has no debt, there cannot be any default-driven wipeout.[18] Again, the seemingly perfect solution of all-equity financing comes with its own set of disadvantages. This time, it is the Return on Equity (ROE) that suffers. This is a highly relevant metric for shareholders as it indicates the profitability of their investment in the firm (as opposed to the profitability of the entire firm, which ROA captures). There is a mechanical and negative effect on ROE from increasing the proportion of equity financing because the earnings of the company are spread out over a larger equity base.

Again, as with excessive cash, there are indirect effects from debt avoidance that also point to lower performance. Feeling safe and protected by a big layer of equity means that cost discipline and efforts to create profitable growth could take a turn for the worse. The presence of risk actually has a benefit in that it sharpens performance, because there is less room for mistakes. When there is significant risk, execution has to be better. This is a general principle, true not just in the context of running a company but in all areas of life.[19] The threat of

---

[18]Even in the absence of debt, the firm can of course end up in bankruptcy due to a failure to honour other contractual commitments, such as trade payables.

[19]Not long ago I watched my son go for some soup at the dinner table. He did not push his plate up to the casserole dish, despite having been told to do so incalculable times. While this saved him the trouble of moving the plate, risk was now higher since he had to move the ladle across the table with soup in it. It could work, but it would take better focus and execution than normal. This did not happen and we had to mop the soup off the table. Either accept more effort (and/or cost) or live with the risk.

a wipeout keeps managers sharp. Finally, there is of course the tax advantage from debt – the firm can deduct interest payments from taxable income but not dividends. There are therefore several undesired side effects from these broad, generic strategies aimed at keeping the firm out of harm's way.

To summarize, the Black Swan problem is created by an unfavourable set of incentives and biases that discourage a serious discussion about tail risk, let alone actions that would serve to mitigate it. There is a fundamental lack of visibility with respect to these abstract possibilities, so any benefit from risk mitigation is heavily discounted by decision-makers. What we cannot visualize properly, we tend to neglect. When we struggle to describe something, to put together a coherent picture of what it might be like, we do not internalize its consequences. There are general risk management strategies – use cash, avoid debt – that help us deal with tail risk without having to spend organizational capital trying to come up with elaborate countermeasures. However, they also come at a price in the form of reducing ROA and ROE. In the perennial struggle between short-term efficiency and tail risk mitigation, the former tends to win out, which leaves us vulnerable.

The Black Swan problem is therefore that firms fail to visualize and prepare for improbable high-impact events and that generic strategies for risk management, i.e. those not targeting any specific event or risk factor, reduce return on equity in the vast number of scenarios in which no calamity happens. The later chapters of this book will be about how we can make some progress on this issue and try to devise some tactics for mitigating the problem by recognizing the factors standing in the way. We need to use the limited mental bandwidth and resources available for tail risk management to the greatest effect possible.

Before we move on with that, though, we cannot help but note that all three points of differentiation mentioned earlier – truly inconceivable events, tails in flux and self-imposed Swan blindness – have something in common. It is that we assign a probability of *effectively zero* to the outcome in question. When we assign a probability of zero to something, an interesting thing happens: the cost of risk also goes to zero (because it is the product of probability and impact). When the cost of risk goes to zero, there is nothing to justify risk mitigation actions! The implication would be that firms are right not to invest in measures to prepare for unknown risks with massive consequences. We are, it might seem, relieved of duty.

While the conclusion seems to follow an impeccable logic, the conclusion that it is okay just to shrug one's shoulders and carry on as usual does not seem quite right. Curious about how academics would respond to this conundrum,

I sent an email to colleagues and friends, all professors of finance or expert-level professionals. The question I posed was as follows:

'Firm value is the expected (probability weighted) free cash flow discounted at the cost of capital. Black Swans are impactful events outside our collective imagination and are therefore attached a probability of zero. Therefore, Black Swans do not affect firm value and firms are not justified in spending any resources in preparing for such events.

Is this correct? Please explain your answer.'

I will come back to what the professors answered in the next chapter. The background for my question was that, in the several hundred valuations that I have seen, Black Swans or tail risk have been incorporated into the analysis a grand total of *zero times*. Not even once. It simply does not seem to be a feature of the standard valuation process as taught in business schools around the world. One is in fact quite lucky to get any scenario evaluated other than the forecast itself (i.e. the 'base-case' projection). Many valuations are lightning-quick applications of rote formulas. Given this lack of interest in tail risk, there seems to be no mechanism whereby firms would be rewarded for their efforts to counteract severe but presently unknown events.

To see what I mean, imagine an airline in early 2019, just prior to the C-19 pandemic. What if they communicated to the rest of the world that, 'hey, we are going to hold back on growth for a while and refrain from paying dividends. Instead, we will build up some cash, just in case, you know, something inconceivable happens'. Would the market, robbed of its lifeblood (growth and dividends), really have bestowed a higher valuation on this company, praising its prudence and sound policies?

Most of what we know about the stock market suggests that the answer to that question is 'no'.

# CHAPTER FOUR

# Greeting the Swan

I F YOU ARE GOING to operate a business, it is surely a good thing to be realistic about the fact that we live in a world of wild uncertainty. Remaining ignorant about tail risk is not an acceptable state, as it implies acting as if the world is more benign than it really is. It furthermore implies us being caught by surprise and consternation when something serious goes down, placing us firmly in the 'sucker' category. The first order of business is therefore to make sure that this does not happen. This is what 'Greeting the Swan' is about: facing up to and getting realistic about the wild nature of randomness in this world, and seeing more clearly the organizational biases that get in the way of having reasonable conversations about tail risk. It is also about seeing the trade-off that exists, on a broad level, between moving towards a goal (i.e. perform) and devoting time and attention to preparing for outlier events.

Being Black Swan aware is not the same thing as being fatalistic. The attitude that 'yeah crazy stuff can happen, what can you do about it' is not especially productive. Instead, a Black Swan aware organization means that its key decision-makers take an interest in tail risk and explore its ramifications for corporate strategy. As importantly, they must not think the job is done and pat themselves on the shoulder just because they have implemented tools that create an impression of control over risk. That is to step right into the Platonic fold. Promoters of risk management tools like to sell them as foolproof fixes to all your problems, which is inviting trouble when wild uncertainty is what we are dealing with.

Greeting the Swan means that the organization should embrace tools that improve the firm's ability to make tail risk more 'visible' to the firm's decision-makers. Importantly, however, it has to remain humble with respect to the limitations of the knowledge thus generated. We walk a fine line between finding simplified representations of the world that help us function and becoming overconfident from their seeming perfection.

 ## RANDOMNESS REDUX

The first step on the journey is to reconcile ourselves with the fact that we indeed live in a world of wild uncertainty. That is, we need to get our basic view of randomness in this world right and start taking for granted that large discontinuities occur much more frequently in the world than what the lull of our everyday lives would have us believe. We must avoid the temptation of thinking that long stretches of calm and routine cannot be punctured at the drop of a hat. Perhaps our experience as an organization so far has been one of relative stability and prosperity. It would be easy to take this as confirmation that we are beyond the ordeals affecting lesser firms. The Swan-astute manager never assumes things like this. Taking past stability to suggest a benign world and a carefree future is precisely what Taleb warns us against. Continuity and prosperity may well be highly likely and what we plan for, but it is not an excuse to ignore the possibility of drastic discontinuities altogether. Greeting the Swan involves a commitment never to lapse into that comforting place where we just assume that nothing bad is going to happen.

Our basic assumption is therefore going to be that uncertainty is of the wild sort, but how should we, thus enlightened, think about random processes more specifically? Let us revisit the Black Swan conundrum posed in the previous chapter. The conundrum was that if the probability of a Black Swan is effectively zero, then indeed it is not worth taking it seriously because the cost of risk also tends towards zero and committing resources to deal with tail risk has a very weak case. Something *has* to be wrong with this proposition if we want to argue that it should be on the leadership agenda.

I mentioned posing the question to various finance professors. Their answers varied greatly, but they were united by two things. One was the undying belief, so typical of their profession, that the market gets everything right in the end. Somehow, it is able to process all the information fairly and correctly, including tail risks and Black Swans, so that prices are right in the end. This habit dies hard among finance professors. The other unifying theme was that the 'true' probability of a Swan is not zero. Some may, out of ignorance, act as if it were, but it only takes a few enlightened investors to get asset prices right overall. The DCF model for valuation, employing multiple scenarios, which I referred to when posing the conundrum, is not how astute traders go about determining what a stock is worth.[1] In the end, however, a price is obtained *as if they were.* If there is something in the world giving rise to tail risk, as long as it is relevant to the firm in question you can count on the market to factor it into the price, one way or the other – or so say the finance professors.[2]

When I talked to financial analysts about the same issue, the answer was quite different. It was more or less obvious to them that the hypothetical airline that chose to boost its ability to resist tail risk through conservative financial policies in 2019, just prior to the pandemic, by reducing the rate of expansion somewhat, would see its stock price *fall.* Protecting against inconceivable calamities (or even conceivable ones, like a pandemic) is not the story the stock market wants to be told. Furthermore, it seems safe to assume that stock market participants have the same blindness as everyone else to outlier events, on top of their obsession with growth rates in the baseline scenario. We know that mispricing of shares can go on for substantial periods of time, both for an industry as a whole, e.g. the IT bubble in the late 1990s, and for specific firms, e.g. Enron, whose lack of substance in the form of positive free cash flows did not stop it from reaching stratospheric valuations. Valeant Pharmaceuticals is another example of a fast-growing stock market darling, in which risks were hidden from view for an extended time, only to cause a

---

[1]One professor, however, maintained that the DCF template can and should be equipped with an entry called 'failure probability' to account for tail risk.

[2]The issue is quite involved. The professors like to point out that firm-specific tail risk gets diversified away when holding a diversified portfolio and that any premium for tail risk is implicit in the equity risk premium and the beta coefficient, which captures the systemic risk of a stock. These are elements that determine the discount rate and by extension firm value. However, firm value is also a function of the expected (probability weighted) value of future free cash flows. Tail risk mitigation can raise the mean of future expected cash flows, primarily through eliminating the expected costs of wipeout or strategy disruption (but also if the expenditure related to mitigation is less than the future discounted benefits, in which tail risk mitigation has a business case in its own right even without considering wipeout or disruption). My argument is that firms are not necessarily rewarded for efforts to mitigate tail risk due in part to severe information asymmetries – it can be difficult for market participants to assess the consequences for strategy execution from performance tail risk. This is also, then, because they have a fetish for growth that biases them to focus on that number in the most expected scenario, i.e. the growth forecast. The argument is that they place too much weight on the growth forecast and consequently downplay the value consequences of tail risk scenarios. As a result, they will champion growth even when that expansion drives the firm towards high levels of vulnerability.

remarkable implosion once they became impossible to ignore any longer. The company's new strategy, ushered in by former McKinsey consultant Michael Pearson, involved reducing traditional R&D (which created growth at too slow a pace). Instead, they went shopping for companies with established product portfolios. Following each new deal, the prices of those products were swiftly raised. This generated growth and a sense of excitement in the stock market, but the strategy was executed using a raft of sketchy practices, which built up the risk that later became the firm's undoing.

The whole issue could easily be resolved by simply ignoring whatever the stock market is currently doing and instead choose the policies that we believe will maximize long-term firm value, a concept quite distinct from the short-term share price observed in the market. Long-term value is indeed given by the discounted expected value of future free cash flows, as illustrated in Chapter 3. It may well be that long-term value increases from tail risk management because we can expect to fare better in a tail risk scenario, even when this comes at the expense of a slightly reduced growth rate (for some limited time) in the business-as-usual scenario. Because of the market's bias towards growth stories, however, the stock price may still take a tumble on the announcement of such a policy. The advice would be to go for the policy that we believe will improve firm value the most, and not think so much about whether the stock market's immediate reaction to that is positive or negative.

True, one of the benefits of being a listed firm is getting feedback from the market on the strategy's performance. A steadily declining stock price signals that the strategy is not working, which should prompt action. It is important, however, that we do not let fear of short-term market reactions – the tyranny of the market – stop us from doing what we feel is in the best interest of the firm. If the best way forward includes mitigating tail risk because we believe it could either wipe us out or seriously wreck our strategy, then we should calmly proceed to do so even though it may change the market's (short-term) view of growth prospects negatively. In the end, and over some time, the market tends to get prices broadly right – the wisdom of the crowd should ensure this outcome. That is, give them enough time and a fair price will be obtained as the fundamentals are (re)discovered. If there is an immediate negative reaction and some disappointment among analysts because of their prior expectations, or because of a temporary market euphoria rewarding only growth stories, then so be it. Managers in private firms have the luxury to ignore the stock market on an everyday basis and can focus exclusively on long-term firm value. For managers of public firms, however, it can be devilishly hard to take their eyes off the screen showing the latest share price. Such an obsession can distort corporate policy in all sorts of ways if the game deteriorates into second-guessing what the market wants today.

An important part for us of the professors' response is that the 'true' Swan probability is not zero. Indeed, many of the extreme events listed in Table 1.1 have historical precedents and respectable probabilities according to the relevant expertise. An electromagnetic pulse happened in 1859 with devastating consequences for the technology of the day (telegraphs). October 27 is the day we raise a glass of vodka to commemorate Vasili Alexandrovich Arkhipov, who was the only commander on board a Soviet nuclear submarine (B-59) who dissented to execute a nuclear strike, thereby preventing all-out war. It might also interest the reader to know that experts in the field have considered the probability of nuclear terror to be significant. The author of a book published in 2004 estimated the odds of a nuclear terrorist attack before 2014 as *higher than even* (meaning more likely to happen than not).[3] Legendary investor Warren Buffett endorsed the idea, referring to nuclear terrorism as by far the most important problem of our time – and so on. Ignorance and emotional detachment are the real reasons we assign a probability of close to zero, implicitly or otherwise. When we take those elements out of the mix and actually give it some thought, the conclusion is bound to be different.

In fact, the probability of a Black Swan happening is probably closer to 100% than zero. We simply need to extend the time horizon to see why. Swans are a sure thing if you give them enough time. It is just a matter of when, regretfully, that a large enough volcano erupts, blackening the skies and causing crop failures around the world. Of course, if we also talk about the probability of *a* Black Swan (any Swan), it is clearly far from zero. We can be absolutely sure that something unanticipated and shocking, with major consequences, will happen, and we probably do not have to wait very long either. Even inconceivable events, the unknown unknowns, are a given in this perspective.

If an extreme event happens with only a 0.5% probability in any given year (i.e. we expect it to happen roughly once every 200 years), the probability over a 10-year horizon is just shy of 5% for that risk factor alone. Consider the large number of sources of extreme uncertainty and it is not hard to see why the probability of at least one of them occurring over 10 years approaches 1. It is probably enough with a five-year horizon for the probability to get close to 100%. Looking back at the most recent centuries, when was the last time that the world went for a full five years without something dramatic and

---

[3]Nuclear terrorism: Did we beat the odds or change them? PRISM, National Defense University News (ndu.edu).

'unprecedented' going down that changed everything we thought we knew about the world? I am sure that someone willing to pour over the records will ultimately be able to find a few of them. But a 10-year period? Then it gets really hard to find.

Take note, however, of the perspective we are applying here. The discussion has revolved around high-level, "civilizational" Black Swans from the vantage point of a reasonably educated and up-do-date individual, interested in world affairs but not privy to any privileged information. These high-level Black Swans, however much we enjoy talking about them, are not our focus. We are practical men and women interested in how *firms* should approach wild uncertainty and in how many resources they can legitimately spend on tail risk mitigation. As such, we are only interested in random events insofar as they connect with corporate performance. It is our firm's vulnerabilities, we shall become convinced, that dictate which sources of randomness are relevant to consider and the appropriate "level" at which we try to define and measure them.

Given the corporate perspective, an opportunity to grasp randomness opens up. We could go back to data on Corporate Swans introduced in Chapter 2, there defined as an unexpected drop in revenue of 30% or more, and let that rate stand in as an indicator of the probability of a Swan in any given year. After all, it covers 65 years of data on the corporate sector. During this time, many 'real' Black Swans presumably happened, in the sense of inconceivable high impact events on the civilizational level, the kind of events that drive history and come as a complete surprise for the great mass of humanity. There have also been countless firm and industry specific Swans, which is to say those that arrive unexpectedly but had a huge impact only on certain organizations. This will be reflected in the data insofar as these events had an effect on corporate performance through some exposure mechanism.

By using a large sample of financial data, we also move away from the pitfall of just looking at our own firm's recent history, which may be perfectly tranquil. Instead, we pool large quantities of data on firms *like* us over 65 years. How frequent are large performance shocks in that perspective? Across decades of business cycles and competition, how often do firms that are doing roughly similar things to us take this kind of hit? Of course, utilizing data points for other firms and from other time periods involves a leap of faith of a different kind, in that we assume they are representative. While the world changes, and the details are impossible to pin down, the way wild uncertainty drives corporate performance on a broad level may be changing more slowly. However imperfect this approach may be, it is surely a better alternative than looking at a few years' worth of recent history for our own company. It will incorporate much more wild uncertainty and extend our estimation of the tail accordingly, so at the very least we err on the side of caution. You can think of it as a corrective to one of the core sucker mechanisms, which is the practice of inferring a sense of safety from our own recent track record.

Using this perspective, we can get a grip on Swan rates for different sub-samples of firms. The oil and gas industry, for example, stands out as the most Swan-prone line of business with a rate of over 10%. Its storied cycles of boom and bust indeed show up in the data. Firms in the consumer non-durables industry, by contrast, see a comparatively low Swan rate of 2.6%, a materially lower tendency towards large performance shocks. Looking across industries, a reasonable working assumption is that the rate, with a one-year time horizon, is in the 2–10% range, depending on your line of business. This approach gives us a flavour of the wild uncertainty in our vicinity and lowers the temptation to infer too much from our own recent past, which might indicate that the probability of such an event is rather close to zero.

Apart from an industry classification, one can add dimensions like size and profitability and create cohorts of firms that resemble our own even more, while still utilizing the power of large samples over long periods of time. We want to make the comparison based on firms that are reasonably like us because their experiences can illuminate our thinking about the scope for randomness. As long as we preserve the power of large datasets, a higher degree of similarity in the peer group is desirable. While we assume that the relation between the wild uncertainty of the world and corporate performance is reasonably stable, of course things do change on a structural level. For this reason, we may be advised to use more recent data, say from the year 2000 onwards.

Naturally, we are free to work with other definitions of tail risk than the revenue shocks between 30% and 90% that I have used here, which represent a particular part of the tail of the distribution. To the extent that other definitions of tail risk fit better with the purpose of the exercise, this is of course possible to do with the data. Zeroing in on a narrower range, for example, could make sense in a practical application. We will come back in Chapter 5 to an extended discussion about this possibility.

Revenue shocks, to sum up this perspective, are one of the key mechanisms through which extreme events in the economy and broader society filter through to corporate bottom lines. It offers a way to work practically with randomness using the power of data in a way that does not do any obvious injustice to the lessons that the Black Swan framework teaches us. We look at the ultimate impact of wild uncertainty on something we can measure and relate to. In a way, looking at percentage drops in revenue means that we reign in the Moving Tail because it cannot go below –100%. We have created, therefore, a context in which we can begin to decide how far we want to go in building up defences against extreme outcomes.

The approach outlined above gives us a framework for thinking about wild uncertainty on the enterprise level and even putting some numbers on it. The bigger picture approach using performance numbers is useful as it lets us address the risk profile of the firm as a whole. However, this does not mean that we can just leave it at that. Many decisions on the operating level are affected by how we think about randomness. Also in this case, wild uncertainty should be the baseline assumption – how we think about things. Yet we frequently find that the data is not there to provide even a starting point for an assessment of the probability of highly consequential events. It is clear that our approach will have to be less data driven and rely more on subjective estimates.

Here we run into some issues. Many, including Taleb, are distinctly hostile to attempts at quantifying possibilities under conditions of wild uncertainty. Pay no attention, however, to those who argue that it is epistemologically arrogant to attach probabilities when they simply cannot be known. It is epistemologically ignorant to not even try. Obviously, it matters for decision-making if we consider something to be highly unlikely, unlikely, likely, or highly likely. I invite the reader to think about what the alternative would imply. If something is considered extremely unlikely, of course that does diminish the scope for actions designed to mitigate the consequences of that something. Unfortunately, some degree of quantification will be necessary to ensure that we are talking about the same thing and to ensure that our response is ultimately proportional and reasonable. Using traffic light colours or verbal descriptions suffers from the drawback that my interpretation of the colour red, for example, could be very different from yours.

In most cases, what we can discern are *possibilities* for the future rather than well-defined probabilities. Based on experience, observations and reasoning, we may grant certain outcomes as possible in the first place, and some of these possibilities we will also consider more likely than others. In the literature on the subject, this is referred to as 'degree of belief' or 'degree of certainty' – a subjective estimate of the plausibility of an outcome given what we know. A subjective probability is essentially a relative frequency on a forward-looking basis: the number of outcomes in which the risk 'happens' divided by the total number of possible outcomes we have taken into account – *all subjectively determined.*

The position taken in this book is that subjective estimates, as long as the process for generating them meets certain criteria, have a natural place in the decision-making process.[4] If someone has a problem with the word 'probability', just substitute it with 'subjective degree of belief' and you will be fine. Therefore, instead of 'the probability of event X', think of it rather in terms of '*our* subjective degree of belief in the plausibility of event X'. It is nothing more than a qualified guesstimate by the best brains in the organization regarding how plausible a certain outcome is. As such, it is perfectly legitimate as input for decision-making. This is true even in a world of wild uncertainty.

##  THE ROADS NOT TAKEN

It should be clear from our discussion in the previous section that there is enough randomness of the wild sort out there to take it seriously as an issue, whether we prefer to call it Black Swans, tail risk, volatility or just plain old variability. The question of tail risk is important because it implies a possible wipeout or a severely damaged strategy. The idea is for the firm's leadership to take certain measures that will improve the odds that the firm survives and thrives come (almost) what may. Now, we need to start thinking about how to work with the tail risk question in our organization and, so to speak, find a home for it.

First, let us agree not to overdo it. We do not want to replace a Black Swan-blind firm with a Swan-obsessed one. It is by no means obvious that the organization is well served by extensive investigations into remote possibilities. There is a quality-of-life issue involved when approaching the question of tail risk. By spawning a large number of potential disasters, taking each of them very seriously and devoting considerable resources to preparing for them, we become, well, preppers. Granted, true preppers seem to take enjoyment in their craft and once society breaks down they will have their moment and thrive (compared with the rest of us, that is). It is not a lifestyle that most of us envy, however, and does not seem conducive to human flourishing. Just as risk and return must always be calibrated, the need to protect our firm against Black Swans must be balanced against the overall cost of prepping. We get it wrong when we obsess about disasters and let it take over our existence. While the basic problem is one of tail risk getting too little attention, there is, as we have seen, also the potential to overspend on risk management.

---

[4]The interested reader is referred to my previous book for an extended discussion about subjective probabilities. Jankensgård, H. and P. Kapstad, 2021. *Empowered enterprise risk management: Theory and practice*, John Wiley & Sons: Hoboken, New Jersey.

On the same note, there seems to be little point in holding Black Swan workshops throughout the company where just about any staffer is encouraged to speak out about possible extreme events. It would only generate a heap of absurdities that would be filed away minutes upon completion. It could also spook people into spontaneous prepping activities, like developing contingency plans that cater to their personal risk aversion but make no economic sense for the firm.[5]

Another idea we can dispatch is to have the risk manager assume responsibility for Swan-watching. Yes, letting him or her do so would have the advantage that the rest of the organization is allowed to feel less bad about carrying on as before. It would not work, however. Styling oneself in terms of a Swan detector is about as bad a career move that any risk manager could make. Anyone who insists on pointing to various potential calamities and bringing them up for discussion is likely to fade quickly into irrelevance. Nobody wants a risk manager who cries Swan at least once a week. Once that is part of your job description, it is easy to get caught up reading about something and thinking that this has to be the next one. It sends our minds off in a very futile direction all too often.

A Swan-minded risk manager back in, say, 2005 who wanted evidence that the US dollar was about to collapse would find plenty to support that view. Already at that time, much was being written on the reckless deficits and mountains of debt building up in the US. It also seemed well-researched, pointing to legitimate sources and authorities. All that just had to spell doom for the US dollar, which, being the reserve currency of the world, would bring untold turmoil. Let us say that our Swan manager writes up a dossier on this, brimming with arguments, graphs and statistics that all point to this being a Black Swan about to be set loose on the world. The document gets passed around to people in the organization, some of who might glance over the executive summary and pause to think for a few minutes. Then, obviously, nothing happens. The next week, the same risk manager discovers that China has been growing at break-neck speed, all driven by vast quantities of credit. According to the historical record, no economy has ever expanded at such a pace without

---

[5]Researchers in corporate finance spend a lot of time studying executive misuse of corporate resources, or what is referred to as 'the agency problem'. Executives might have their companies pay for luxury apartments or hunting cabins, for example. An interesting extension of this research would be to investigate agency costs related to prepping, i.e. the use of corporate resources in setting up bunkers for their executives to utilize, which increasingly might be seen as the luxury good of an uncertain future. I hereby name this 'the executive prepping' hypothesis.

suffering intermittent episodes of chaos and crisis. If that were to happen in today's interconnected economy, imagine the consequences. So, another Black Swan waiting to happen! A memo just as impressive as the first one is written up and circulated. This time, no one even bothers to look at the summary. Instead, eyebrows are likely to be raised and some will start to wonder what this so-called risk manager is really up to. Eventually, the question will be asked: 'Does it really make sense to pay someone to sit around and be paranoid?'

Another road not to be taken is that of pouring more resources into forecasting. A team of qualified forecasters, one might think, could help us predict events and navigate more safely. However, this is not the message of the Black Swan framework. Once we acknowledge that we live in a world of wild uncertainty, it follows that attempts at forecasting are bound to have little accuracy. If anything, maintaining a delusion about being able to predict outcomes successfully is only making us an even bigger sucker. Taleb is at pains to point out the astonishing extent of our failure to forecast the future. Our collective track record in this department is remarkably poor. Forecasts, in Taleb's view, are just noise from pundits without skin in the game. The surprising part is not that forecasting fails, but that few in this world are ever held accountable for their previous attempts through rigorous evaluations, meaning that there is no penalty involved for being wrong (Taleb, 2007, Prologue). The pattern can just repeat itself indefinitely.

While mundane forecasts, like exchange rate forecasts, are routinely wrong, the truth of our inability to get forecasting right is particularly evident when the time horizon is extended several years into the future or, horrors, decades. Even some of our greatest minds have succumbed to the temptation of making long-run forecasts and got it spectacularly wrong. Herbert Simon, polymath and Nobel Prize winner, was not exactly right when he claimed back in 1960 that we were 20 years away from when machines can do anything that humans can do. Nor was the highly respected economist Paul Samuelson when he predicted, in the 1980s edition of his economics textbook, that the Soviet economy would overtake that of the US by 2012.

Why do forecasts fail so often? The general opaqueness of the complex systems that generate wild uncertainty are reasons enough for forecasting to be deeply problematic as well. The cardinal error in many of the classic cases of forecasting failure, though, seems to be extrapolating trends from the recent past into the future, or over-playing some aspect that has been in focus lately and thus caught our attention. An even more fundamental reason for the failure of forecasting is that you can be wrong in countless ways, but only right in one. For many non-trivial stochastic processes, the odds are therefore stacked up quite badly against any single point forecast coinciding exactly with the observed outcome. The forecast is really only one out of a large number of scenarios, or paths, that are possible beforehand. It may only be marginally more likely to occur than other possible outcomes, yet we tend to fixate on this particular number.

It would be wrong to conclude, however, that forecasts should have no place even in a world of wild uncertainty. In a business context, it is hard to function without some sort of a plan, and a plan must be underpinned by some assumptions. The most logical assumptions to plug into a plan are the ones we consider to be most likely to happen, i.e. the forecasts. We need a sense of the overall direction of things and an idea of where we think we are headed. Without that, there is hardly any basis for decision-making. At the end of the day, most organizations need forecasts in order to function. It is more a matter of where we put the emphasis.

An approach that gets the emphasis wrong is to set up a big forecasting department and perhaps a trading desk on the side to make some money based on all the superior insights generated by it. This arrangement is sure to increase costs, as some highly paid individuals are now immersed in what amounts to a low-productive sideshow. Forecasting units and trading desks are quite obvious signals that the firm has a cost discipline problem and that it is naïve enough to think it can beat the market. In addition, we now also have to live with the risk of rogue traders and trades going very wrong. Thankfully, forecasting departments and trading desks have become less common in the corporate sector over time. Most likely, this is a reflection of some of these drawbacks having been found out the hard way.[6]

A more sensible approach realizes that unbiased forecasts help us function, but that the marginal utility of putting more resources into them diminishes quickly. We only need a forecast that is good enough, meaning that it cannot be improved in any obvious way. In some cases, simple algorithms can be used to generate decent forecasts.[7] In the FX market, for example, a rule that equates

---

[6]The habit called 'selective hedging' is alive and well, having so far escaped the clutches of corporate governance. Selective hedging is when the company hedges an underlying exposure, but does so in an opportunistic way in accordance with views in the market. The premise is still that they can beat the market, except that it now takes place under a veil of respectability, since it can be presented to the world as 'hedging of risk'.

[7]Also known as a 'random walk', a stochastic process with no 'memory', free to wander over time with no mechanism that pulls it back towards a stable mean or some other reference value.

the forecast of the exchange rate with the most recent observation does surprisingly well in forecasting competitions. Today's exchange rate carries a lot of information about where the price is likely to be on some future date, i.e. it cannot be improved easily.

What we want are earnest and open discussions about the implications of extreme events involving the people best suited for the task. Greeting the Swan is about finding ways to make these conversations happen naturally and regularly. Conversations are crucial in the risk management process, as risk expert John Fraser has pointed out in several publications.[8] Only then, John argues, can we make the right prioritization with respect to the use of corporate resources. The idea is to trade viewpoints, bring up new perspectives and ultimately work out differences of opinion to arrive at a policy that people can get behind. It is by having such discussions that a topic gets the attention it deserves and the wisdom of the group is enlisted in the endeavour to keep the firm safe. To support these conversations, we also want the relevant information to flow freely. Good information is essential in shaping a realistic response to tail risk, and all employees should be encouraged to share what they know about critical exposures. The risk manager/risk function typically has a central role in facilitating this flow of information and processing it so as to provide solid inputs to the discussions.

Tail risk is ultimately an issue for the firm's leadership. A Black Swan by definition has massive impact and deals with existential matters like surviving and executing strategy. Therefore, these conversations need to be held in the same venues where corporate strategy and financial performance are discussed and be an integral part of that process. The full extent to which Black Swans bear down on corporate strategy will be explored in Chapter 6.

 ## FUNCTIONAL STUPIDITY

The challenge we face is to get tail risk on the agenda in the first place. We run into a set of by now familiar problems. The diffusion of responsibility that is so typical of firms means that nobody really feels compelled to champion this cause. Not only is the would-be Swan manager bringing up a problem, it is a very abstract one at that, lying somewhere in the distant future, overwhelmingly unlikely

---

[8]Fraser, J. R. S., 2014. Building enterprise risk management into agency processes and culture. In Stanton, T. and D. W. Webster (Eds), *Managing risk and performance: A guide for government decision makers*. John Wiley & Sons: Hoboken, New Jersey.

to happen. Therefore, we never seem to get round to discussing it, let alone formulating a reasonable response. The issue of highly consequential events with low probability, when this is the case, falls through the corporate cracks.

It might be tempting to think that ignoring Black Swans in a world that demonstrably offers wild uncertainty is, well, stupid. By using this term, nobody is suggesting that the people in the organization are stupid, just that collectively, by pretending that tail risk does not exist, they act as if they were. Interestingly, it turns out that there is a case to be made *for* a certain kind of organizational stupidity. Why? Alvesson and Spicer (2012) argue that it can be functional.[9] They define functional stupidity as follows:

> 'Functional stupidity is [the] inability and/or unwillingness to use cognitive and reflective capacities in anything other than narrow and circumspect ways. It involves a lack of reflexivity, a disinclination to require or provide justification, and avoidance of substantive reasoning.'

The thrust of their argument is that when people just do what is expected of them, and work towards a shared goal, harmony prevails and the organization performs well, at least in some narrow, short-term sense. Thinking critically and challenging taken-for-granted assumptions about how things are to be done creates frictions and disturbs 'the flow'. Therefore, any initiative along those lines is actively discouraged in the name of getting on with the job. Mantras like 'Don't think about it, just do it' and 'We want solutions, not problems' are markers of organizations characterized by functional stupidity. Needless to say, inserting the issue of Black Swans into this flow of goal-oriented activities constitutes a kind of friction. Black Swans fit right in when Alvesson and Spicer discuss the benefits of avoiding intellectual resources being diverted into nonproductive uses like 'critical thinking, existential anxiety, and other miseries'. Dealing with them calls on us to do some substantive reasoning with respect to some pretty existential miseries – so hint taken.

The number one priority is indeed to get people to perform their best and implement the plan. Firms are on a mission and should be wholeheartedly innovating, improving and, as Jack Welch put it, just 'implement like hell' in order to get the most out of the firm's resources and capabilities. We want the firm to be striving wholeheartedly towards reaching its goals and realizing its full potential, so the culture should primarily be conducive to that. If the culture is aligned with the organization's mission, as we have all been told,

---

[9]Alvesson, M. and A. Spicer (2012). A stupidity-based theory of organizations. *Journal of Management Studies*, 49, 1194–1220.

it can be an important catalyst towards achieving that mission. Corporate cultures, for natural reasons, gravitate towards generating and sustaining near-term performance rather than risk thinking.

The orientation of corporate cultures towards short-term performance has important consequences for our purposes. It means that even when several individuals have discovered the potential for tail risk to wreck the company's strategy, they might be stopped in their tracks by the very culture they operate within. The organization is, in such cases, not capable of registering or processing that kind of input. It does not compute. There is resistance to the very notion of disruptive events that would end the status quo, so the firm never gets to where it has the kind of discussions we would like. The organizational capability for dealing with wild uncertainty will consequently be low.

Greeting the Swan involves a bit of introspection to help us see more clearly the extent to which the firm's culture prevents having serious discussions about extreme events and our preparedness for them. While Alvesson and Spicer speak about organizations in general, there is of course some variation in practice as to what are the dominating cultural traits. Some cultures will be more hostile to the idea of tail risk than others. A bit of self-diagnosis is therefore in order. In our quest for understanding, we will consider two practically important management styles that can influence the culture in a big way: fear and optimism. They represent starkly different ideas about how to bring the best out of the employees and to achieve maximum success for the organization. Management-by-Optimism stresses that people do best when moving towards something positive (a vision, success, possibilities) and Management-by-Fear that they do when moving away from something negative (pain, failure, humiliation).[10]

Our concern is that both approaches distract from having useful dialogues about tail risk, but in different ways. Whenever either is found in excessive amounts, it should serve as a red flag to the BoD that the firm is undermanaging its exposure to extreme risk. So let us dig into the mechanics behind each. First, we consider Management-by-Fear. The upper echelons of Volkswagen, for example, believed in fear as a motivating factor. ('Give me the result I want in six weeks or you are history.') For whatever reasons, they had come to believe that if you want results, make people realize the consequences of failure. According to this philosophy, then, fear is functional because it shakes

---

[10]It has been noted that managers who disseminate fear are not always aware that they do, and few would ever confess to practising a management approach based on the principle of fear. It may therefore be more correct to describe it as a 'style' rather than a philosophy. Some people may have a sadistic streak and take pleasure in the exercise of power, in which case it is not a philosophy at all either, just a way of life.

people out of their comfort zones and gets them working with a laser-sharp focus. In turn, this should translate into higher performance, the realization of objectives and higher firm value.

The proponents of Management-by-Optimism,[11] in contrast, assume that people perform best when they feel support and receive encouraging feedback. In this view, optimism is functional. Professor Kim Cameron (2012) reviews considerable empirical evidence suggesting that a positive tone achieves better organizational outcomes.[12] How does optimism achieve this? The message, according to the literature on the topic, is that humans flourish when presented with a picture of an optimistic and meaningful future, and when they believe that they are part of the community that is about to make it happen. Interestingly, data from clinical studies involving scans show that the brain performs better in a positive condition, which is observable in that more parts of it are activated when in an optimistic mood. In other words, we become smarter and more creative when optimism rules. According to Cameron:

> 'Negative emotions narrow people's thought-action repertoires and diminish their coping abilities. In other words, inducing positive emotions (such as joyfulness, love, and appreciation) enlarges cognitive perspectives.'

Insofar as you have a meaningful degree of influence over the situation, it seems that any notion of management by fear is the wrong way to go. Our agenda is to make firms less prone to Black Swans while preserving maximum upside, and fear is completely contrary to two of the things that are most effective in preventing disasters from building up: the free flow of information and open, honest conversations about future possibilities. In these workplaces, one dares not speak up for fear of the consequences, which effectively shuts down the lines of communication. Fear-based management also seems hopelessly out of date, like a recipe for transgressions that can only bring bad press and lawsuits. If anything, it makes fertile ground for Corporate Swans. The line between fear and abuse of power is a thin one. Today, thanks to the internet, the fury that can be unleashed online in response to perceived wrongdoings is formidable, putting that most precious of assets – a company's reputation – on the line.

The case for a certain degree of positivity seems more solid. A reasonable conclusion, considering the evidence, is that optimism is functional and

---

[11]Alternatively referred to as 'positive leadership'.
[12]Cameron, K., 2012, *Positive leadership: Strategies for extraordinary performance*. Berrett-Koehler Publishers: San Francisco.

raises organizational performance, at least in organizations where creativity and initiative are considered conducive to long-term success. It has the added bonus of reducing the risk of reputation-trashing transgressions that come with a culture that tends towards fear. In workplaces where optimism is the norm, people are more likely to be on their best behaviour.

If we adopt the view that positivity is functional and generally risk-reducing, all we have to do is ensure that it does not get excessive. Positive leadership has come under fire for leaning towards new age-ism and self-help approaches designed to make people feel happy about their lives. Some slap the epithet 'Pollyannaish' on what they find to be excessively cheerful cultures, hinting that these organizations suffer from a delusional belief in the inherent goodness of everything around us.[13] This is when a generally positive attitude and healthy dose of organizational confidence pass into more cult-like behaviour. In its more extreme forms, a Pollyanna culture produces some of the same detrimental results in regards to Black Swan awareness as a culture of fear. Supreme cheerfulness implies, in much the same way, that there is no time or place for serious discussions about how to best prepare for things that could go wrong.

Greeting the Swan involves seeing the connection between performance-enhancing 'stupidity' and optimism, on the one hand, and shutting down discussions that open our eyes to the potential for serious disruptions, on the other. In a way, we need both positivity and negativity. Negative feedback is a crucial part of any dialogue because it identifies areas of improvement.[14] Asking, for example, if we really have done enough to prepare for the eventuality that the high-impact but highly unlikely event X happens, might come across as negative to some. Not only is that person pointing to a scary possibility, he or she is also alluding to the fact that we have not done a good job in preparation. As an organization, we are in trouble if people cannot speak out about things that could be done better. Negative feedback, however, should not become the norm, because the end station is a dysfunctional organization where people spend their energies trying to avoid being blamed. We need a generally optimistic attitude because it supports goal-achievement, but one that allows for constructive feedback loops even if they bring up 'negative' and scary perspectives.

---

[13] As in the irrepressible optimism of the girl Pollyanna in the novel from 1913 by Eleanor Porter.
[14] Some take the view that there is no such thing as positive or negative feedback, only constructive and non-constructive. That is a healthy attitude that actually resolves many of the issues we are talking about here. It can be hard to live by, however, if we are emotionally vested in something and take any non-positive feedback personally and as evidence that the other person is never happy and always on our backs.

An interesting idea that has been advocated is to think in terms of the ratio of positive to negative expressions. According to Cameron, high-performing cultures do not have zero negativity. Instead, they have a healthy balance between the two, skewed in favour of positive statements. What it means is that there is no fuss about bringing up something that could be seen as potentially threatening. Nobody is penalized for it and certainly not ridiculed. In other words, it is psychologically safe to introduce the topic. This is the challenge in a world of wild uncertainty: to maintain a generally optimistic mode and push forward, yet create a space for constructive dialogue about how to achieve a modicum of preparedness for worst-case scenarios.

As a practical matter, to generate these conversations, try adhering to the 1% rule. This rule was originally proposed by a 'merchant of dread', Bradley Garrett's preferred terminology for individuals profiting from solutions that cater to people who dread what the future might bring (Garrett, 2020, cited earlier). The rule says that people should spend 1% of their net worth on preparing for a major calamity. It would mean that corporates devote at least 1% of their resources *and time* on the issue of how to prepare for extreme events. This does not seem excessive in a world where, if anything, uncertainty only appears to be getting wilder. By following the 1% rule, we ensure that there is a basic awareness and a proportionate response in place. The rule de-individualizes the issue in the sense that no single person should be put on the line by bringing attention to it. It takes the career risk of pointing to extreme events out of the equation. Instead, it becomes a shared responsibility, something we do as a matter of course ('just following the rule here').

In practice, it might mean that the leadership of the firm holds a certain number of workshops or meetings per year dedicated to the topic or, perhaps, that they even convene for a 1-day retreat somewhere on an annual basis to really dig into it. Think of it as retreating into a war room (Black Swan room?) under the assumption that we are under attack from wild uncertainty and that we need to overhaul our defences. As we shall also see in later chapters, perhaps we could also entertain the possibility of going on the counteroffensive.

 ## THE SWANMAKERS

Say, for the sake of argument, that we have succeeded in normalizing conversations about tail risk and in establishing a forum, involving senior decision-makers, in which this takes place on a reasonably regular basis. What should we fill those conversations with? We could talk about the Black Swans themselves, or at least the known unknowns. The list produced in Chapter 1 (Table 1.1) provides a list of potential high-impact events or situations. We could spend some time exploring how they might play out and how they would affect our firm. For many, like all-out nuclear war, we might quickly conclude that we have no way of really dealing with those consequences, and therefore we have no option but to immediately accept them. It is part of the risk of being alive in the twenty-first century, one might say.

An alternative topic of conversation, which directly gets down to business, is to start with our own situation and ask, *what would it take* to do some serious damage to crucial aspects of our value chain? The emphasis is now less on the details of the Black Swan event itself and more on understanding points of failure in the business model. As noted, extreme events can only be high impact insofar as there is a meaningful exposure to it somewhere in our business. The four questions in Table 4.1 connect extreme events with possible consequences somewhere in the value chain.

Armed with some answers, we could then work backwards to ask *what type* of Black Swan event has the potential to create that situation. Specific extreme events can be sorted into generic categories based on the kind of consequences they could bring about, like 'a shutdown of international trade', 'a breakdown of the power grid' or 'a breakdown of the internet'. This helps convert broad existential dread, which is not very productive, to specific questions that more clearly relate to our ability to do business. More often than not, this can be expressed in terms of a basic function, or system, in society ceasing to work for some period of time. Which of the high-level Swans is the root cause, or trigger, of these outcomes may be less relevant than the fact that something like that could be the consequence.

In our conversations, we can also search for mechanisms on a more firm-specific level that are conducive to losses that do not have any clear upper

**TABLE 4.1**  Value chain vulnerability

---

■ What could cause a (massive) deterioration in the ability or inclination of our customers to spend money on our products?

☞ What could cause a (massive) deterioration in our ability to deliver our products or services to the end-customers?

■ What could cause a (massive) deterioration in our ability to produce products or offer services?

■ What could cause a (massive) deterioration in our ability to procure the goods we need to manufacture our products?

---

limit, or at least whose practical limits kick in too late to save us. I will refer to such high-impact risks as Swanmakers. They, just like the Black Swans themselves, have three attributes. First, there is a specific mechanism that is initially hidden from view, at least to the uninformed. Second, they are triggered by some external contingency, which is rare and unexpected. Third, they have a certain potential for losses that are, if not uncapped, then at least without a clear boundary that would keep the firm at a safe distance from wipeout or strategy disruption. It is prudent to scan the environment for possible Swanmakers to ensure we do not blindly walk into a situation with serious wipeout risk. We can quite possibly uncover both the mechanism and the trigger event if we just look in the right places. So let us talk about that.

Our first example of a Swanmaker is the third-party liability law in the US. This law regulates corporate liability in case of an accident that causes harm to the livelihood of others. If there is an oil spill, for example, and this leads to a shrimp fisher losing his ability to support himself and his family, the company responsible for the accident is liable to compensate him for his loss. The damage, and consequently the liability, is assessed over the time horizon it is considered to last – which can be decades. The legal liability will be proportionate to the damage caused for any number of claimants involved. In contrast to other legal regimes around the world, the US version of this law is not capped – *it does not have an upper limit*. Already here we begin to sense the tail risk. The potential for such legal liabilities to take firms down should be clear. When the Deepwater Horizon exploration platform, located in the Mexican Gulf, suffered an explosion in April 2010, it caused a tragic loss of life. It also created the largest marine oil spill in the industry's history and an environmental disaster of corresponding magnitude. BP, the company that, together with various subcontractors, operated the platform, found itself looking at a whirlwind of lawsuits and the wrath of the general public. Thanks to the nature of the third-party liability law, the liabilities just kept piling up. At the end of the process, they had been handed the largest legal bill in US history ($62 billion). It took a massive toll on BP's business model, which was disrupted in various ways, including by having to sell the US arm of the firm.[15]

---

[15]The true tragedy here is, of course, the environmental and human consequences. Eleven people lost their lives. One could well argue that BP deserved to go under as a company for what they did and that we should not treat their possible demise in this situation as a worthy issue. I agree to that. It is revolting to think that chasing financial targets had a role in creating the catastrophe. However, I am only using the example to clarify the principle that uncapped exposures have a special standing in the risk management process due to the collateral damage involved.

Derivatives are also potential Swanmakers. While in principle a device for sharing risks efficiently, they in fact have a legendary status as generators of terrible surprises. During the 2010s, for example, a number of Spanish companies sued Deutsche Bank for the mis-selling of derivatives. Pitched by Deutsche as a low-cost way of hedging FX exposures, the losses on some of these positions pushed clients into acute financial problems and even sent at least one company to the brink of bankruptcy.[16] Black Swans, we recall, are a function of ignorance and of putting too much faith in the benign intentions of the world surrounding us. Not just any derivative qualifies as a Swanmaker, however. Buying a put option is safe. You pay the premium and from that point on you hold an asset that, if you are lucky, generates a payday at expiry. By construction, you cannot lose more than the premium. The problem is when we *sell* derivatives to somebody else. Being on the selling side of a derivative means that you are effectively selling insurance (and receiving a cash premium for it). That is, you create a liability that you are now legally committed to honouring. Crucially, *it is liability without a cap.* If you have sold a call option on the EUR/USD exchange rate, for example, the liability grows every time the US dollar appreciates another cent. If the euro weakens outside its historical range, sending the exchange rate well above the strike price, the value of the liability would rocket. In an extreme case, investors could completely lose faith in the euro and its value collapses. Such an exploding liability could be the end of the party that sold the call option if they have not made any provisions for that eventuality. The Spanish firms in question, of course, did not suddenly decide to make a bet that they could collect a premium based on a view on how the markets would develop. They were most likely reassured that the package sold to them represented a sensible way of putting together a combination of derivatives, and that the risk was limited. Therefore, it has all the ingredients we need: an uncapped exposure, a specific conditional mechanism (the reference rate reaching the strike price in the derivative contract) and a blindness to the Black Swan potential stemming from a lack of relevant information and/or capability of evaluating it properly.

Our third and final example is the experience of Griddy Energy, a Texas-based retail electricity provider, in the wake of the Texas Freeze covered in Chapter 1. When the price of electricity soared to its maximum level and remained there for days, Griddy found itself with liabilities related to power purchases that exceeded its ability to pay, and ended up petitioning for Chapter 11.

---

[16]Deutsche Bank under pressure over derivatives sales in Spain, *Financial Times* (ft.com).

The mechanism was that the Texas grid manager, Ercot, had the ability and right to increase the price to that legally mandated ceiling for as long as it deemed fit. This was a built-in feature of the market that Griddy operated in. It only took a severe enough shock to trigger it, which the extreme winter blizzards provided. A relevant circumstance pointing to uncapped exposures is that power plants and natural-gas providers in Texas, unlike neighbouring states, are not required to winterize their facilities. There was thus a vulnerability. When a system or market with a vulnerability experiences a stressor, risk travels through it and pops up where there is an unmitigated exposure. Griddy was on the receiving end, but it was not alone. Many retailers were forced to purchase electricity in the spot market at sky-high prices in order to deliver on their commitments to customers with fixed rate utility plans. Several of them went bankrupt or exited the market altogether.[17] Again, we have that combination of an outlier event, a mechanism, and terrifying consequences. There may have been little that Griddy or other retailers could have done given the business model they had chosen, but we had better be good at identifying these exposures because, otherwise, it is not a calculated risk – it is a Black Swan waiting to strike.

 ## ON TOOLS AND MODELS

A possible response at this point is to say that many firms already have this covered because they have been thinking systematically about risk for a long time. What I am talking about is the so-called risk map, which summarizes and visualizes a firm's top risks, 'the risks that really matter'. To come up with one, firms engage in a process aimed at identifying and assessing risks on a firm-wide basis. The risks that have been identified are then compiled into a 'risk register', which is an inventory of sorts of the risks that could materially affect the firm. The risk map is a visual rendering of the most important risks in the register and typically characterizes each risk in it according to its probability and impact.

Risk mapping exercises are a staple of most contemporary risk management programmes, usually under the banner of 'Enterprise Risk Management', or ERM for short. ERM got underway in the late 1990s and has had a considerable impact on corporate practice since then. It has been described as 'a board-supervised process for integrated risk management across the firm'.[18]

---

[17]Griddy argues it was, in fact, a Champion of Consumers, *Texas Monthly*.
[18]Gates, S., 2006. Incorporating strategic risk into enterprise risk management: A survey of current corporate practice. *Journal of Applied Corporate Finance*, Vol. 18, No. 4, pp. 81–90.

Integrated risk management suggests that one manages a firm's net exposure to a certain risk factor and co-ordinates the risk response at the corporate level. This is in contrast to a situation in which various so-called 'silos', i.e. business units and corporate functions, are allowed to go about this task as they see fit from their more narrow perspective. The reference to 'across the firm' suggests that all the various units in the firm engage in the risk management process, mapping out their risks using a common methodology and 'risk language'. Finally, the reference to the Board of Directors implies a level of board involvement that previously was not there.

ERM and its risk maps take us into the fascinating territory of management tools. Managers often resort to various conceptual models that help them organize a decision-making situation. Academia has been a willing accomplice, delivering a steady stream of concepts, models and tools that not only purport to describe the world, but also to inform managers in their quest to optimize firm performance. Michael Porter's five-forces framework, which identifies factors that should determine the attractiveness of corporate strategies, is an excellent example of this.[19] Drawing on theories of industrial organization, it summarizes important principles into something than can be applied by management teams to arrive at policy decisions.

Models provide a simplified representation of reality. A good model captures the essence of the phenomenon and points to key causal relationships and mechanisms. The usefulness of models and theories lies precisely in the fact that they abstract away from so much real-world complexity. Models help us *see* what is going on because they remove much of the clutter. Apparently, there is value in reducing the number of dimensions of the phenomenon at hand. Which sounds like the opposite of the message Taleb has for us, which is that crisp and elegant models are fundamentally Platonic, and that putting our faith in them is bound to lead us into trouble (Taleb, 2007, p. 157). In fact, inevitably, the pet theories we fall in love with, and then try to prove, are going to be overwhelmed by messy reality and the Black Swans it offers up.

Theories and models thus have the potential to both enlighten and help us function *and* make us vulnerable because we ignore so many things that lie outside them. This is an interesting lens through which to view some of the tools that have been developed explicitly for the purpose of dealing with risks. In fact, the risk management industry is all about the tools, and risk maps have a prominent role in it (we will discuss quantitative risk models in the next chapter).

---

[19]Porter, M. E., 1979. How competitive forces shape strategy. *Harvard Business Review*, May 1979, Vol. 57, No. 2, pp. 137–145.

The question we are going to ask is whether the risk maps have succeeded in helping firms give appropriate attention to tail risk or do they just serve to bring a modicum of attention to easy-to-identify risks, thereby lulling us into a sense of safety that makes us *more* vulnerable to the real Black Swans that continue to reside outside the maps? It seems undeniable that, taken as a whole, the risk mapping exercises have raised the risk awareness in the corporate sector and made information about risks circulate more widely. When a major risk is detected and understood, it moves on to the map and becomes visible to the organization. Whenever that is the case, it is a triumph of the imagination over our tendency to stick our heads into the sand.

A considerable effort has been made by many corporates to map out their risks, and it is talked about in a way that would have been hard to imagine going back to, say, 1990. I have heard stories from people who were part of the early push for ERM who say that they struggled to bring up the subject of risk because managers did not even want to admit that they had any! These days, in contrast, making some sort of an inventory of risks is fairly routine and much less associated with a stigma. While far from perfect, the risk map represents a kind of progress, at least when compared to the situation of denying that the business faces any sort of risk and therefore refusing to talk about it.

Efforts at ERM are sometimes called out, however, for being superficial and tending towards box-ticking. Some managers, the claim goes, merely want to be seen as responsible in the field of risk management, for which there is now considerable external demand. This could be a problem if the firm's independent directors take the risk map to mean that the tail risk issue has been covered, and feel good about leaving it at that. If the risk map is the beginning and the end of the conversation about risk-taking in firms, we could be in for some surprises.

For a risk factor to transit from a Black Swan status (surprises, unknown unknowns) to tail risk (calculated risks, known unknowns), it is not enough for it to be identified and listed in some risk register. Sometimes one hears that a Black Swan becomes a Grey Swan in the moment one thinks of it, because it is no longer unknown. However, it should not be that easy to get off the hook. If a risk appears as a dot on some risk map it means nothing by itself. There is a sense in which a Black Swan ceases to be one when it is identified, assessed and *internalized* by key decision-makers in the firm. We have desuckered the organization when the question is taken seriously and paid due attention, and posed in the context of the firm's financial performance and strategy. That is when a high-impact risk effectively ceases to be a Black Swan, not when we merely give it a fleeting thought.

Whether firms are ultimately successful in transforming Black Swans into tail risk is an empirical issue. For that to be argued, it would have to be demonstrated that risk maps are able to flag what later turned out to be major disasters.[20] To my knowledge, no empirical investigation of this has been carried out yet. We can glean some insights, however, from the risk disclosure of airlines in the annual reports pertaining to 2018. These reports were published in early 2019 – well before anyone took notice of the C-19 virus. We now know the devastating impact that pandemics can have on the travel industry, so it is interesting to have a look at how much weight firms in this industry seemed to attach to the risk of a pandemic at the time. It makes for a useful case study because pandemics *can* be approached like a tail risk issue. As noted, there is much information on pandemics to be found, and calls to take them seriously have been issued repeatedly by respected institutions. Yet it is exactly the kind of phenomenon we find so easy to go into denial about, to prioritize away, which makes them more like Black Swans.

Let us start with Norwegian ASA, one of the most badly affected airlines. Headquartered in Norway, it experienced a brush with bankruptcy in 2020 as travel came to a standstill (at the time of writing, it is still unclear if they are going to survive as a company). In its report from 2018, it talks extensively about risk, which is mentioned a full 128 times. The report speaks at length about various kinds of risk, including jet fuel risk, credit risk, safety risk, liquidity risk, and foreign exchange risk. The risk of a pandemic is not mentioned.[21] Delta Airlines also did not mention the threat of a pandemic in its report from that year, despite including a section with the heading 'Risk factors relating to the airline industry'. This section does, however, speak of risks such as terror and geopolitical conflict. Southwest Airlines, for their part, talk of cyclical risks in economic activity and risks affecting their cost competitiveness negatively – but the word 'pandemic' gets no hit in their report. The winner in terms of the number of mentions of the word 'risk' must surely be Finnair,

---

[20]This is what we would have any chance of testing. We would like to be able to argue that the firm would have remained ignorant about the risk in the absence of the risk map, but this is unknowable. Putting potential high-impact events in the risk map that never materialized is also consistent with best practice but that does not lend itself to any form of testing. Of course, in reviewing annual reports we must acknowledge that some firms are aware of and have discussed pandemics without finding it necessary to discuss it in the external report. For the airline industry, however, this is a risk that very much ties into its revenue-generating ability with precedents in the not-too-distant history (SARS etc.), so it is not unreasonable to expect some level of preparedness.

[21]Of course, we do not know if a pandemic featured in the company's internal risk assessments. It may be that the company did evaluate such a risk scenario but chose not to disclose it externally. The same comment applies to the other firms mentioned in this section.

whose annual report returns no fewer than 401 hits. The number of hits on the search term pandemic? Nil. As should be clear by now, this is the general pattern. Perhaps somewhat surprisingly, Ryanair, the no-frills, hard-charging airline based in Ireland stands out positively. From their 2018 annual report:

> 'The Company believes that if any influenza or other pandemic becomes severe in Europe, its effect on demand for air travel in the markets in which Ryanair operates could be material, and it could therefore have a significantly adverse impact on the Company. A severe outbreak of swine flu, MERS, SARS, foot-and-mouth disease, avian flu or another pandemic or livestock-related disease may also result in European or national authorities imposing restrictions on travel, further damaging Ryanair's business. A serious pandemic could therefore severely disrupt Ryanair's business, resulting in the cancellation or loss of bookings, and adversely affecting Ryanair's financial condition and results of operations.'

Finally, an airline that was attuned to the risk of a pandemic! They talk about restrictions of travel, cancellation of bookings and a severe impact on financial results that rhymes well with what we later observed. We have no way of knowing, of course, whether this was internalized by the management team or just the words of some unusually insightful controller or lawyer. As would befit a company aware of such tail risk, however, Ryanair seems to have made certain provisions for it in terms of having a cash balance larger than the industry average.

The fine exception of Ryanair notwithstanding, we must concede that the litmus test of a pandemic risk in the airline industry does not point to any favourable conclusions with respect to the ability of risk mapping exercises to capture tail risk meaningfully. What is evident from these risk disclosures is instead the tendency to gravitate towards the concrete. People, it seems, would much rather talk about credit card losses, exchange rates and similarly tangible risks that satisfy our need for verification, and which we can talk about with some degree of expertise.

 ## A SWAN RADAR FOR THE BOARD

In this book, the vantage point for Corporate Swans is the Board of Directors (BoD). That is, outlier events occur relative to the expectations and knowledge of the firm's independent directors. This, as we concluded earlier, has the effect of increasing the number of Black Swans. The primary reason is that these directors are at an information (and time) disadvantage compared to the executive team. Another reason is that there *are* more things that could go wrong from their point of view. They are one level further up in the corporate hierarchy, so there is one more layer in which Black Swans can arise. We know from our discussions in Chapter 2 that more than a few CEOs have a narcissistic streak, partly because it takes that kind of person to reach the top. Wildly ambitious, they pursue attention-generating acquisitions and set goals that are a stretch in order to bask in the glory (and personal wealth) that comes from realizing them.

All of this makes them potentially dangerous. It points to the following conclusion: *we cannot entrust the Black Swan problem entirely to the CEO because he or she might be one*. It is a higher-level issue, one for the BoD. Taking a realistic view on these matters is what allows the board to graduate to an effective bastion of strength in the ongoing effort to keep the firm out of harm's way. The BoD can be rightly viewed as the last line of defence in the struggle against the Black Swans. Only they can exercise some control over the CEO and reign him or her in while there is still time. Greeting the Swan is a matter of operating with a realistic, fact-checked base assumption about how the world works, which includes appreciating the wild nature of consequences that can arise from mis-steps by executives. As always, people and institutions that are naïve, ignorant and overgenerous in terms of assuming good intentions by others are in for more Black Swans.

Recall that whenever you let somebody take possession of something on your behalf, you need to be realistic about some of the possible consequences of diverging interests. Chief among the potential problems is that the management team starts behaving as if it was their firm, engaging in various forms of self-dealing and indulgences. A Swan-astute BoD, recognizing the many historical precedents of this phenomenon, is *aware* of the potential for serious abuse by executives and considers the possibility. The BoD, in this scheme of things, takes to heart the fact that they represent the firm's owners and that it is their duty to hold the CEO to account, and to make sure that personal ambitions do not put the company at undue risk.

For reasons that are complex, many board members do not see it in this way and may not even be aware of this intended role of the board. To be appointed to a board is rather like being admitted to an exclusive club that gives you an opportunity to share your advice and wisdom. It is a very visible sign that you are somebody important, and once your status has been elevated to this level, the priority is being invited back. The compensation is fair, amounting to some nice disposable income. Moreover, many of them are part of a not-too-large circle where most people know each other, and therefore are on a friendly basis.

While not quite the golden old boys' club of yesteryear, the community of directors remains a fairly small one. Sitting on many boards is quite common and some members even make a career out of it. Further contributing to board meekness is the logic that failing together, as a board, might be the preferable risk to the career complications that could result from standing out in terms of how seriously one takes the oversight role.

All of the above translates into a preference among directors for not rocking the boat or displeasing the CEO. Instead of the board holding the CEO to account, in some firms the opposite seems to be closer to the truth: inconvenient board members that probe too deeply into red flag issues might not be invited back. CEO-dominated boards almost by definition lead to higher risk, because we are talking about unfettered power. This is a very unfortunate state of affairs, because it means that the board fails to perform its most important function, which is to ask tough questions and make sure that the risks being taken are proportionate to the potential rewards.

Executives are, of course, unlikely to think of themselves as risk factors. For natural reasons, they are rarely found on corporate risk maps. The risk management frameworks have a CEO centric view of risk, and therefore remain remarkably silent with respect to potential conflicts of interest and reckless behaviour on the part of executives. In fact, I venture to guess that the concept of a rogue executive has never been put on a risk map. For the consultants selling risk management, suggesting something along those lines would be, you know, awkward. Traders and clerks can be designated as potentially rogue and dangerous, by all means. But executives? No way. The risk management function, and the consultants assisting with the implementation, have zero incentive to suggest that the executives themselves could constitute a major risk. You do not bite the hand that feeds you.

Instead, the frameworks make out risk management to be a harmonious process in which all levels of the organization work together to achieve a better outcome. In reality, when risk considerations clash with a keenly felt desire to do business, chances are it is the latter that wins out. Having a first-rate risk management function may mean nothing the day executives decide to risk it. We were reminded of this in 2021 when managers at Credit Suisse chose to ignore the concerns voiced by its risk managers about the bank's exposure to an entity called Archegos, which had built up a highly leveraged $100 billion portfolio. As its trades misfired, Archegos went on to default on margin calls related to its borrowing, leaving destruction in its wake. Credit Suisse suffered losses in excess of $5 billion and, along the way, earned its place in the history books of risk management failures.

Due to their CEO-centric viewpoint, contemporary risk maps exclude several important Swan mechanisms. It is therefore appropriate for the BoD to take it upon itself to construct an extended risk map, or a Swan radar if you will. What, besides rogue executives, would the BoD put there? We have met many factors conducive to Corporate Swans already. A culture of fear and intimidation is one thing to look out for, as it obstructs the free flow of information and open conversations. Acquisitions also have a certain Swan potential, especially if large and financed with lots of debt, or if it means diversifying into businesses or geographical areas where the company has little in the way of experience. High-powered incentives, and the stretched performance targets they bring, have also been implicated in corporate disasters and therefore need to be on the Swan radar. These elements have been summed up in Figure 4.1.

As they contemplate the Swan radar, the directors should realize that they can exert influence on all of them. To begin with, they hire the CEO, so there is every possibility to assess any tendency towards narcissism-fuelled ambition. If the CEO rules by intimidation it could quickly trickle down the hierarchy and change the entire culture of the company. By controlling the CEO, the BoD indirectly determines the tone at the top. Furthermore, the BoD is responsible for negotiating the CEO's compensation package, and ultimately signs off any incentive programmes that are rolled out in the organization. As part of this

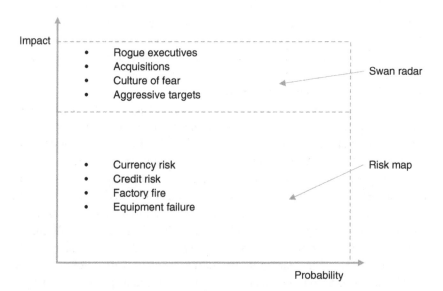

**FIGURE 4.1**   The Swan radar

process, the directors need to see clearly the power of incentives and targets to generate not only performance but also risk. There is a discussion to be had as to whether the targets in place push people too hard and induce a stress that could cause people to cross lines that should not be crossed.

The growth rate targets, for example, so crucial for the kind of performance pressure that executives find themselves living under, is shaped in the process of setting objectives and designing incentives, which the BoD is (or should be) heavily involved in. A simple but useful way of looking at it is this: the growth rate is like a gas pedal. The more aggressively we set the targets, the faster we can expect the firm to grow. Set ambitious goals that inspire maximally and the firm is likely to find itself travelling along at a brisk pace. With that comes increased risk, however, because people will do increasingly desperate things to reach the goals, and the firm will consequently have to tolerate more in the way of failures, accidents and losses along the way. An incentive scheme that is clearly more of a stretch than those of competitors, as was the case with Wells Fargo, should trigger some soul-searching. In conclusion, if the BoD wants to influence Black Swan risk, it has the levers to do so. It is just a matter of seeing it that way.

In a world of wild uncertainty, an empowered BoD is an asset. What we need are strong boards that are willing to assert themselves, ask tough questions and act on red flags. There is a need for a balance, obviously. The goal is not to abruptly reign in the degrees of freedom of the CEO, or to treat him or her with great suspicion. There is that issue of functionality again and we do not want the medicine to be worse than the ailment. It bears repeating that the great majority of executives are decent, hard-working people who want only well for their company in every possible way. A spirit of collaboration and common purpose is more productive. Like its brethren, the Chief Executive Swan is a rare animal. However, it is out there, and we must keep an open mind. The proverb 'Trust, but verify'[22] can serve as a useful guideline, where 'verify' refers to the need to confirm, on a regular basis, and as quietly as possible, that none of the items in the Swan radar seems to be emerging as a major threat. In the rare event that indications are that one of them is, the BoD needs to take a deep breath, suppress its misgivings and do the right thing.

---

[22]An old Russian proverb popularized by former US President Ronald Reagan.

# CHAPTER FIVE

# Taming the Swan

A VERY BASIC OBSERVATION is that the same Black Swan can affect two otherwise similar firms very differently depending on their resourcefulness going into the event. One may come out of it largely unscathed, whereas another may be badly decimated and reduced to a shadow of its former self. Whether or not consequences count as massive or not is a function of the firm's ability to withstand the shock. We are going to frame this issue in terms of fragility versus resilience. Fragility means that something breaks easily and crumbles when exposed to a stressor. Resilience, in contrast, denotes a capacity to quickly recover and bounce back to a level of performance similar to the one enjoyed before the shock.

Taming the Swan is about achieving the vaunted state of resilience. The resources accumulated, and the actions taken to prepare, will decide how well we fare when confronted with a shock to performance. In simple terms, the more a firm engages in proactive risk mitigation, and the more risk capital it has, the more resilient it is going to be. These strategies are costly, however, and we run into the organizational forces that resist them in favour of maximizing short-term performance. We have to design our Black Swan response mindful of the limited resources and patience available for tail risk management and try to ensure that we get the most out of whatever resources we commit to it.

## DRAWING THE LINE

Taming the Swan is, on one level, about fortifying business operations so that continuity is assured in the vast majority of scenarios. What we would like is for the value-creation process to go on in as many circumstances as possible. The basic philosophy is that the best approach in a world of wild uncertainty is not to obsess about the details of specific Black Swans but to shore up our weaknesses until we do not have any. There is something deep and reassuring about Taleb's decision rule that we decide primarily on fragility, not probability (Taleb, 2012, p. 260).

We will take his axiom to heart. What we would like is for identifying and addressing vulnerabilities to be a core organizational capability. Because we have committed to viewing wild uncertainty as self-evidently true, it is also second nature to run thought experiments, or scenarios, to 'pressure test' these exposures. If a scenario points to disastrous consequences, we should, if the cost of doing so does not strike us as outrageous, probably just proceed and do something about it. Maybe there are better ways of doing things that will reduce or eliminate the exposure. Some measures may be within reach inside of what might be considered 'ordinary business' – not a killer cost, so nothing much to speak of. We just do it to rid ourselves of a vulnerability that could be a problem one day.

Unfortunately, however, we cannot, much as we would like to, plough endless resources into an effort to achieve maximum resilience. The affordability issue discussed in Chapter 1 prevents this approach. Strategies for accomplishing resilience on the operating level are united by the fact that they will typically drive costs higher, either through upfront investment or in the form of higher running costs. What are the measures at our disposal? We will consider three generic ways of increasing resilience: *invest in buffers*, *invest in flexibility* or *invest in quality*. Increasing buffers essentially means keeping higher levels of inventory, whereas investing in flexibility means creating a 'Plan B' or a continuity plan. Investing in quality means that we opt for solutions that come with lower failure rates. Sometimes the cost is considerable and would have a noticeable effect on operating margins.

The premise is therefore going to be that there is limited patience in organizations for accepting costs related to the management of highly improbable risks. We therefore want to bring managerial attention, and the corporate purse, towards the *most critical points of failure* and pursue risk mitigation on *a targeted and selective basis*. Once the major weaknesses in the firm's value chain have been identified, we direct the scarce attention and money available for tail risk management that way. Great progress in building resilience can be made if we are able to identify such points of failure in good time and do something about them.

The experience of a real-world industrial company (they prefer to remain anonymous) provides a nice illustration of a highly targeted form of tail risk mitigation. Its managers undertook a systematic mapping of its value chain on a global basis and the flow of activities it encompassed. The analysis revealed that one node in the network was crucial to its whole operations as almost all its goods passed through it, supplying various production sites. This was a point of failure, the disruption of which would entail serious collateral damage. Seeing this exposure clearly in these terms was enough to get its managers to overcome any tendency towards inertia. They realized they had to shore up the firm's defences and therefore opted to increase the inventory of finished goods manufactured at this particular site (i.e. the strategy of investing in buffers). While this naturally increased costs, the action was considered proportionate in relation to the damage that could have been triggered throughout the value chain by a failure at this site. The firm had detected and acted on a crucial vulnerability, thereby turning a potential Black Swan that could have seriously disrupted the firm's strategy into a well-understood tail risk. As in other companies, the tolerance for accepting increased costs in the supply chain may have been limited, but this approach ensured that whatever resources were available for tail risk mitigation were used *with precision*. By staging proactive risk mitigation where it mattered the most, it had taken important steps towards Taming the Swan.

Risk expert Gary S. Lynch offers some insightful perspectives on the affordability issue and its effect on resilience in the supply chain context (Lynch, 2008, cited earlier). His point is that our pursuit of lower costs can sometimes backfire because it makes us too fragile. The more we suppress costs, the more risk is likely to pop up in places where we do not want it. According to Lynch, outsourcing over large geographical distances is a recipe for fragility – and, in due time, higher costs:

> '. . . a frenzy of off-shoring was touted as promising cheap labor and higher profit margins. But the reality has been quite different. The costs of labor, transportation, warehousing, insurance, and lean everything have grown to levels not imagined when the simple cheap labor motive first arose. But all of these costs are only the obvious ones. *A far greater cost occurs in the risk arena.*' (Emphasis added.)

This goes to the heart of the trade-off between chasing low costs and living with increased fragility. In many cases, the real cost of outsourcing has turned out to be higher than expected. When the cost of risk is factored in, outsourcing may well be more expensive, not less. Lynch argues that many supply chains, to reduce fragility to acceptable levels, need to shrink, i.e. become more local and streamlined (i.e. the strategy of investing in quality). Streamlining refers to reducing the complexity that comes from having a large number of overlapping suppliers. It is better, in Lynch's view, to go for a select few and pursue a higher level of integration. With a deeper level of integration, there is better communication and a chance of co-ordinating risk mitigation efforts. In supply chains, everyone is in it together, in the sense that the risk of a supplier's supplier is our risk too. Resilience is increasingly about taking that kind of holistic view and aligning risk management expectations across the various players involved. In this way, points of failure are minimized throughout the supply chain in a concerted effort that benefits everybody.

Of course, there can be too much of a good thing. Streamline too far and there may be too little geographical diversification of supply, and consequently too strong a concentration of risk. With a single supplier, the risk of a shutdown due to, for example, local extreme weather, which is steadily increasing, may be too much to bear. Many outlier events have an impact in a confined geographical space, so in a world of wild uncertainty, geographical diversification has a role.

We face similar trade-offs when it comes to production facilities. Operating a single plant at full capacity is of course a bonanza from the point of view of efficiency and margins. However, it also means we are sitting on a single point of failure and that we will be highly susceptible to extreme events that could cause major discontinuities in that geographic area. Adding another facility (i.e. the strategy of investing in flexibility) just for the sake of business continuity may be a stretch given the cost of the investment. If the firm is already contemplating such a move, however, the reduction in tail risk may be the factor that tips the scale in favour. Risk considerations are frequently part of a broader investment calculus, rather than a stand-alone decision.

We now turn to another aspect of Taming the Swan, namely the role of information and knowledge. Turning Swans into calculated tail risk, and mitigating risks on a targeted basis, requires high-quality information on risk exposures. Without the element of surprise stemming from ignorance about our vulnerabilities, we rob the Swans of a tactical advantage. Recall that Black Swans depend on expectations (or lack thereof), which in turn are a function of information and knowledge. Therefore, if we upgrade our ability to gather and process information (which is what generates knowledge), we are much more likely to arrive at the kind of fact-based decision-making that accounts for tail risk exposures. Basing decisions only on gut feelings and a lust for expansion increases the chances that we run into one of the Swanmakers unawares.

To appreciate the role of information and knowledge in Taming the Swan, consider the experience of Equinor, the Norwegian energy company. The company at one point contemplated drilling for oil in the Mexican Gulf. The location of the operations meant that the operations would fall under US jurisdiction, which made that country's uncapped version of third party liability law a big factor to consider. The business model they looked at would have the oil extracted from the drilling site transported to the refineries on the east coast of the US by way of tanker ships. Did Equinor also have legal responsibility for what happened during this transport? Their inquiries into the legal framework revealed that the responsibility for leakages could fall also on the owner of the oil (as opposed to the shipping company), so they would be on the hook. Lawsuits would be highly likely to pile up in case of an accident given the litigious nature of the US system, and the company would be sure to look at years of legal processing. They also learnt that the Obama administration had, in order to make stalling tactics a less effective weapon, enacted a law that would have forced the company under investigation to forward in advance an amount proportionate to the legal claim. The money would be placed in trust in an escrow account until the legal responsibilities had been sorted out. Because of this rule, any legal liability was likely to become cash effective upfront, something which, depending on the circumstances, can overwhelm a company.

The legal risks were mapped out and thoroughly discussed in relation to the venture. Questions like: 'Do we even want to do business here given these exposures?' were vented and discussed. The company tasked its engineers to evaluate countermeasures for mitigating the risk of an accident, and the probability of it happening given that these measures were implemented. They went for the strategy of investing in quality to mitigate risk. The measures they came up with included using tankers equipped with a double bottomed hull and the best radar technique available, and manning them with only highly competent crews. Their conclusion was that, given these countermeasures, an accident was an exceedingly distant possibility. On the basis of such diligence by the engineers, the company decided that the potential rewards were enough to motivate the venture, even with the tail risk that came from the legal situation. The company walked into the situation well advised about various high-impact contingencies. What could have turned out to be a complete shock to be discovered by the directors back in Norway, if an accident did happen, instead was fully internalized by key decision-makers in the organization. This level of engagement is what it takes to make a Swan grey, i.e. turn it into a reasonably understood tail risk as opposed to a completely unheard of Black Swan.

Note that the final decision involved an assessment of the probability of the event. While the primary focus is on detecting exposures to massive consequences, and taking countermeasures where we can, we cannot absolve ourselves completely from the probability aspect. As discussed, what is an appropriate risk response is determined partly by our subjective belief as to how likely the risk is to materialize. The risk management team in Equinor has long insisted on the quantification of risks to improve comparability and connect it with the bottom line (earnings), and over time it has become part of its culture. The lack of verifiable data did not faze them because they had accepted the notion that a best-effort estimate by their top engineers was the best they could do.

Taming the Swan also hinges critically on the integration of existing knowledge into the corporate decision-making process. Because of the ethos to optimize on costs and hope for the best, there might still be some reluctance to get these initiatives underway despite solid information pointing to a critical point of failure. A crucial question is therefore what it takes to galvanize an organization into taking concrete actions that aim at preparing for low probability high impact events. What is it that makes some firms prepare responsibly whereas others prefer to remain passive and try their luck? How can we jolt senior management into action based on these vague possibilities?

It helps to think of the lack of proactive action as a problem of low visibility. As noted, to get people to rally behind any forward-looking action, it is essential that people share a common view about what problem we are addressing in the first place. Taking practical steps becomes much more likely if we can formulate the risk in terms of a problem that everyone can see and understand. If enough heavy-hitters in the company are exposed to the vulnerability and deem it credible, the tail risk problems of inertia and inaction might be possible to overcome. It needs to solidify into an issue that is widely seen as deserving proper attention. So begin by putting it on the agenda as a problem worthy of solving. Articulate it as a critical point of failure in the clearest terms possible, so that no-one can later say that they thought it was somebody else's responsibility. Few can resist a challenge, so why not present it as one: How can we optimize our cost structure *given* the presence of tail risk? That is the mental frame we want to get into. Compare it with merely being satisfied with 'how can we produce at low cost with an acceptable level of defects', which, according to Lynch, is a common mindset in practice.

The BoD, as the guardians of the company's well-being, should throw their weight behind this agenda. While they do not have an operational role, they can change expectations. They may observe that the executives of the company have little time for investigating points of failure, preferring instead the more gratifying pursuits of expansion and acquisitions. In these cases, Black Swan-minded BoDs should request that key vulnerabilities are mapped out so that a consensus can form regarding the firm's soft underbelly. An even more concrete step is to tie CEO compensation to the implementation of best practice business continuity plans. Once those incentives are in place, everyone else in the organization is soon about to be made aware of them. Also, pay attention to the powerful effect of incentives and the way profitability targets can stand in the way of proactive risk mitigation. If the firm's KPIs create strong incentives to this effect, see if they can be rewritten in a way that resolves the tension between the desire to collect the bonus and doing what is right in the long term.

Moreover, the BoD should look for evidence that the executives are not just going for a rock-bottom effort. What passes for risk management on paper may not be very effective when push comes to shove. Risk mitigation actions need to be checked to ensure that they are not paper tigers. If the firm operates two factories, for example, managers might conclude that if one suffers a severe disruption, they will rely on the second and increase output there. This sounds like a nice Plan B that guarantees continuity, but may be entirely ineffective in countering tail risk if it turns out that the second plant is already operating at close to full capacity. Continuity plans have been known to fail due to unrealistic assumptions, like taking for granted that the power grid will function, when in reality there could well be an outage. Likewise, insurance programmes should be critically assessed so that the coverage really adds up to something meaningful. Insurance contracts that are outside routine areas are legally very complicated documents and the insurance company may well dispute the claim if the nominal amount is large. In these situations, it comes down to the fine print, and the insurance programme may end up giving much less protection than the company thought based on reading the sales material.

What we are talking about here is the *effectiveness*, in the hour of need, of the measures aimed at mitigating tail risk. It is easy to feel better about oneself after having done *something*, however inadequate that something might be, and stop there. The action, however under-dimensioned it is, resolves the cognitive dissonance that existed between the previous state of inaction and the sense that something had to be done. Ideally, the BoD should be presented with some convincing evidence that, when it hits the fan, the thing works. The limitations of key mitigation measures taken should be keenly appreciated, or else the Black Swan will sneak through the defences and take us in despite of all the effort. We should not be content with what might at first glance seem like risk mitigation: 'Oh, so you bought a business continuity plan and some insurance? Good then!' Risk mitigation actions that do not withstand the pressure in a real emergency turns those who believed otherwise into suckers, taking us back to square one.

It is up to the BoD to draw the line and make sure that there is always an adult in the room. By drawing the line, I mean not accepting any risk that threatens to wipe out the firm or lead to serious strategy disruption. They should consider which exposures simply cannot be tolerated, on account of the collateral damage they would entail. For drawing the line, it would be quite useful to get a sense of roughly how *close* we are to the point where such consequences would begin to happen. This will be the topic of the next section.

However, before leaving this section it is worth reflecting for a few moments on what companies think makes them resilient. In my conversations with business leaders, one theme keeps coming up. What they say is that having the right people is what makes the difference. They describe it in terms of having competent people in leadership positions, giving them close to full autonomy and responsibility so that they can act quickly and forcefully when there is drastic change. Their ideal is to empower good people and avoid diffusion of responsibility. Engaging the full, drawn-out corporate decision-making process is seen as a luxury you cannot afford when the world is thrown into a full-blown crisis. Empowerment of good managers is a message that is more pronounced in companies favouring a decentralized business model, but it has general appeal because it seems to put people first. This kind of agency is a more deeply embedded organizational quality that goes outside the three generic strategies of investing in buffers, flexibility and quality. We must not forget, however, that even highly competent and empowered people can struggle to produce good outcomes when acting from a position of overall (and perhaps avoidable) distress, pointing to the continued importance of the three generic strategies. Let us not also forget another deeper organizational capability relevant for resilience – that of communicating across different parts of the firm and of co-ordinating actions. Silo-effects are real, and everyone in the company going it alone may not be the right way to do things in a turbulent situation, no matter how talented they are. We will touch on this subject again in Chapter 6.

 ## DISTANCE TO WIPEOUT

To learn how we might become resilient as an enterprise, we must first see what makes us fragile. The way we are going to understand firm fragility is in terms of closeness to certain *pain thresholds*, which are performance levels at which we have good reasons to believe that some very damaging consequences would occur. We need to think about consequences beyond the mere monetary losses, which takes us back to our earlier discussion about collateral damage.

We will consider two pain thresholds: one associated with wipeout, the other with strategy disruption. The wipeout threshold, if breached, implies either bankruptcy or outright liquidation and the likely loss (to shareholders) of any option value that would have materialized in case of a rebound. The strategy disruption threshold is the point at which the strategy starts to break down. Signs of a compromised strategy include excessive cuts in costs and investments, making asset fire sales, experiencing deteriorating terms with suppliers and customers, and so on. The pain thresholds thus indicate the outer limits of our ability to survive and thrive. Whereas before we were talking about these consequences in general terms, now we are interested in pinpointing more exactly the circumstances that would trigger them.

The goal is to understand how big a performance shock it would take to end up on the wrong side of the thresholds. We capture this notion by introducing two measurements: 'Distance-to-Wipeout' and 'Distance-to-Disruption'. A fragile firm finds itself already close to the thresholds, so it would not take much of a performance dip to send it over the brink. Conversely, a firm that has managed to put a greater distance between itself and the thresholds has a better chance of getting through a period of turbulence unharmed. We can obtain a representation of the firm's current risk profile if we craft scenarios, apply them to our firm's performance and observe the distance-to-thresholds that results.

Scenarios are primarily a tool for opening our minds to (extreme) possibilities and generating good conversations about the right way to proceed in the light of those. It represents a more flexible and versatile mindset compared to the rigid process of compiling forecasts and budgets, and is therefore more aligned with the realities of wild uncertainty. There are a multitude of different ways that the world can unfold, many of which have stark implications for our strategy and financial health. For our present purposes, we can make further progress if we express scenarios in terms of their impact on financial performance. The usefulness of this approach is that it offers us a way to identify rather precisely the circumstances under which the thresholds would be in danger. That is, every scenario that we come up with has to be translated into effects on financial performance: cash flow, profit, balance sheet and financial ratios. This is how we make sure that the things we talk about are ultimately relevant and comparable.

In the end, wipeout and disruptions are functions of cash flow generation in relation to cash needs. It is when a large enough imbalance between these two build up and we struggle to cover the gap that painful consequences are likely to follow. Accordingly, to begin with, we will express scenarios in terms of operating cash flow ('supply of liquidity') and cash commitments ('demand for liquidity'). Cash commitments are all cash outlays that are needed in order to stay alive and execute the firm's strategy. To simplify things, capital expenditure will be used to denote the investment needed to execute the strategy ('thriving') and debt servicing to denote the interest payments and repayments of loans needed to avoid default ('surviving'). Cash commitments, in this stylized approach, is the sum of capital expenditures and debt servicing.

The difference between operating cash flow and cash commitments, as it appears in our financial forecast, is a rough first indicator of how removed we are from the pain thresholds. Whenever operating cash flows are insufficient to cover cash commitments on their own we have what amounts to a *potential* disruption of the firm's strategy where capital expenditure *might* have to be scaled back. The shortfall may or may not be a problem, depending on the firm's resources. The firm might be able to shrug it off (a resilient firm), but it might also be doomed by it (a fragile firm). We just need a structured way to think about which of those two outcomes is more likely to happen, which brings us to the topic of risk capital.

 ## RISK CAPITAL

The most basic approach for increasing resilience is to make sure that the firm has enough *capital* around to deal with any contingencies that might arise. Risk capital, broadly defined, encompasses any resource that helps a firm get through a rough patch without experiencing negative consequences. It is the old idea of having a buffer against risk, of saving up for a rainy day. We are essentially talking about 'shock absorbers', a cushion of resources that allow the firm to get through worse-than-expected scenarios largely unharmed. The concept of risk capital can be given a broad interpretation that includes things like reputation, political connections, government interventions and managerial resourcefulness – basically, anything that helps the firm pull through. In order to keep the story tractable, however, and in keeping with the literature on the subject, I will focus on *financial* resources. Maintaining a healthy balance sheet will be a big part of the answer to how firms can become resilient.

To develop some perspectives on risk capital, consider that doing business and investing are inherently risky activities and some capital is required to protect the firm against unforeseen shocks that could affect their performance.

For example, let us say a start-up firm intends to earn a profit by lending to small businesses and raises $100 million by issuing a bond. How much equity must the owners contribute to keep the company safe against credit losses? An insurance company sells insurance against natural disasters to firms and other entities. How much capital does it need to ensure its survival in case one or more disasters occur over the next 12 months? A trading desk has a new investment strategy that it thinks will generate superior returns. How much capital does it need as a buffer to ensure that it does not suffer a complete loss of capital through some blitz of market volatility that occurs along the way?

The trading desk example illustrates the point that risk capital is distinct from transaction capital, where the latter signifies the money needed to launch an investment or carry out a transaction. If a firm wishes to buy plant, property and equipment to set up a cash flow generating business, those purchases must be financed up-front. This is the financing of a venture. Risk capital is needed *in addition to that* until the day the project is brought to fruition. It serves the purpose of providing a cushion against adversities that occur in the meantime, thereby allowing the venture to continue undisturbed. One way to think about this issue is that risk also has to be financed. We need to put enough money in a venture to allow it to carry out all the necessary purchases *and* keep some money as a buffer for eventualities.

Risk capital offers an attractive way of dealing with Black Swans. It represents a generic approach for absorbing performance shocks regardless of their nature and source. We do not have to try to predict various calamities or devise elaborate risk mitigation strategies. Instead, we rely on these buffers to bail us out if anything goes wrong. This saves us precious mental bandwidth, allowing us to focus our energies on getting ahead, generating growth and becoming a more formidable competitor. The reason we want risk capital is that there is a value in surviving and in being able to see the strategy through periods of turbulence. Short-term shocks to performance are a threat to both those objectives and risk capital can make the difference regarding how such shocks end up affecting the firm.

Risk capital, as envisioned in this book, is a function of two balance sheet decisions: how much equity to use as part of the overall financing of the firm and how much of liquid assets to keep as a portion of total assets. Both equity and liquidity function as buffers, but in different ways. Equity does so by reducing the amount of fixed cash obligations in the form of interest payments and instalments on loans. Having more equity also makes it easier to obtain new financing if need be, as there will be fewer conflicts of interest to account for compared to a balance sheet already burdened with lots of debt.

The risk-reducing effect of having more liquid assets, such as cash in the bank, around as a precautionary measure is straightforward. Rather than relying on capital markets to keep us going by injecting new funds, we have stockpiled some liquidity internally.

To understand and manage resilience it is important to have a working knowledge of risk capital and make it part of our toolbox. We will therefore explore two different ways of conceptualizing risk capital: *Economic Capital* and *Risk Capacity*. Economic Capital deals with the potential for losses and their consequences for solvency. It is a concept that has been implemented primarily in the banking and insurance sectors, where financial stability is of the utmost importance. Risk Capacity instead deals with the potential for cash flow short-falls and their consequences for strategy execution. While these subjects may have an air of complexity to them, the ideas underpinning them are quite simple and intuitive.

Economic Capital can be thought of as the capital a bank needs to survive in a worst-case scenario. The word capital is somewhat nebulous and can mean different things to different people. The easiest way to think of capital, in this context, is in terms of *loss-absorbing equity*.[1] When losses occur, they deplete equity, and if the accumulated losses become large enough, the firm is at risk of becoming insolvent (technically, this occurs when the value of assets falls below that of liabilities). In order to qualify as loss-absorbing equity, the financial claim issued by the bank has to fulfil two basic criteria. First, there is no fixed and con-tractually binding principal to be repaid. Second, the firm has full discretion over any payments made to the claimholders. That is, the payments can be cancelled or postponed without any negative consequences being triggered (the same is not true for debt and other legally binding debt equivalents). Perpetual preferred shares, for instance, typically qualify as capital, because any dividends paid are at the board's discretion and there is no principal that ever needs to be repaid.

The basic way of thinking is that the larger the initial base of equity capital, the lower the likelihood of insolvency. Framing it in this way introduces the notion that any given amount of capital is associated with a certain *proba-bility* of insolvency. Indeed, a more formal definition of Economic Capital is in terms of the capital a bank needs to survive with a targeted probability (alter-natively, the capital consistent with an X% probability of insolvency). This is

---

[1]Some equity is considered to be of higher quality than others. Share capital (paid-in capital) and retained earnings are considered to be of the highest quality, for example, because they can be assumed to reliably absorb losses (this is 'Tier 1' capital in the regulatory jargon). Other sources of equity, such as various revaluation and hedging reserves, are considered more flighty and driven by accounting considerations, and therefore less reliable ('Tier 2' capital).

an important conceptual step, because it means that we are going to *accept* a certain possibility of insolvency. Ensuring survival in all possible scenarios would be inefficient, because it implies relying 100% on equity and devoting a disproportionate amount of the company's resources towards survival. Some risk is therefore to be accepted, and Economic Capital is what makes sure that this targeted probability of insolvency materializes. If our assessment is that the insolvency probability is too high, we add capital until we reach the desired level. Likewise, if it is virtually zero, we might retire some capital (pay it back to investors as a dividend).

Risk Capacity is also based on the idea of a buffer against risk, but conceptualizes it a bit differently from Economic Capital. Here, the focus is on liquidity. Risk Capacity is understood as a buffer of highly liquid assets that help to absorb cash flow shortfalls. This is where we reconnect with the point made in the previous section, which was that risk is a function of imbalances between cash generation and cash needs. Whenever such a shortfall occurs, wipeout and strategy disruption may be real prospects unless the firm has the means to cover the difference. As long as it has enough liquid assets at its disposal, it can continue to cover the shortfalls and keep executing the strategy.

The most obvious source of Risk Capacity is cash-at-hand. Going into a situation, any excess cash (i.e. cash not needed for operational purposes) will be available to deal with unexpected shocks to performance that create shortfalls. However, there are also conditional forms of liquidity that add to Risk Capacity. The firm may have untapped borrowing capacity that makes it easy to cover a shortfall. The undrawn part of a credit facility, for example, can serve to smooth out temporary imbalances between cash generation and cash outlays. Finally, we also count cash flows from contingent claims such as derivative contracts towards Risk Capacity *on condition* that these payoffs reliably occur in situations where there are cash flow shortfalls. That is, if there is a scenario in which operating cash flow is 75 and cash commitments are 100, a contingent claim adds to Risk Capacity if and only if it yields a cash flow in that scenario to help cover the difference. Contingent claims are qualitatively different because we are talking about a risk transfer, i.e. using markets to lay off risk (while obviously paying the counterparty for that privilege). Relying on existing cash to sort out shortfalls, in contrast, is to self-insure rather than use markets for risk absorption.

Risk Capacity is about corporate survival in worst-case scenarios, but, unlike Economic Capital, it also targets strategy execution. Recall that the definition of cash commitments includes capital expenditure, broadly defined as any expenditure associated with the successful implementation of strategy. In a sense, by making strategy execution across scenarios a stated objective, we raise the bar compared to being content to verify that the firm will not be wiped out. It is a more ambitious agenda. Making provisions to ensure survival in a worst-case scenario takes fewer resources than making provisions for thriving in addition. When things head south, we do not just want to survive but would also like to keep implementing the business plan. The value-creation process, if we are truly resilient, should go on regardless of the circumstances we find ourselves in. If we want to protect the strategy as well, we need a bigger buffer. Risk Capacity is about making a conscious decision about how much liquidity, whether at hand or contingent, we need to keep to ensure this outcome even in worse-than-expected scenarios.

Risk Capacity increases the distance to the critical thresholds, which is the same thing as saying that it leads to a lower probability that the critical thresholds are reached. Any given amount of Risk Capacity is associated with a certain probability of strategy disruption. The resources we have available will absorb many shortfalls but quite possibly not all of them. Because capital expenditure is typically the first cash commitment to be scaled back, this disruption risk can often be interpreted as the probability of not being able to invest optimally. Some risk of disruption may have to be accepted due to the cost of keeping Risk Capacity. Recall in our discussion in Chapter 3 that liquid assets lower the return on assets and using more equity capital reduces the return on equity. As always, *there is that tension between resilience and efficiency,* so we want to create some transparency around this and make an informed decision. Figure 5.1 illustrates how Risk Capacity shifts the critical threshold towards the left, but that there is still some probability of strategy disruption (underinvestment) associated with it.

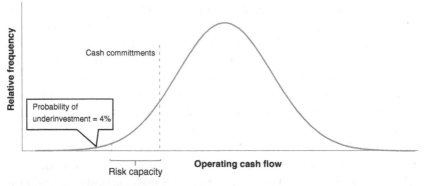

**FIGURE 5.1**　Risk Capacity

At this point, someone may wonder why the firm does not just go to its owners for more capital when they are in trouble. If they believe the business has potential, they will support it with more capital – correct? Well, the thing about Risk Capacity is that, to count as such, it has to be available on *pre-agreed terms or terms that can be assumed to be efficient*. Risk Capacity is only meaningful to talk about if the liquidity can be obtained on reasonably efficient terms, while times are still good(ish). When assessing spare borrowing capacity, we need to have solid reasons to believe that we can access the funds without being subjected to punishing conditions. When the latter is the case, we are already paying a certain price since we have no choice but to accept the terms that are dictated. That is, we are experiencing negative consequences of variability in performance, as opposed to coming out on the other end unscathed. To understand Risk Capacity, an effort must be made to anticipate what kind of conditional sources of cash we can get access to *as things would appear in a worse-than-expected scenario*. It should be clear that we are talking about what we can accomplish in unfavourable scenarios here. Extrapolating from today's situation and assuming we can access money on the same terms would most likely be unrealistic.

As for issuing equity to shore up a balance sheet during a crisis, that almost certainly counts as a negative consequence of variability that we would like to avoid. Contingent equity issuance is therefore not generally part of Risk Capacity. To begin with, it will tend to be incredibly expensive, as the uncertainty surrounding a troubled firm would necessitate a huge risk premium. Another problem is that, if the firm is in outright distress, most of the proceeds will merely serve to make existing debt safer. This is the classic debt overhang problem in corporate finance, which explains why equity is a costly measure of last resort and not a handy way out of distress. Because of the low value any equity investor would attach to the shares being issued, the dilution of existing shareholders can be stupendous. For example, when troubled air-carrier Norwegian Air Shuttle issued equity in 2020 in a do-or-die fashion, it did so at an 80% discount to the price at which its shares were trading. If it means that some groups of investors lose control or influence, it is all the more reason to try to avoid getting into that situation in the first place (fiduciary duty implies that managers are supposed to choose the policy that is in the best interest of existing owners).

To sum up so far, Economic Capital deals with loss-absorbing equity capital and the risk of insolvency, whereas Risk Capacity deals with cash flow shortfall-absorbing liquidity and the risk of not being able to execute the strategy. Which of these versions of risk capital is appropriate for building resilience and navigating a world of wild uncertainty? For a non-financial firm, not motivated by regulatory demands on solvency, it primarily makes sense to manage liquidity. As our discussion in Chapter 3 showed, negative book equity has no clear-cut interpretation and may not matter much. The bankruptcy process is much more likely to be triggered by an inability to meet ongoing cash obligations. We learned from the Hertz episode that this sets in motion a dangerous process that may end up in a shareholder wipeout, i.e. a scenario in which the firm is liquidated or where shareholders emerge from the process with a greatly reduced stake in the firm's future performance. As we have already noted, liquidity-driven bankruptcy from short-term shocks to performance is primarily what should be feared.

An important part of Taming the Swan, therefore, is to make a qualified assessment about the firm's Risk Capacity and its ability to absorb cash flow shortfalls, thus keeping the firm at a safe distance from the pain thresholds. This is not to say that the solvency dimension is unimportant. On the contrary, understanding a firm's solvency is usually necessary to assess refinancing possibilities (spare borrowing capacity). The firm's ability to cope with cash flow shortfalls is weaker if the firm's balance sheet is burdened by debt, because it largely determines whether capital markets are open to it on good terms. Wipeout risk and strategy disruption can usefully be thought of in terms of scenarios in which the firm's liquidity is down *and* its solvency is depleted to the point where easy refinancing can no longer be taken for granted.

On a related note, it might seem strange that we consider borrowed money to be part of Risk Capacity. Is not adding debt normally the same thing as increasing risk? This is true (unless the proceeds are kept as cash, which is not our case – we assume that it is used to plug cash flow shortfalls). However, the concept is built on the premise that a firm could have an underleveraged balance sheet and thus some ability to get through short-term turmoil, which is the main objective here, with the help of the bank. It is not imprudent to borrow money to avoid a breakdown of the strategy if there is spare borrowing capacity, because the term itself implies that long-term competitiveness is not undermined by it. We can borrow at practically no risk of becoming Zombies, to put it that way. The very term 'spare borrowing capacity' implies that the firm is fundamentally viable and its balance sheet is strong enough to cope. It furthermore implies that we can avoid a strategy disruption now in exchange for a miniscule increase in future wipeout risk, which is a fair deal. That is, when we borrow, the needle on future wipeout risk hardly moves. That is the condition for being part of Risk Capacity.

Risk Capacity always refers to the ability to avoid disruptions in the present planning period (as defined) with little or no detrimental consequences on our future ability to manoeuvre. However, the opposite can also be true, which is when borrowing does increase future wipeout risk. Because we plugged the cash flow gap with debt, we may, when we repeat the analysis in future periods, alternatively find that the risk of future financial distress is now decidedly higher. There is a trade-off involved that we should not be blind to. Many commentators worried about the 'mountain of debt' that built up during 2020 as firms scrambled to keep themselves going, suggesting that the systemic consequences were merely delayed. Indeed, some of those firms may be doomed to Zombiehood and low competitiveness due to the extensive borrowing they had to resort to in order to survive. Surviving now, for these firms, comes at the price of thriving less in the future, because the debt load crowds out investment and expansion. If you subsequently went into Zombiehood, it means that you overindulged and that the borrowing was not covered by pre-existing Risk Capacity. Rather, by borrowing more in that situation, those firms were mortgaging their future competitiveness. In fact, falling into Zombiehood could be viewed as another form of strategy disruption, one that will make itself felt in future periods.

Because we take an interest in tail risk, one more point is worth elaborating. It is as follows: since tail risk refers to severe but rare events, an efficient way of buffering that risk is to arrange for cash to be released in exactly those circumstances. This means that, out of the three sources of Risk Capacity that we have considered, conditional cash from risk transfer is the most attractive in principle. Keeping a buffer of cash or arranging for a sizeable credit facility are strategies that are in place regardless of which scenario plays out. In all the scenarios in which times are good or even fantastic, they will still sit there and generate a cost. An enticing possibility, then, is to use risk transfer to zero in precisely the circumstances in which a wipeout or strategy disruption is on the table. What if we could execute the financing of tail risk with some precision?

Take an oil firm, for example, that is currently enjoying robust profits at an oil price of $70. It figures that if the price took a steep dive down to $30 over the next year, it would have to make some tough cuts in its operations due to substantial cash flow shortfalls, from which it would not easily recover. This represents a strategy disruption that would erode its long-term competitiveness and ability to thrive. For this firm, an efficient way to strengthen Risk Capacity is to buy put options (the equivalent of buying insurance) with a strike price of $30. Here we face the usual issue that tends to stop proactive risk management in its tracks, namely that such a position would have to be continually renewed over time, causing an outflow of money on account of the premium that must be paid. This outflow would soon become unbearable to some of the managers. To avoid this, the firm may decide that it is preferable to sell some of its upside potential to finance the purchases of the put options (i.e. writing call options on which it has to pay out money if they end up in the money). Let us say it sells call options at a strike price of $110, such that it fully finances the put options. It has now dealt with its tail risk and has done so in a way that imposes the least amount of psychological pain on the organization. Selling calls is out-of-sight, out-of-mind, which cannot be said when the put options are cash-financed. We have sacrificed some upside potential, yes, but we have done so *just enough* to accomplish the goal of making us resilient to tail risk. This is an elegant and efficient way of going about tail risk management.

There is a second, and easy to overlook, advantage of conditional payoffs from risk transfer when it comes to the financing of tail risk. Payoffs from risk transfer have the benefit of *dynamically adjusting* to the size of the cash flow shortfall. Compare the following strategies for buffering against tail risk: keep cash-at-hand versus using the same cash to buy put options. Besides the usual inefficiency of keeping cash, which is that it sits on the balance sheet across all scenarios, including very positive ones, we should also pay attention to the fact that it becomes depleted, or overwhelmed, if the cash flow shortfalls reach a certain point. When the cash runs out, that is the end of that buffer. With the put option strategy, in contrast, the size of the cash injection it generates keeps getting bigger the more serious the cash flow shortfall gets (this happens because the underlying spot price that dictates the payoff is what simultaneously drives the operating cash flow lower). This dynamic feature means that it keeps buffering shortfalls 'all the way down', and that it does not get overwhelmed in the same way that a cash balance can.

Cashless option-based strategies therefore have a certain appeal from a tail risk perspective. It serves as a nice mental model for what we are trying to do: take the edge out of tail risk, while causing the least amount of friction in the corporate decision-making process, and while giving away the least amount of upside potential possible. Perhaps for this reason, so-called collar strategies (long puts combined with short calls) are a very popular strategy among commodity producers. It is a pity that such contracts are not widely available for general performance risk because that would allow the broad mass of firms to deploy similar strategies.

##  STRESS TESTING

A cornerstone in the framework for resilience proposed in this chapter is the pain thresholds. Whenever we fail to defend our cash commitments, we feel 'pain' as the strategy begins to be disrupted and, in particularly bleak circumstances, we may even default on our debt obligations. In practical terms, it means that we have to establish the liquidity requirements that are associated with both surviving (debt servicing) and thriving (capital expenditure). To understand the implications of potential cash flow shortfalls, we complement the analysis with an assessment of Risk Capacity (cash and conditional sources of cash) that serve to absorb the shortfalls. In doing so, we come around to a decent appreciation of the kind of financial resources we can muster in worse-than-expected scenarios. The analysis of Risk Capacity is therefore a second cornerstone in building up an understanding of our resilience.

At this point in our narrative, the missing ingredient is some estimate of the tail risk scenario itself. The questions we are trying to make some progress on are the following: 'How bad can get it get – realistically?' and 'What residual tail risk are we willing to accept?' We can try to use our data and imagination to come up with a scenario that really puts the firm's survival skills to the test. Such exercises, usually called stress tests, make for great advances in terms of the firm's tail risk awareness. Importantly, these tests should refer to the welfare of the enterprise as a whole. What we are stress testing is the performance at the level of the corporate group and the focus is on whether the firm is resilient enough to withstand truly awful circumstances. Enterprise stress testing should revolve around assessing whether one or both of the pain thresholds are reached, as they signal the limit of our ability to survive and thrive. The learning experience that enterprise stress testing promises is that it allows us to become familiar with the firm's breaking point and the distance to it, now versus how it would look under extreme conditions. The insights generated by this exercise should then loop back to the process of setting corporate policies so that we achieve a defensible balance between tail risk and upside potential.

As should be clear from our earlier discussions on risk mapping, the BoD should be under no illusion that all of this is somehow covered just because the firm has an impressive-looking register describing a vast number of risks. A register is for the most part just a static compilation of risk factors. A stress test, in contrast, is a specific scenario with a major impact on our firm. In rare cases, it might be assessed that a single risk factor in the register could break the company on its own, like a sustained spike in the price of electricity in the case of the energy firm Griddy. In these cases, the realization of that single risk is so consequential that it effectively becomes the stress scenario. If such a killer risk has been identified, the stress test follows the following steps: (1) take performance as it looks today, (2) assume that the tail risk event occurs, (3) overlay its impact on performance and (4) observe whether the impact is bad enough to push the company below the pain thresholds, while factoring in any risk capital it might have.

Risk registers can sometimes be put to use, due to the fact that the stress test can be 'informed' by the risks that have been compiled in the register. However, there are no hard rules for what constitutes an appropriate stress test or how to put one together. When we devise one, it can revolve around a specific event if impactful enough, but often we face chains of interconnected events. We should always have a certain sensibility towards any dynamics that could create a perfect storm. An exceptionally poor way of implementing a stress test, however, is to assume that all of the risks in the register magically materialize at the same time, as this tends to lack in realism.

This brings us to the sensitive topic of whether or not a stress test should be realistic or not. When the US Treasury rolled out its SCAP programme in the midst of the financial crisis in the late 2000s, widely hailed as a watershed moment in the use of stress testing, they characterized it as a 'severe *but plausible*' scenario (emphasis added.) For some reason, they did not refer to it as a 'severe and inconceivable' scenario. We clearly want some degree of plausibility here. If revenue drops by 100% and we all die, who cares? Push it too far and people will think you are ridiculous and lose interest in the exercise. Push it too little and you are not respecting the Moving Tail. Of course, this balancing act makes it more of an art than science. However, we should at least raise the issue of the Moving Tail and get some kind of discussion going as to whether what is on record can be exceeded by a material amount and what that would mean for the organization.

Stress tests are fundamentally linked, I would argue, to the concept of the Moving Tail. Our first priority is not to be lulled into inaction because we have seen nothing but mild fluctuations in performance in the last, say, 10 years. This goes back to the sucker's problem of trying to infer the future from the recent past. Using only a limited period of history, concerning our immediate surroundings, to come up with an idea about what a stress test might look like could severely underestimate the potential scope of what could happen.

Again, the C-19 pandemic serves as a useful backdrop. Take a company with operations in East Asia that, in early 2019, wondered about the potential for pandemics to inflict havoc on their business model. Hopefully, it would have been wise enough to see that the absence of such outbreaks affecting its business in the 2010s meant little. The company could instead start by assuming that something like the H1N1-virus or the Hong Kong flu might happen again (the latter occurred in 1968 and killed over a million people).

If a few decades worth of data was gathered, these data points represented the tail of the distribution. If we extend our view beyond a few decades, we will discover that the tail has moved several times in the past. When the analysis covers a larger span of human history we find more realistic indications of how bad things can possibly get. Our stress test would now be informed not only by H1N1 and the Hong Kong flu, but the likes of the Spanish flu, which reached a global spread (it affected about a third of the world's population in four successive waves, and tens of millions of people died from it). It would be clear that such a tail event is at least to be considered a once-in-a-century risk, and therefore plausible enough and something we might want to make some provision for. Then there is the Moving Tail: things can get even worse than anything we have observed in the historical records. The reason is simply that things can change. Viruses can get more contagious and deadly, and the connectivity of the global economy is much higher than in the past.

The above reasoning leads to the following conclusion as to how to use stress tests in a world of wild uncertainty. Good practice is to fit our stress test not to recent history, but to a longer stretch of observations that include more episodes of severe stress. That gives us the appropriate view on what the tail actually might be like. Then, we need to acknowledge the idea that it is possible that the tail will move yet again. The general idea is to take the worst episode on record and move beyond that (unless it is clear that the worst on record is devastating enough, in which case it already serves its purpose). To keep the shift in the tail economically meaningful yet still within the realm of the possible, consider a 20% mark-up relative to the tail risk on record. Ultimately though, circumstances will have to dictate the appropriate design.

Any successful attempt at managing tail risk on a regular basis must walk another fine line, which is to not become perceived as too burdensome. Patience quickly wears thin with analytical techniques that come across as too complicated. Stress tests certainly have no free pass. They too have to prove themselves useful in the face of a limited corporate attention span. Becoming tangled up in detailed drill-downs is not always the way to go. A more economical approach, which covers a number of bases, is to implement the stress test using financial performance numbers directly. The position taken in this book is that a suitable baseline structure for the analysis of enterprise risk is to start with the corporate top line, which is to say revenue. Then, we ask what impact revenue shocks would have on some bottom line of interest (i.e. the pain thresholds), mediated by various buffers or shock absorbers that are under management's influence (i.e. risk capital). This structure is also applicable to stress testing exercises.

If we start by zeroing in on revenue, the question simplifies to: What happens to the company if there is a very large and sustained fall in revenue? Such a large drop in revenue stands in for the more precise dynamics that would be identified in a granular type of stress test. How big the loss in revenue should be for the purpose of a stress test will vary, but the 30% threshold for Corporate Swans discussed earlier could serve as an initial reference point. Losing a third of one's sales is a very serious situation for most companies. As our analysis of the empirical data showed, it is a rare event, well placed in the tail of the distribution. Using this approach, the East Asian operator we mentioned earlier would substitute the analysis of how a pandemic might play out with a large enough revenue shock that it assumes would follow. When we look to develop risk responses on an operational level, the financial approach has its obvious limitations, but it goes a long way toward a basic understanding of resilience at the enterprise level, i.e. the ability to survive and thrive (we will come back to the operational response later in this chapter).

Stress tests are indispensable for Taming the Swan. The main lever in affecting the outcomes in the tests is Risk Capacity, by which we can bolster our resilience. The goal is to calibrate the amount of Risk Capacity so that a sensible tail risk–return balance obtains, i.e. one that cannot be improved in any obvious way. Practically, it means that we repeat the stress test many times assuming different levels of Risk Capacity. The company could choose to take actions to either boost it (if resilience is found to be uncomfortably low) or decrease it (if found to be grossly excessive). This kind of proactive evaluation produces a before and after view of the firm's resilience also *under different policies*. For example, managers might consider withholding a dividend payment to boost the cash position or put in place a derivative that is likely to produce a payoff coinciding with falling revenue. Its Risk Capacity, and resilience, would therefore be higher. It can now submit the firm's expected performance to the same stress test to learn what difference this extra Risk Capacity does in terms of the company's distance to its pain thresholds. Doing this for various configurations of Risk Capacity might lead to an appreciation of how much of it would be necessary to arrive at the desired level of resilience.

As part of this process, any costs related to committing more resources to Risk Capacity would have to be appreciated as well. We are, as always, in the business of trading risk against upside. This does not change just because we are talking about tail risk. While a basic goal is to keep the wipeout risk as close to zero as possible, there is only so much one can do. There are times when pushing it towards zero would be counterproductive.

While plenty can be learned from stress tests, even without attaching probabilities, once more we face the fact that some kind of probabilistic assessment is going to be necessary.[2] A stress test could easily shake everyone and push a lot of buttons on our risk aversion, prompting a risk response that swings into overmanagement of risk, which is not ideal either. The probability aspect is, as we know, a key determinant of the cost of risk, which determines the scope for resilience-boosting actions. Recall that earlier we defined risk capital in terms of the financial buffers associated with a certain probability of a negative consequence. We are going to tolerate some possibility of failure, but would like to know roughly what it would take to end up there and to have some idea about how likely that outcome is.

There is a tension here between acknowledging that the world offers wild uncertainty, implying that the odds cannot be known, and our desire for some kind of probabilistic approach that lets us determine whether our Black Swan response is underdimensioned, proportionate or excessive. This is what is so maddening about Swans and the Moving Tail: there is no way of really knowing how bad it can get or what the probabilities are, so how can we 'optimize'?

Despite the seeming hopelessness of this situation, there are a few things we can do. At the very least, we will enlighten ourselves in the process and reach our goal, which is a policy that is not obviously inadequate for dealing with tail risk, nor obviously excessive. Again, we can use the power of data, but target the probability aspect in a more direct way. Instead of fixing the magnitude of the shock (30% in our example), we could go for using the revenue drop associated with a predetermined probability. In this case, we would take the historical distribution of percentage changes in revenue for a sample of firms that resemble our own and look up the change that represents the 99th percentile. This informs us that in only 1% of cases do we observe negative revenue changes larger than this. Put another way, it indicates that the probability of experiencing an even larger negative drop is 1% in any given year. Ending up so far out in the tail could be thought of as a once-in-a-century type of risk *as it applies to corporate revenue.* For example, for US manufacturing firms, the percentage drop in revenue associated with a 1% probability is −45%. Going by that number, the probability of losing roughly half our revenue over the next year is 1%. Then we can apply a negative change of that magnitude on our firm and observe the kind of outcome it would generate on various bottom lines.

---

[2]Some would say stress tests are fundamentally a non-probabilistic exercise and that the point with it is to escape the overreliance of probabilistic approaches. I think this view needs to be qualified in that the analysis of risk should never be completely detached from the notion of likelihood, however subjective.

There are good reasons to accept some risk of failure and just leave certain extreme possibilities to rest. We may ignore an extreme possibility because the probability is, while not zero, so close to that number as to make the cost of risk miniscule as well. This goes for all the asteroid impacts, mega-volcanos, and so on. Many Black Swans will forever go on lurking in the shadows with a non-zero probability, but it does not affect how we go about things. The same thing can be said for the unknown unknowns that could change the world as we know it but of which we have yet to hear. There are plenty of those unnamed possibilities with massive consequences out there and some day, for all our efforts to stave them off, they will bring us down. Over the next hundred years, we should probably count on something like that happening at least once. Let us, therefore, just for the sake of heeding this philosophical point, never let the probability of a worst-case scenario in which the strategy breaks down go below 1% (another 1% rule!). Setting the probability to 1% on a yearly basis means that the probability of enterprise failure over a 100-year horizon is 63.4%, which is to say that we consider it more likely than not that the firm will fail (go under) at some point during the next 100 years. This is an entirely reasonable assumption – very few firms that existed a hundred years ago are still around.

Reporting a zero probability of enterprise failure would indeed be epistemologically unfortunate because it signals overconfidence in our ability to control wild uncertainty. Therefore, whenever we estimate (subjectively, yes) the probability to be higher, we communicate that. If it goes below 1%, we overrule that and communicate 1%. We are fine with that risk – it comes with the territory. In the extreme end of the tail, managers are right to shrug their shoulders.

## The Exit Option

In the previous section, a structure for stress testing that starts with the top line, revenue, was favoured. Going for operating cash flow directly in the stress test might seem to simplify things even more, because the pain thresholds are expressed in terms of the level of cash commitments we need to defend in order to survive and thrive. Cash flow relates to that in a more direct way than revenue. However, this approach misses the point that the firm's cost structure is a critical determinant of resilience, and one that is to some degree under management's control. When there is a sharp fall in revenue, one of the big questions is what happens to costs. How quickly can we adjust our cost structure to the new circumstances? Are we stuck with lots of fixed costs that are hard to scale back or can we make adjustments so that the fall in revenue is matched by a swift reduction in costs? The latter is clearly the less risky situation.

Targeting operating cash flow is to gloss over these crucial dimensions of enterprise risk. It harks back to the idea that flexibility is one of the most fundamental ways of managing risk. Flexibility means that we are not stuck in one mode of operation – we have the freedom to change things. Flexibility serves a similar risk-dampening function as risk capital. When a Black Swan hits, the issue of both buffers and flexibility come into sharp focus. We are going to need every bit of them we can muster and they should be accounted for in the stress test. When we underestimate our flexibility, we might be tempted to stock up more on risk capital than what we actually need, thereby reducing return on equity unnecessarily. This suggests that risk capital and flexibility are deeply interconnected. In fact, they are functionally equivalent from a risk perspective. The more flexibility we have in managing our cost structure, the less risk capital we need to buffer against any given level of revenue risk.

Flexibility emerges as an issue as soon as we move below the revenue line. For costs that are variable, purchases can be scaled down quickly in response to falling demand. If a drop in demand effectively finishes off the prospects for a certain product line, it is rational to exit that position and discontinue the associated fixed costs as well. If, in our analysis of enterprise risk, we assume that costs will go on indefinitely at their baseline level, we get risk and resilience very wrong: resilience will be understated and risk will consequently be overstated. Dynamic analyses of cost structure are something corporates do too little of today as part of their risk management programmes. Most firms today operate with unrealistic cost assumptions in their planning tools, which virtually assures that they get cost assumptions wrong in stressed scenarios. Essentially, the more a cost structure naturally adjusts to changes in revenue, the more resilient the firm is because it is less likely that the pain thresholds will be reached. Operating flexibility therefore needs to be anticipated and incorporated into the analytical framework for resilience.

A deeper point with flexibility is that the optimal level of costs is not the same across all scenarios. We can divide costs broadly into the value-adding and the non-value-adding (wasteful) kind. We accept costs because we believe they allow us to generate revenue that earns us a positive margin, so they are considered as value-adding. In the baseline forecast, presumably all costs are in this category (why else would we plan for them?). However, as revenue deteriorates and margins are squeezed, more and more costs will start to look non-value-adding. The world has changed and in the new house we live in, some costs are no longer defensible. We should therefore consider using the exit option, which restores the margin to some extent. The better this cost adjustment mechanism is mapped out, the more realistic our appreciation of resilience becomes.[3]

We can take this train of thought one step further. It turns out that the pain thresholds themselves, just like operating costs, are not fixed across different scenarios for revenue. As revenue drops substantially, chances are that what counts as the optimal strategy also changes. Just as fewer costs are value-adding in these new circumstances, the same may be true for many of the firm's strategic initiatives. That is, in light of the scenario we find ourselves in, we may well decide to rethink our strategy. The strategy 'shrinks', if you will. Most likely, given that the overall outlook has worsened, we are no longer interested in pursuing some of the projects we had in our pipeline. Since we have less of an interest in growing and innovating now, we also have less of a need for capital expenditure, so the pain threshold automatically adjusts downward. As that happens, the need for risk capital is also less. This mechanism acts as a natural hedge.

This point was elegantly made by Professors Kenneth Froot, David Scharfstein and Jeremy Stein in a publication from 1993 (cited earlier). They argued that the need for hedging (risk transfer) is lower in firms that suspect that their investment needs have a high degree of co-variation with their revenue risk. In these firms, the supply and demand for liquidity self-coordinate without any intervention in the form of hedging. When revenue is low, the need to invest is correspondingly low. When the co-variation is less strong, revenue can drop without an offsetting reduction in capital expenditure requirements. If so, hedging can be used to improve this co-ordination by strengthening internal cash flows in low revenue scenarios. They use oil and gas firms as an example of an industry where the adjustment mechanism is economically meaningful: the value of exploration decreases with a falling oil price. Firms in the pharmaceuticals industry, in contrast, see much less of a co-variation between the value of their investment pipeline and current revenue streams.

The second pain threshold, debt servicing, may also correlate with changes in revenue. Creating some visibility on this issue is also highly desirable as it has significant implications for overall risk. In fact, a goal of corporate policy, in the name of increasing resilience, should be to increase the degree to which its debt servicing costs move together with changes in revenue. Whenever there

---

[3]Take note that a negative margin does not automatically indicate that costs are non-value-adding. We have to factor in the possibility of a rebound and future congestion costs that might occur if costs are reduced here and now. When we say costs are non-value-adding, it means that we have considered the possibility that demand growth might resume and *still* conclude that it is not in our best interest to keep the costs.

is a shock to revenue, we would like a mechanism whereby these expenditures are automatically reduced. If we manage that, it becomes a shock absorber along the same lines as the exit option, and similarly reduces the overall need for risk capital.

The case of Hertz illustrates the unfortunate consequences of having debt servicing costs that move in the wrong direction when revenue takes a hit, which makes a company *more* fragile. The terms of the loan agreement were such that collateral requirements increased as the value of the fleet of cars began to show signs of falling. This is precisely what happened, and in the worst possible moment Hertz saw its cash commitments increase. Of course, the creditors were just looking after their own interests. If the value of the car fleet drops, as it does with deteriorating revenue prospects, their collateral is worth less, and the margin calls were meant to compensate for that to maintain the risk at an acceptable level. For firms, however, this kind of mechanism virtually guarantees fragility in a worst-case scenario. While they may not be in a position to negotiate it away completely, it is something that firms should fight tooth and nail. The idea is instead to design the firm's liability side, whenever possible, in such a way that payments of interest and notional amounts are reduced when the firm's revenue is down. A simple example are loans to companies in the gold mining sector in which the level of interest is tied to the price of gold. Whenever the gold price is falling, squeezing margins and cash flows, the firm gets a relief in the form of reduced interest. Revenue and cash commitments in this case correlate positively, not negatively, as with the margin calls that sent Hertz into administration.

To further drill down into the concept of building shock absorbers into the liability structure we can consider 'contingent capital', more affectionately known as CoCos. These instruments have the express purpose of reducing the burden of liabilities in times of stress, this time targeting not only ongoing payments but also the notional amount. A CoCo is essentially a bond with a series of coupons attached to it, but differs from other bonds in that it is converted into equity *automatically*, contingent on some trigger level being reached. When this conversion takes place, two things happen. The first is that the coupons are cancelled. The second is that there is no nominal amount to be repaid any more. Consequently, the firm's cash commitments go down precisely when the firm would otherwise have struggled to meet them. In contrast to a normal rights issue, which would be done on very unfavourable terms (given the plight of the company), the conversion into equity under CoCo is done on reasonable and pre-negotiated terms.

As far as reducing tail risk is concerned, the structure of CoCos seems like a godsend. Despite its attractive features, however, these instruments have met with limited success in practice. A handful of banks have used them as a way to meet regulatory demands for capitalization in an efficient way, but outside this narrow sector there has been very little interest. Part of the problem has been agreeing on what should trigger the conversion. Variables that are under the influence of the firm itself, like revenue or net income, do not work because management may decide to play games and manipulate the outcome. Triggers that are outside the influence of managers yet still capture firm-specific distress sufficiently well are in short supply. Perhaps even more problematic from the point of view of establishing a functioning market is the lack of an investor clientele that is attracted by the specific payoff structure in CoCos. Getting a lower coupon now in return for the chance of investing in the equity in distressed firms is not how a lot of investors approach things.

To summarize this section, we can look at things in the following way. The firm generates revenue. It has three sets of cash commitments: operating costs, capital expenditure and debt servicing (interest and principal). Maintaining capital expenditure and operating costs is necessary for strategy execution (thriving) and debt servicing for staving off wipeout risk (surviving). Because debt servicing is associated with survival, one of the other two will have to give when there is a negative shock to revenue. Some of the changes in these elements will be a natural adaptation to new circumstances, so these cuts are not to be considered 'risk' or something we should resist. The true pain threshold is when we start having to make cuts in operating costs or capital expenditure that we believe are fundamentally value adding. Then we have crossed the pain threshold and started to incur collateral damage. We increase resilience to the extent that we can make any of these cash commitments coincide positively with revenue. The more we do so, the less risk capital we need to stock up as a buffer against performance shocks.

##  RESILIENCE VS ENDURANCE

When implementing an enterprise risk analysis, an important design parameter is the time-frame. Let us say that we have decided to use a one-year time horizon. We now want to learn how well we would cope with a 30% fall in revenue over the next 12 months, considering the risk capital and flexibility we believe ourselves to have. Would stressing revenue to this level lead to a situation where we struggle to maintain a positive distance to the pain thresholds? If our conclusion is that we are not even close to wipeout or strategy disruption in that scenario, the firm is coping well with tail risk and we might be inclined to consider it resilient.

However, what if the situation lasts? The duration of a crisis could easily extend for longer than one year. Mid-level shocks that drag on can finish us off just like a larger but more short-lived one. How long could we cope in this state of depressed performance? By considering for how long we can withstand a shock of a given size, we introduce the notion of *endurance*. This term can be roughly understood as the ability to go on doing something for a long time without losing way. Implied in the word is that this process is somewhat unpleasant or challenging, and thus a test of our stamina.

Discussions often revolve around resilience, a very popular word to throw about these days. However, it is also worth reflecting for a bit on the endurance aspect. If we are going to make some provision for tail risk, we may want to factor in for how long the worst-case scenario will be dragging on. Now the distinction between resilience and endurance is by no means clear. One might say that resilience refers to the ability to cope with a shock during 'one unit of time' and that endurance comes into the picture when we add units of time to the analysis. A unit of time has no fixed meaning, however, as corporates could be using multiple-year horizons when looking ahead and deciding policy. For what it is worth, though, in what follows I will use a one-year time-frame when referring to resilience and endurance will mean that we extend the horizon beyond that in increments of one year.

The duration we can expect in a crisis is of course one of the big unknowns, contributing heavily to the Moving Tail. There may be a recurrence of a certain kind of event, but the magnitude of its consequences and its duration can vary greatly. The C-19 pandemic and its impact on the airline industry can be viewed through this lens. As the travel restrictions kicked in, the majority of airlines saw their revenue drop by about 60–70% over only a couple of months. The focus of the industry quickly came around to the issue of how long will this go on. When will demand recover and things return to some kind of normal? At that point, the financial implications of C-19 had just started and the race for survival was on. It was clear that the companies in the industry faced a gruelling battle to avoid bankruptcy, as the downturn had left revenue insufficient to cover costs. Some would last whereas others would not, depending on their cash burn rate and risk capital.[4] As the year

---

[4]Actually, government support turned out to be one of the most decisive factors in this race for survival. Because of this support, there was, surprisingly, fewer bankruptcies in 2020 (43) compared to the record year 2018 (56). However, there is the suspicion than many bankruptcies have merely been delayed because of the huge increases in debt that took place during 2020.

wore on, getting through the winter became the great preoccupation. As one analyst explained:

> 'Many airline failures typically occur in the final few months of the year. The first and fourth quarters are the hardest because most of the revenue is generated in the second and third quarters . . . The goal for airlines now is to survive at any cost and see if the summer of 2021 brings solutions or higher demand.'[5]

The Factor X in enterprise risk analysis is what happens, as the crisis drags on, to the strategy that we are trying to defend. What we would like risk capital to do is to buffer against temporary shocks that are likely to pass without affecting the fundamental viability of our business model. A true and most unfortunate risk management failure is to fold due to liquidity issues shortly after some turmoil has erupted, only to see demand resurge a few months later. The oil and gas industry, for example, regularly suffers through violent price collapses. This happened in 1986, 1998, 2008, 2014, and 2020, just to take some recent cases. However, these price slumps generally do not last much more than a year, after which the oil price returns to levels where profitability is possible. In general, as an owner of oil and gas assets, you do not want to be wiped out during one of those short-lived episodes. Therefore, firms dealing with that kind of wild uncertainty should want to create buffers that are adequate for lasting somewhere between a year or two. Certainly, in a world of wild uncertainty there is nothing to say that the next one would not last much longer. However, we may conclude that this outcome lies so far out in the tail that, given the cost of prepping, we are going to consider it a risk we accept. Resources consistent with being able to sustain a crisis with a duration of around 18 months would be an eminently reasonable approach.

As a crisis continues, there is always the concern that the business model itself will break. The fear of airline executives would have been that the Corona virus and its many mutations are here to stay, hampering travel well into the future. At the onset of the crisis, many were quick to take the view that the crisis would fade quickly, that it would just 'go away', reflecting general optimism (denial?) and perhaps an unbending faith in the capabilities of science. If so, the travel industry would spring back to pre-pandemic levels relatively shortly. Others looked to history and concluded that pandemics typically last some 18–24 months, and used that as a benchmark. Yet others were beginning

---

[5]Over 40 airlines have failed in 2020 so far and more are set to fail (cnbc.com).

to say that versions of the Corona virus might be with humanity forever. Hard answers as to the likely length of the crisis were elusive. The information environment at the time was highly volatile and confusing.

Our perspective, however, is that of decision-makers *before* anything has happened, wondering how many resources can justifiably be committed to risk capital. For this purpose, we can modify our stress-testing framework to elaborate also on the endurance aspect and, so to speak, tighten the screws a bit. If the conclusion was that we can weather a 30% decrease in revenue without much ado, we might move on to consider a scenario in which it declines by 40% and investigate whether the conclusion changes. Alternatively, we could deepen our stress test in terms of a revenue shock that is 30% but *stays at that level for another year*. That is, the 30% drop lasts two years rather than one. This also puts more stress on the firm compared to the baseline test. The duration of a shock is now formally incorporated into the test. We might continue to stress the firm's performance by pushing it even further, for example by investigating a 40% drop over two years, and so on. As always, our interest is in how the firm stands to cope with these scenarios, using the distance to pain thresholds as reference points. As we extend the time horizon, perhaps we will start to see some signs of cracking, i.e. outcomes in which the strategy is disrupted yet survival is not in doubt. This iterative process can go on until we have identified the breaking points for both strategy disruption and survival. Perhaps it is found that, if a revenue drop of 50% occurs and stays that low for two years in a row, the company would have depleted all its risk capital and have very little chance of survival.

Figure 5.2 shows a resilience-endurance matrix that summarizes whether the pain thresholds are met for different combinations of magnitude and duration. It informs us, at a glance, where the breaking points are for the two thresholds. As for obtaining likelihood estimates associated with the breaking points, we can always consult the database and draw on a subsample of firms similar

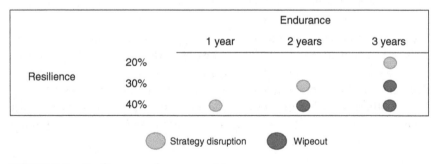

**FIGURE 5.2**   Resilience-endurance matrix

to ours and observe the frequency with which revenue shortfall of that magnitude occurs (and remains that low if we use time horizons longer than one year). That is, we fit the data-driven probabilities to our own specific breaking points to gauge their likelihood.

What emerges from this analysis is an improved understanding of our resilience and endurance. Based on the outputs, we can have some good conversations about what kind of corporate policy might be appropriate. Maybe our conclusion is that we believe it is prudent to be able to sustain a situation of a 40% drop in revenue for two years, but, after that, we will just have to see. At that point, we will be at the mercy of greater forces, but so be it. After two years, we may surmise that the information environment has stabilized so that we have a clearer picture of the extent to which the fundamentals of the business model have been undermined. At some point, we will have to put the firm's fate in the hands of capital markets, for them to decide whether the business is worth supporting. We cannot hide forever. If the markets decide that they do not believe in the firm at that point, well, then it is good-bye. Risk capital can and should not get us out of that. What we have avoided, however, was a situation where short-term liquidity pressures sold the strategy short by either triggering bankruptcy or leading to all sorts of panicky decisions. That is not a good situation for checking in with the financial markets either, because they may also be in a panicky mood and as confused by the mixed signals as everyone else. A lot of ill-thought-out decisions can be made when panic has got the better of a large number of people. If risk capital helps us avoid the brunt of that toxic situation, all the better, but beyond a maximum of two years, we cannot, in good conscience, continue to burn money any more if the fundamentals are not there.

 ## QUANTITATIVE MODELS

As always, bringing the most talented and experienced people together to discuss policy in a meritocratic fashion remains our best option. This group of people can weigh up the pros and cons of various policy alternatives. The analytical framework outlined in this chapter is meant to generate a structured input that facilitates those conversations. Analysing revenue shocks in relation to cost structures, risk capacity and corporate strategies may seem like a tall order. How can it be done in practice? The answer is that it can only be done successfully using a quantitative (financial) model. The purpose of models is to handle complexity and transform that into something useful for decision-making. Back-of-the envelope calculations can only get us so far.

Before proceeding, it should not be lost on the reader that Taleb warns us against quantitative models *specifically*. It is a familiar story by now. Models, while seemingly sophisticated, could end up making us more fragile because they lead to hubris and a false sense of security, thereby distorting our world view and creating the preconditions for Black Swans.[6] Since a Black Swan is relative to expectations, and those can be shaped hugely by access to a powerful model, they have a potentially critical role in the Swan-formation process. Some of the more entertaining parts of The Black Swan are when Taleb pokes fun at academics who build models based on Platonic assumptions – and who then have the poor taste of actually believing in them. Just to retire anyone's doubt about the Black Swan potential of such model-fuelled hubris, recall the hedge fund LTCM. Operated by an intriguing combination of academic masterminds and star traders, it was said to be a close shave from bringing down the entire financial system, despite using the finest risk management techniques academia had to offer.

The main culprits behind the Great Recession of the late 2000s were likely to be the astonishingly aggressive lending practices of financial institutions, handing out mortgages to people who clearly could not afford them. However, it seems clear that model-fed overconfidence was a significant catalyst. The investment-grade credit ratings assigned to bundles of mortgages instilled a calm among market participants that was crucial in the lead-up. It explains why the risk was able to infiltrate so many institutions despite their dedication to quantitative risk modelling. The hapless rating agencies fed assumptions into their models that basically ruled out mass defaults on mortgages, and everyone took them on their word. It is a school-book example of how Black Swans can be *made* by collective arrogance.

Watching people surrender to a model and then starting to view it as the bringer of truth is something that I have seen happen many times. Convincing managers that a quantitative model effort is in their best interest can be hard, but once something like that gets underway, the attitude often changes to one of absolute faith, as if the model can do no wrong. It happens very easily if the people responsible for the model are seen as clever and are good at talking themselves up. Before you know it, the model has acquired an air of mystique, keeping people in awe while they wait for its next utterance, like some kind of modern-day oracle.

---

[6]Taleb is a harsh teacher. First, he admonishes us for making forecasts. Then we are rebuked for not risk-adjusting our forecasts one bit. When we do, using some reasonable-looking bell-curves, we are again slapped in the head.

Once you start building models, it is very easy to be seduced by the elegance of it all. The experience is very rewarding and carries you away. The model is never finished and you always want more. Perhaps you started out concerned about the firm's resilience, relatively embedded in the firm's business, but now you find yourself immersed in the details of the model and just preoccupied with making it even better. The model itself consumes a disproportionate amount of mental energy that could be used in better ways, like engaging with the real world and the decisions that are about to be made in the company. Speaking from my own experience, when you are in model-constructing mode, your mind-set does become more Platonic by the day. Model development is a comfort zone. There is that siren song, the lure of allowing oneself to become stuck in it, indefinitely. Be warned.

Does all of this suggest that models should not be used and are best done away with? Absolutely not. On the contrary, models have an essential role to play in a world of wild uncertainty. Believing blindly in any model is treacherous, but not using one at all is even worse. *Black Swan blindness is not about the tools you use, it is about how you use them and the attitude with which you approach them.* They are only dangerous if you *allow* them to corrupt your thought processes. This occurs when you place an unwarranted amount of faith in its outputs and you proceed to take decisions without reflection on the assumptions that went into it (and without giving any thought to the Black Swans that remain outside it). If we hold ourselves to be better than that, things should be fine.

The case for a well-designed model is a strong one. The analytical rigour and learning process delivers benefits that are real and very tangible. The complexity of firms is such that getting a good overview of their financial position and risk profile is very difficult without a model to underpin the effort. A model can be like a torch that lights up the dark, and if you handle it with respect, it will not burn down the house. In fact, as part of their risk oversight, BoDs should demand that one be put in place.

At this point, it is important that we clarify what kind of model we are talking about. The model we need is a very different one compared to the ones emphasizing advanced statistics, which is what Taleb primarily takes aim at. Value-at-Risk models exemplify the latter category of models well. They provide information about the level of market risk inherent in a portfolio of financial instruments. With them, we can assess the maximum loss in value associated with a certain probability. The statistical intricacies know no bounds here, so people who are into that sort of thing can have a jolly good day. For operating companies with long-term strategies, however, they are completely meaningless. What sense is there for a company that operates projects that span decades to engage in the modelling of the behaviour of financial instruments over the next few days? It has zero ability to inform about whether the firm could be wiped out or see serious disruptions to its value-creation process. A Value-at-Risk model, therefore, should offend the sensibilities of Black Swan attuned directors of the board.

What we want is a very different kind of model, one that is purpose-built to provide feedback on how resilient the firm is. Again, this can only be done if we express risk using financial numbers – net income, cash flows, balance sheets and financial ratios. That is the only way we can capture the risk of the firm as a whole and evaluate our ability to withstand significant shocks to performance. Now there are plenty of models out there that deal with financial forecasts. Unfortunately, most of them fall short of describing enterprise risk well, lacking as they are in the level of analytics and integrity needed to support such an effort. Things need to be taken to another level. The model framework that I am about to discuss is the centre-piece of Risk Budgeting, an approach tailor-made for the analysis of enterprise risk. The framework is described in more detail in my previous book *Empowered enterprise risk management: Theory and practice* (Jankensgård and Kapstad, 2021, cited earlier) and summarized below.

A reliable decision-support tool is distinguished, first of all, by its analytical and accounting integrity. Together, they ensure that the model gives a realistic representation of the firm at all times. Analytical integrity means that the model contains realistic dynamics, notably with respect to how the cost structure, liabilities and capital expenditure adapt to shocks to revenue. Accounting integrity is when the model is, under any assumptions made about the future, capable of representing the firm's financial statements in a way that correctly reflects current standards, such as IFRS or US GAAP. This integrity is the bedrock of the model. Thanks to it, the model will come to earn peoples' trust. It warrants a different level of faith compared to traditional spreadsheet-based financial models, notorious as they are for their many inconsistencies and errors.

At the core of an enterprise risk model is functionality that allows us to evaluate different scenarios and policies with great ease. These two features are what truly makes it function as a decision-support tool with respect to risk management. Scenarios can be constructed in terms of revenue shortfalls directly, or in terms of specific risk factors whose impact on performance has been specified (e.g. 20% increase in steel prices => 10% increase in costs). The policy functionality means that one can change the assumptions regarding policies and immediately receive feedback on how that drives the firm's risk-return profile. Policies that can be evaluated include acquisitions, capital expenditure, leverage, dividends, hedging and others. It is often forgotten in risk mapping exercises, but one of the main drivers of corporate risk is actually strategic decision-making. A debt-financed acquisition, for example, can move the risk profile in a major way, yet somehow tends to bypass the typical risk maps.

One more feature is necessary to complete the transition to a fully-fledged tool for the analysis of enterprise risk. We need to overlay the financial forecasts with a structure for risk analysis, such that we obtain formal risk indicators that inform us about the Distance-to-Wipeout and Distance-to-Disruption. Risk in the Risk Budgeting framework is expressed primarily in terms of the distance to the pain thresholds. Therefore, we have to agree on how to best apply these ideas to the firm in question. Taking care to map out cash commitments related to strategy execution and debt servicing is a good starting point for understanding the thresholds and makes for another round of useful discussions. We also have to think through what Risk Capacity we have and incorporate those elements explicitly into the model: the cash position, contingent cash flows from risk transfers and spare debt capacity.

Formulating balance sheet constraints is usually important because they determine our spare borrowing capacity. To this end, we can review credit facilities, credit rating targets, financial covenants and other proxies for balance sheet strength to infer what borrowing opportunities are likely to be across scenarios. A covenant may stipulate, for example, that the Debt-to-Equity ratio must not exceed 1, lest the firm be in violation of the agreement. Then we may assume that borrowing can continue only up to this point and instruct the model to interpret any cash flow shortfalls beyond it as underinvestment. We have now identified a pain threshold in the model that captures strategy disruption and we can keep track of how it develops in various scenarios and under different policies. Likewise, the point at which we would be forced to default on our debt obligations (and thereby risk a wipeout) can be defined and *tracked as an output in the model*. This means that the risk indicators will be sensitive to (respond to) changes in assumptions about external risks *and* corporate policies.

A model thus equipped will give a fair picture of the current distance to pain thresholds and what it would take for us to end up on the wrong side of them. There is, I feel confident in saying, great value in this kind of decision-support tool for almost any kind of firm. Contrary to Taleb's assertions about the dangers of quantitative modelling, this value is *especially* great in a world of wild uncertainty. What Taleb has a problem with, though, is primarily the assumptions we make with respect to randomness, of which we have said nothing yet. He seems particularly incensed by the tendency to use recent and limited data, as in most Value-at-Risk applications, to infer something about future risk. This practice is indeed fraught with dangers when uncertainty is of the wild sort. However, a model showing future financial performance that contains realistic dynamics and correct accounting relationships, connects that with scenarios and policies and has a theoretically sound structure for analysing enterprise risk, is something very different. Such a model is geared towards understanding our resilience to shocks and the consequences that our own decision-making carries for that resilience. It need not involve any unsafe assumptions about the nature of randomness.

Now, we *can* add a probabilistic dimension to the model and implement a form of automated scenarios referred to as 'simulations'. Doing simulations involves making assumptions about the underlying stochastic processes that corporate performance and/or various risk factors affecting it follow. Once a description of these processes is in place, the computer generates a large number of scenarios, say 10,000 or more. We no longer have to create scenarios of our own: they are wholly implicit in the simulated outcomes. Furthermore, once the model is specified, we obtain a whole new set of ways to analyse risk in corporate performance. We can derive any sort of risk measure based on simulated outcome distributions in, say, EBIT or funds from operations, and learn from what we see. We can also derive risk measures that indicate the probability of breaching the pain thresholds, which adds the probabilistic dimension to Distance-to-Wipeout and Distance-to-Disruption.

The simulation approach actually has several things going for it. Just like financial models generally, it also brings analytical rigour to the risk management process and sets in motion a learning process that can be impressive. It forces a more integrated perspective as we have to ask questions about how different aspects of the business relate to each other. Quantitative risk modelling of this sort makes it possible to heed some of the most fundamental principles of risk. For example, we can combine several risk factors in an integrated framework, taking into account the ways in which they tend to co-evolve over time. To get risk right for some superordinate entity, like an investment portfolio or a portfolio of cash flow generating businesses, we have to give some thought to how the constituent parts move together. That tendency to co-move can be an important determinant of overall risk and simulations create opportunities to incorporate this dimension.[7]

---

[7]A Black Swan attuned observer might remark that these tendencies to co-move are another Platonic construct, the belief in which makes us suckers. Taleb abhors any mention of correlation, a linear measure of co-variation often used in practice. It is true that correlations sometimes break down spectacularly, but any sensible approach to modelling would take this kind of model risk seriously and investigate the consequences of a breakdown in historically observed relations. Robust tendencies to co-move should inform risk management strategies. It is just a matter of not forgetting that in the tail of things, everything goes towards the extreme.

For all these benefits, taking the step to do simulations is where it gets more sensitive, because now we *are* making assumptions about randomness into our decision-support tool. All the potential pitfalls Taleb warns us against therefore resurface. When we debate whether simulations and probabilistic exercises make things worse or better, it depends on what we are comparing with. In some ways, and rightly approached, it represents progress compared to a situation where the firm's decision-makers are largely unaware about certain core principles of risk. If we use simulations, we explicitly grant that the future is uncertain and that wildly different things can happen than what is assumed as part of the budget. We open our eyes to the fact that the tail may inflict some serious pain and that we had better pay some attention to it. All of this has the power to make us less of a sucker; we are contemplating a whole range of outcomes in a very active way rather than being content with a narrow set of soon-to-be-outdated forecasts. We start to "see" risk in a different way and it becomes part of our thought processes.

Simulation models, looked at in this way, represent an improvement if managers are otherwise stuck in a 'budget' mindset that is poorly attuned to randomness and contingencies. Because of the ability to visualize risk and to express it in terms of important bottom lines, it holds the potential to lead to a completely new way to looking at the firm. The problem is rather one of taking it too far, of thinking that the job is done and that we are now safe because the model says so. Even though tail risk has been, to the best of our abilities, incorporated into the model, some Black Swans are still lurking outside of it (by definition). It is when this is forgotten that we are possibly making things worse because it might cause us to overestimate our resilience and underprepare for what the future might bring. When we pretend that the model is perfect and that its simulated distributions fully and adequately capture tail risk, we have started down a dangerous path. When complemented with stress testing, simulations start looking pretty good, however, because stress tests force us to face a bigger picture view and to recognize the limitations of whatever assumptions we have made about randomness. This reminds us that the simulated tail of the performance distribution is not the end of the story with respect to how bad it can get. That is, we remain humble rather than overconfident even when we have put some sophisticated modelling in place.

Simulations, then, can be made to work for us and not against us. It can effectively serve as a red flag device. If a robust simulation framework is put in place and not tinkered with too much over time, any material change in the risk signalled by the model may tell us that something is going on that needs our attention. In one company that operated such a model, there had been a long stretch of rather low risk. Then, from one quarter to the next, the model indicated a substantial shift in the risk profile that caught the managers' attention, as illustrated in Figure 5.3. Upon investigation, it turned out that three things had happened that altered the risk of the firm as a whole. There was a proposed increase in the dividend, an expansion of the investment programme and a deterioration in the main product markets. Combined, they served to shift the risk profile is a way that could not be ignored. The feedback from the model prompted the managers to revise their policies and come up with a way forward that implied a less aggressive risk profile.

Two points are worth noting. First, the model's feedback triggered these discussions. None of this would ever have happened if it were not for the model. The dividend policy, the investment expansion and the market risk were the domains of different departments in the firm that never had conversations about the joint impact of their policies. The model had brought everything together into an integrated framework. Second, the signal from the model led to proactive actions, thus helping to overcome the inertia that so easily locks us into a certain path. The power to visualize is key here. Because simulations allow us to visualize risk, they change how we think. Actions are usually only taken when enough people can *see* the problem, and when they start seeing it in a similar way. It hardly matters whether the risk probabilities delivered by the model were accurate or not. It is a moot point, in fact, because there is no way of knowing because they are subjective in the first place. The *change* in the

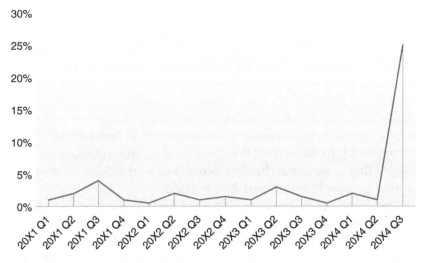

**FIGURE 5.3** Shift in risk profile (risk measure over time)

risk profile, however, had real meaning to it and the model visualized it and therefore supported proactive action.

The risk manager in a world of wild uncertainty must try to take the golden middle path. We embrace the power of financial models designed for analysis of resilience, and in some cases even simulations, yet we resist the temptation of congratulating ourselves for being so good at it and having everything covered. We need to be model-builders, but humble ones at that.

The goal, in the end, is simple. It is that the BoD is duly informed about the firm's resilience to shocks, as captured by stress tests and similar exercises. Recall that it is of no use if a deeply skilled and philosophical risk manager somewhere in the organization has all the right insights about all of this. To have any impact, it must be clear to the directors how far we are from the pain thresholds, whether any proposed policy change moves us closer or further away from them and what kind of shock it would take to breach the thresholds. There should be a continuous discussion as to whether Risk Capacity is appropriate, given the goals of ensuring resilience and pursuing business opportunities across a large number of scenarios. When the BoD is reasonably enlightened on these matters an important milestone is reached. It is when the company's directors see and internalize both the possibility of and most of the possible consequences from tail risk scenarios that the firm can safely be said to have reached the status of a non-sucker. Contrary to what you might have been thinking, a model is also instrumental in getting us there.

##  LIQUIDITY IS KING

Along the way, we have identified several determinants of resilience. Cash-at-hand, equity, and operating flexibility all serve to strengthen a company's defences. To this list we can add the ability to generate cash internally, or the 'cash margin', defined as revenue less operating costs. This also represents a kind of buffer: the more cash we can generate per unit of revenue, the larger the drop in revenue that is required before we run into problems. Cash margins are not the same thing as operating margins, but are related. You might say that being profitable, or keeping a good cost discipline, is also good risk management because it means that the drop height will be higher the day that trouble arrives. Thanks to high margins, we will be at a larger distance to wipeout and disruption.

So, what is, at the end of the day, the most effective way of cushioning performance shocks? Given that strategies for increasing corporate resilience are costly, we would like to know how effective they are in coping with tail risk.

To find out which of the various forms of buffers are better at absorbing shocks to performance, we might consult the data. Together with co-authors Christie and Marinelli, I set out to address these questions using the decades-spanning dataset of US listed firms described in Chapter 2. Our empirical definition of a Black Swan is an unexpected drop in revenue between 30–90%. The bottom line we work with in this analysis is the number of employees, which proxies for strategy execution. The premise is that the more a firm adjusts its workforce in response to revenue shocks, the more fragile it is. This is in keeping with our earlier argument that excessive cuts in operating costs are a form of strategy disruption. We take relatively larger cuts to a shock of the same size to indicate fragility. That is, if two firms in the same industry experience a surprising 30% drop in revenue, and one adjusts its workforce by 10% and the other by 20%, we would infer that the latter is more fragile.

To summarize, we examine firms' resilience to tail risk by examining how shocks to the corporate top line (revenue) impacts the bottom line (number of employees) as mediated by four different buffers – cash balances, cash margins, equity capital and operating flexibility. The expectation is that all of them act as buffers and cushion the blow from revenue shocks, but would it be possible to establish a 'winner'?

Our results, based on over 140,000 firm-year observations from 10 industries, point unanimously to the conclusion that liquidity is king. Cash reserves are, by a wide margin, the variable that most consistently reduces the sensitivity of employment to revenue shocks. Being in the top third in terms of cash reserves decreases fragility by about half (the baseline sensitivity of employment to a revenue drop between 30 and 90% is a decrease of about 15%). Cash margins also reduce fragility, but with less statistical and economical significance. The managerial implications of these results would be to emphasize financial strategies that support the provision of liquidity in worse-than-expected scenarios and to maintain cost efficiency in good times to maximize the risk-absorbing buffer from cash margins.

As part of our empirical investigation of resilience, we also investigate a conjecture made by Taleb about the relation between size and fragility. He essentially, and curiously, argues that size is conducive to fragility. Taleb's assertion with respect to size is not developed into a coherent thesis, but he states that 'size hurts you at times of stress. It is not a good idea to be large during difficult times' (Taleb, 2012, p. 279) and that 'fragility comes from size' (Taleb, 2012, p. 282). Taken literally, the claim suggests that we should expect fragility, here defined as the sensitivity of the number of employees to large revenue shocks, to be an increasing function of size.

Taleb's size conjecture is not supported by our data. In fact, the data contradicts it. Our findings indicate that small firms are afflicted more by revenue shocks, in two ways. First, they are more prone to experience them. The smallest third of the sample accounts for over half of all Swans, a significant over-representation. Second, they are also more sensitive to them, as evidenced by a larger average cut in employment compared to their larger peers for a revenue drop of a given size. One may speculate that these findings reflect smaller firms' being more dependent on the success of a limited number of innovations and product lines. Large firms, in contrast, tend to have a more established market presence with some proven successes in the product mix at any given point in time.

After this detour into the role of size, let us now come back to our finding that cash reserves most effectively absorb revenue risk. It may suggest that we need to view corporate cash balances a little bit more forgivingly. Contrary to customary accusations that the cash is not 'working' and should be returned to shareholders, the cash balance may well be working in the sense of bearing risk. Is the detrimental effect on Return on Assets really so bad? If we compare RoA for a firm that earns 1% on its cash and 10% on its operating assets, a 2% cash ratio (cash/operating assets) lands RoA at 9.8% compared to 9.1% for a more sturdy 10% cash ratio. If we acknowledge that we are dealing with wild uncertainty and that we find ourselves at a not-too-large a distance from the pain threshold, the BoD should not have too many concerns about going a bit above whatever is considered the minimum cash ratio required for purely operational purposes.

As for investors fretting about large cash positions, perhaps their main worry is not the opportunity cost from clinging to the cash. It might rather be what the firm's managers might end up doing with such readily available money. As discussed, there is a legitimate concern that they might go off making acquisitions or lose cost discipline out of the general comfort that comes from having it in abundance. Investors therefore need to be reassured and provided with evidence that the firm is well governed and that such side-effects of cash holdings are unthinkable. There is that element of trust again. If the market is convinced that there are no ulterior motives from stocking up on cash, they may come around to the view that the cash position really is risk-bearing and that it makes sense to shore up defences given that the next tail risk event is only a matter of time away.[8]

---

[8]Of course, this attitude is likely to wane the further removed in time we are from the most recent crisis, as the market again becomes convinced there is nothing but good times ahead. As Joe Rogan put it, amnesia is the predicament of our species, a point the financial markets have brought home many times over.

This endorsement of cash reserves is not a blank cheque to pile up on it. The case has to be made, using the analytical framework in this chapter, that the cash really is bearing risk. The case of Volvo Cars, the Swedish car maker, is instructive for analysing some of these themes. Back in 2007, investment firm Cevian Capital, led by investor activist Christer Gardell, had taken an ownership position in Volvo and was lobbying for a large extra dividend to the tune of 17 billion kronor. They were arguing that Volvo's cash balance was excessive and sitting unproductively on the balance sheet. It was indeed massive at over 30 billion kronor, which amounted to 11% of revenue in 2007 (a rule of thumb says that the cash needed for operating purposes is about 2%). However, the company's executives and directors stood their ground and resisted the payout – Gardell had to yield. Then the financial crisis happened, and Volvos revenue in 2009 fell by almost 30% as people drastically pulled the breaks on car purchases. This seemingly vindicated Volvo's leadership, and the episode has lived on in Swedish business folklore as a case of a mischievous raider being defeated by wise and far-sighted industrialists.

Except that this neat story does not hold up to scrutiny. In 2009, despite the scary-looking drop in revenue, Volvo's cash position actually *increased* by an eye-catching 13 billion kronor. There was virtually no way Volvo could have depleted its cash and got into a liquidity squeeze even if it had paid the extra dividend as Gardell insisted. The cash position did not bear risk and we should cede the point to Gardell – it was excessive.

# CHAPTER SIX

# Catching the Swan

I N THE RISK MANAGEMENT literature, there is a deep undercurrent suggesting that risk and opportunity go together. We cannot realize opportunities without taking risk, the argument goes, so they are intrinsically linked. Part of this risk opportunity undercurrent is also the notion that risk (a bad outcome) can be *turned* into an opportunity (a good outcome). The pitch is that if we are strong and clever enough, we can take what is at first an objectively bad outcome and make it work in our favour. This suggests that Black Swan events, being extreme risk, might offer an extreme opportunity as well. In this chapter, we explore the idea of Catching the Swan, by which term I mean capitalizing from episodes of turmoil by grabbing opportunities that otherwise would not have presented themselves. Whoever catches the Swan comes out of a crisis having advanced one's position, if not in absolute terms then at least relative to comparable peers.

Certainly, as we have seen, Black Swans are moments in which corporate strategies can fail. We now acknowledge that they also constitute moments in which strategies – and fortunes – can be made. This is an idea that runs through the history of business. For as long as there has been commerce, people have sought to take advantage of the weakness of others. During crises, there is a lot of weakness to go around. We are not going to consider cruel exploitation of individuals who are down on their luck and similar vulture practices. However, if somebody has willingly accepted the risk of doing business without any element of coercion or trickery involved, increasing one's market share and profits at that somebody's expense is fair game. Anyone setting up an enterprise for the sake of profit has to accept that possibility as part of the rules. Catching the Swan, then, is about how to become a more formidable competitor across a multitude of scenarios, one who finds opportunity in Black Swan induced crises. We therefore set out to explore how strategies can be designed to increase the likelihood of doing so successfully.

##  ANTIFRAGILITY

Catching the Swan is just another way of saying that we are able to gain from the disorder created by a Black Swan event. Gaining from episodes of tail risk takes us to a new level. We are no longer merely resilient or robust, but actually seek to improve from shocks. To convey this idea, Taleb introduces a new word, antifragility. According to Taleb, things are antifragile if they:

> '. . . benefit from shocks; they thrive and grow when exposed to volatility, randomness, disorders, and love adventure, risk and uncertainty' (Taleb, 2012, Prologue, p. 3).

Things that are resilient stay the same when exposed to shocks, they resist them. Antifragility, in contrast, implies getting better from them. We should, Taleb goes on to say, try to identify things that 'love' volatility and distinguish them from those that 'hate' volatility (i.e. those that are non-resilient and fragile) (Taleb, 2012, p. 12). Option contracts are a straightforward example of something that loves volatility. When the underlying reference price fluctuates wildly, there is a good chance that the strike price of the option is reached, which makes the option attractive to hold. When the price is very stable, in contrast, chances are slimmer that it ever will become in-the-money, so the option is worth less.

The immune system serves as another nice illustration of the concept of antifragility. Stressors in terms of bacteria and germs that enter our bodies in everyday situations, like eating food, are actually required on an ongoing basis to keep the immune system performing at its best. Take the stressors away and the system starts to decay and lose some of its ability to deflect threats. This has the consequence that, when a real and serious one comes along, the body is no longer able to mount the appropriate response. There is a strong suspicion, for example, that well-meaning parents who keep their children away from peanuts actually contribute to the problem of peanut allergy. Research shows that children thus protected tend to develop allergies at higher rates, making them, despite the good intentions of their parents, more fragile in the long term. For the same reasons, keeping the house clinically free from dust is a bad idea.[1]

The tragedy of modernity, according to Taleb, is that it is overprotective, as if its mission was to squeeze every drop of variability and randomness out of life (Taleb, 2012, p. 242). Society constantly provides us with solutions invented to make things more expedient and comfortable. This process shields us from the elements and artificially suppresses randomness, which in turn fragilizes everything inside the system (and as Taleb points out – the system as a whole, ironically). It deprives them of the stressors that would otherwise have maintained their vitality. Take someone who is spending most of their time at home watching streamed series and eating processed food delivered to their house. That is an environment about as comfortable and shock-free as it can get. The chronic lack of physical challenges, however, means that this person's senses will dull and his or her muscles atrophy. The bottom line is that we need resistance to access and maintain our inner energies.

People, then, are certainly among the things that can become more fragile when deprived of regular challenges. If we live in a protected environment, a bubble, we become overwhelmed more easily by a shock because we develop fewer defences and less of a thick skin – all of which makes the emergence of 'safetyism' in recent decades troubling. This, according to Professors Lukianoff and Haidt, is a culture or belief system in which safety becomes a sacred value and trumps everything else, no matter how unlikely or trivial the potential danger.[2] These authors also point out that today's conception of what it means to be safe includes protection from *emotional* harm, as opposed to the more traditional idea of physical safety. The sentiment today is that nobody should have to have his or her feelings trampled on, and the bar for what counts as a trauma has been getting constantly lower. As a result, there is a 'coddling' of an entire generation of students in the US (and increasingly in other places as well), creating more fragile individuals in the process. Fragility, in this view, is endemic.

To become antifragile means that we need to acquire a very important habit: to accept (expose ourselves to) and improve from adversity. Lukianoff and Haidt cite research showing that most people report becoming, in some respect, stronger and better after going through a traumatic experience, or what is referred to as 'post-traumatic growth'. According to Professor Kim

---

[1]Finally, some vindication for those of us who always felt there were better uses of time than cleaning the house.

[2]Lukianoff, G. and J. Haidt, 2018. *The coddling of the American mind.* Penguin Books: London.

Cameron, cited earlier, all the experience shows that negativity has a place in human flourishing. Some of the best of human and organizational attributes are revealed only when confronted with obstacles, challenges or detrimental circumstances.

Many of us can attest to this on a personal level. We harbour long-term goals about the kind of person we would like to become, and work to reach that place where we truly flourish: generous, kind, happy, social and confident individuals that others trust and respect. However, as time goes by, we are caught up in the distractions served up by our careers and domestic life. During all this hustle, we start forgetting about those core aspirations and stop moving towards them. Consequently, we feel increasingly dissatisfied, often without knowing why. Then something shakes us up. Something triggers a setback and unexpectedly we find ourselves in a hole. At those moments, we start to introspect again, asking those tough questions about where we are headed and what our true values really are. The question of what kind of person I would like to be gains traction again. We collect ourselves and come out better. We are back on the true path, revitalized and more determined. We may even start feeling a measure of gratitude for having been through the ordeal. Individuals who manage to resolve crises and setbacks in this way are antifragile.

The spirit of growing from adversity has been eloquently captured by decorated MMA fighter Conor McGregor. In a sport where suffering a loss can be traumatizing and is known to have broken fighters' confidence permanently, McGregor has a different take on losses. Reflecting on a recent defeat and a chance to redeem himself in a rematch, he says the following:

> 'It went the way it went and I got a setback in there, but setbacks are
> a beautiful thing. Defeat is the secret ingredient to success, I say, and
> it's put me right where I need to be.'[3]

While hardly a fountain of wisdom on most weekdays, McGregor captures the essence of an antifragile mindset. Taleb elevates this trait to be America's one great asset, the taking of risk in a rational form of trial and error *with no comparative shame in failing* (Taleb, 2012, p. 171). He compares this with the cultures in Japan and Europe, where failure is much more stigmatized. Because of the embarrassment associated with it, risks are hidden under the rug, with the result that their societies are less dynamic and competitive (Taleb, 2007, p. 204).

---

[3]Mmafighting.com, 7 July 2021. Conor McGregor: Dustin Poirier is going to get 'taken out on a stretcher' at UFC 264 – MMA Fighting.

However, a caveat is in order. In the sentence 'most people experience post-traumatic growth', the problematic part lies in the word 'most'. It is the same thing as with the fact that history repeats itself – but only for the most part. The devil is in that detail. We have to be careful not to get too romantic about Nietzsche's aphorism that 'what does not kill me makes me stronger'. The prospect of permanent damage is real. Sometimes, a crisis is just that: a crisis, and hardly something we should wish upon ourselves just for the sake of our eventual betterment. However, when a crisis does happen, yes, we had better strive for renewal and growth if those options are on the table. The general idea in the self-improvement community is that we can *choose* to look at it as an opportunity to grow rather than indulge in self-pity and debilitating thought patterns. Antifragility on the individual level is, in this view, largely a matter of personal choice, of applying the right perspectives and of taking a constructive attitude and persevering in that.

 ## RESTORING THE TRUE PATH

Now that we have explored the concept of antifragility as it relates to individuals, we might ask whether it transfers over into the setting of a business firm. Can firms be antifragile and, if yes, what does it take to qualify as such? If we are going to find antifragility in firms, implying that they get better and ultimately benefit from a disaster, one way to argue is that firms, just like people, can start developing bad habits over time – that they can also lose their way and veer off the 'true path'. A firm that has done so is not presently the best version of its corporate self. If so, it might benefit from a stressor from the outside to help it rethink its priorities and to rediscover the true path.

The above account is not too much of a stretch of the imagination. The manager quoted by Wang in Chapter 2 hints at cost efficiency not always being the number one priority. Pursuing growth is much more fun and interesting. In relatively good times, managers do not want to be the 'bad guy/girl' who brings out the knives and fires people, or hounds them on a daily basis to cut back on all sorts of expenses. Cutting costs brings disagreements and conflict, and they may fear it would affect employee morale negatively. This general reluctance to rein in costs suggests that firms, under conditions of business as usual, can get lazy and complacent over time. In other words, they start accumulating unnecessary costs. If the firm is doing well, the threat of ending up in financial trouble one day may feel remote, so discipline wears off. While most firms operate with some kind of profitability target, such targets are set relative to some reference point that may creep downwards over time as cost discipline gradually deteriorates. Talking about corporate life-cycles, legendary entrepreneur Richard Branson makes the following remark:

> '. . . once a company reaches the mid-life crisis stage it easily gets lazy, overweight, set in its ways and, like adults, can spend more time looking in the rear-view mirror than forging new ways forward and trying to see what is around the next corner.'[4]

Another way for firms to stray off the true path is by taking the road of diversifying acquisitions. Acquisitions, as noted, are about as value-destroying an activity as there is. Overpaying is always a concern, in the sense that the synergies realized cannot realistically add up to the 30–40% (of the acquired firm's pre-acquisition market cap) that, given the premium paid, would be needed for break-even. To that, we add all the things that can go wrong in the post-merger integration phase. While the worst days of sprawling conglomerates may be behind us, an acquisition strategy can still leave behind a set of poorly integrated businesses and lots of goodwill on the balance sheet that weighs down profitability. Excessive buying of other businesses, then, is often an indication that a firm has suffered a mission creep and that it has indulged in the wrong kind of pleasures.

For firms that have lost their way, a Black Swan event may offer a way to turn things around, at least to the extent that it puts enough stress on a company to scare its managers into action. A negative shock makes it compelling to take actions that managers may have felt were overdue but found easy to postpone for another day when things were still moving along okay. This is when the willingness to consider change is at its highest. Crises legitimize actions that, under normal circumstances, would meet too much opposition. Hence the notion of 'having a good crisis' – usually understood as a time to trim some fat and get difficult decisions done.

The experiences of Scandinavian Airlines provide an illustration of the principle that adversity can galvanize support for radical change. When the company entered a full-blown crisis in late 2011, the dire circumstances were used opportunistically – some would say cynically – by the firm's leadership. Stories circulated that they painted an extremely bleak picture of the situation

---

[4]Branson, R., 2014. *The Virgin way: How to listen, learn, and lead.* Penguin Random House: London.

in order to cow its powerful and combative labour unions into submission. According to some of the rumours, union leaders had been brought aside and sat down, individually, surrounded by sinister-looking board members and executives. Bankruptcy lawyers were present in the meetings to underscore the near-death nature of the situation. Ultimately, the unions folded, accepting job cuts as well as other terms and conditions, the overall effect of which was to reduce the company's legacy costs. This was all in the name of securing the survival of the company, which emerged leaner and with a chance at being profitable. These structural changes would have been impossible were it not for the hard times that had fallen on the company.

Moments of crises are also times to restore the focus on core operations. It is very convenient to point to spreading attention thinly over too many activities as a reason for the company doing poorly. Getting back to basics is a popular narrative as companies debunk the strategy they have pursued up until recently (especially if a new CEO is brought on board). Had a major shock not occurred, the company might instead have just muddled along indefinitely. Satisficing, or doing just enough to meet some minimum level that is considered acceptable, can work for an extended time. As long as the firm shows *some* profitability, disgruntled stakeholders may refrain from revolt. There may be a sense that things could be better and that something must ultimately change, but we are fine for now. There is a threshold to get over to push that kind of company into action, and it may take a significant stressor to achieve it.

Part of Catching the Swan is therefore corporate renewal. We take action, finally, towards becoming leaner, more focused, and pursuing business opportunities more vigorously. Negativity, if you want to call a stressor that, seems to have a place as well in corporate flourishing in much the same way that many individuals experience post-traumatic growth. During the C-19 pandemic, many trends that were already underway accelerated sharply. Chief among them was the shift towards digitalization. Many businesses launched themselves into online solutions out of desperation, only to find it to be a way to reach whole new segments of customers, thus tapping into new demand. Many also found that digitalization meant that they could do things at a lower cost compared to the physical alternative. We have all learnt that digital meetings or lectures work reasonably well and offer many benefits in terms of being flexible and travel-free. What started out as an act of desperation, then, turned out to bring some unexpected long-term benefits. The willingness to think anew, which is the deal-breaker in generating change, is often born out of necessity.

**BUYING ON THE CHEAP**

Corporate renewal is one way to emerge stronger from a major upheaval, and so will be a certain agility with respect to modifying the strategy during very volatile conditions. If competitors are held down by legacy factors that constrain their ability to adjust, such as being limited to a certain geographical area, this is to the advantage of more 'free-ranging' firms. During 2020/2021, Ryanair and Wizz Air, while certainly not escaping heavy losses, proved more adept at opening and closing routes according to the outlook prevailing at the time and operated flexibly across the entire European scene. Being able to exercise flexibility during this period, in turn, seemed to be predicated on deeper organizational capabilities related to information systems. Having a well-working data infrastructure affords a firm the ability to co-ordinate and communicate across different departments in a way that more rigid peers cannot replicate easily. This agility comes in handy when the rate of change is fast. The CEOs of these companies also liked to point out that they expected intra-European flight capacity to be significantly reduced as more airlines were on the verge of failing, such that their companies stood to gain from the recovery-induced growth that was likely to happen once travel patterns began to revert to the pre-Covid situation. Remarkably, the share price of Wizz Air reached an all-time high during 2021, reflecting, we may presume, its ability to advance its strategic position during widespread industry suffering.

Another and even more opportunistic way of Catching the Swan is to buy assets that are sold at fire sale prices. This is a concept that almost any manager and investor readily confesses to having in their repertoire. 'The time to buy is when there is blood in the street', as people like to say. Asset sales are indeed a common way to resolve financial distress and generate enough liquidity to keep the nose above the water. During major recessions, asset disposals always tend to shoot up, so there does seem, on the face of it, to be some opportunities created by crises.

Selling in panic is generally a bad idea, because one has to accept a lower price than could be fetched in an unhurried sale. A downturn would hardly seem like an opportune time to be selling, so the only reasonable explanation is that it reflects the desperation of companies that struggle to generate the liquidity they need to meet ongoing cash obligations. Assets divested under these circumstances are likely to be sold at a discount to fair value. This happens because the negotiating power of the selling party is weak. For them, money and other strategic alternatives are running out fast. If the distressed sale does not occur as part of an ongoing effort to stave off bankruptcy, but as part of a liquidation, it means that the previous owners have been wiped out and lost for good any upside from a potential rebound. There is thus nobody fighting for control or demanding a premium for it, making it even more of a bargain situation for buyers.

Asset fire sales count as a strategy disruption for the company doing the selling because it represents a rushed and suboptimal adjustment to the corporate portfolio. As we have discussed, a key benefit of building resilience (Taming the Swan) is to avoid losing control of corporate assets in periods of turmoil. A strategy disruption of a competitor is almost by definition a good thing for you, because they are in a defensive mode rather than trying to steal market share. In the extreme case of wipeout, another mechanism that benefits those still standing, as alluded to by the executives of Ryanair and Wizz Air, is that some competition is eliminated and a certain amount of capacity is taken out of the market. This solidifies their market power and increases the scope for price increases.

The situation can be turned into an even better outcome, for the relatively stronger competitor, if it manages to place itself on the buying side of distressed transactions. The fire sale discount that the seller has to accept represents value-creation from the perspective of the buyer because they are getting assets on the cheap. Catching the Swan is to acquire assets that have long-term potential, are a good mix with our existing portfolio, are sold at a discount and, crucially, *would not have been possible to buy were it not for the shock.*

This all sounds very nice, but are these opportunities real? A study by Professor Todd Pulvino asked precisely this question.[5] By their own admission, the airlines use asset sales to provide the liquidity they need to implement their business plans. Analysing the market for used aircraft, Pulvino found that airlines' financial conditions were key determinants of the prices they received in a transaction. Consistent with this hypothesis, the weaker companies sell at a discount of about 14% to the average market price. Roughly speaking, this loss to the seller is value transferred to the pockets of the buyer. Other studies have shown similar-sized value transfers in other market contexts, such as when firms sell minority stakes in publicly listed firms.[6]

The more transient and short-lived the tail risk event can be assumed to be, the clearer it is that such dips represent buying opportunities. We noted in the previous chapter that the oil and gas markets have seen a large number of price slumps over the centuries. During these moments, the industry is plunged into

---

[5]Pulvino, T. C., 1998. Do asset fire-sales exist? An empirical investigation of commercial aircraft transactions. *Journal of Finance*, 53, pp. 939–978.
[6]Dinc, S., I. Erel and R. Liao, 2017. Fire sale discount: Evidence from the sale of minority equity stakes. *Journal of Financial Economics*, 125 (3).

severe financial distress. However, we also took note of the fact that, frequently, the industry remains depressed for a relatively short window of time. For all these flirts with disaster, the industry is, as of the early 2020s, still standing. What this suggests is that there are some built-in mechanisms in the market that will restore prices to levels at which a sufficient share of companies in it manage to make a profit. It furthermore suggests that buyers of distressed assets have a good chance of making an attractive return on their investment.

Precisely such a countercyclical asset acquisition took place in 1999, when the oil market was experiencing one of its slumps. The price bottomed out at close to $10, a level unheard of (in modern times, that is). Saga Petroleum, a Norwegian oil exploration company, had put itself in a precarious situation due to an international acquisition that was not going well. The company had financed the deal largely with debt, so its balance sheet was weak. Therefore, the company was vulnerable to the collapse in the oil price that was unfolding. It did not help that it had a poorly executed derivative portfolio that started to lose substantial money when the oil price finally began to recover. (Yes, you read correctly. They forgot to take tax differences between off-shore profits and the derivative payoff into account, so the derivative position ended up being long in the oil price.) Burning through cash at an alarming rate, the company explored various strategic options, but in the end had no other choice but to accept a bid from one of its larger Norwegian peers. This happened to be Norsk Hydro, a mighty industrial conglomerate with deep pockets. Owing to the stressed condition of Saga, Norsk Hydro was able to negotiate favourable terms. As the deal was being completed, the oil price had already begun to climb back up towards pre-crisis levels, so the cash flows the combined entity was raking in afterwards were colossal. It was probably the best acquisition in Norsk Hydro's long history, carried out smack in the middle of a crisis.

Large-sample evidence provides further support to the notion that buyers can benefit from the financial weakness of the company they are buying.[7] Professors Meier and Servaes found that acquisitions of distressed sellers are associated with an announcement day return that is about 2% higher than in the average acquisition. In dollar terms, this translates into an average improvement in market value of $30 million compared to the baseline. Interestingly, the authors found no statistically significant improvement in the operating performance in the acquired company, nor did they find any change in the overall value created by these acquisitions. They therefore put their findings

---

[7]Meier, J.-M. and H. Servaes, 2020. The benefits of buying distressed assets. *Journal of Applied Corporate Finance*, 32, pp. 105–116.

down to the weak bargaining power of the sellers. Out of the total value created, which remains largely the same, the buyers of distressed firms are able to capture *a larger fraction.*

 ## OPPORTUNITY CAPITAL

If we look at what is going on here, we find that what the countercyclical buyers are doing is to act as *providers of liquidity.* There are times and places where liquidity is scarce and comes at a huge premium. In these cases, the marginal value of an additional dollar (or other currency) is supremely high. Whoever sits on liquidity can dictate the terms. As the rule has it, he who has the gold makes the rules. Well, during slumps, liquidity is gold. The distressed sellers do not have it, but need it, desperately. Therefore, we should internalize the idea that the marginal value of one extra dollar is not the same across firms and it is not the same across different states of nature.

This observation makes liquidity a strategic issue and something that should be analysed on an industry-wide basis. The way it fits into corporate strategy is as follows. Take measures to ensure that you have critical liquidity when it is most needed, which is when there is a general scarcity of it in the industry, because this is when you might be able to capitalize on strategic opportunities induced by the weakness of others. Which is to say, design your financial policies in such a way that they generate cash in those scenarios in which you can *assume* that there will be wholesale distress and that others need to resort to fire sales to survive.

This strategic view of liquidity implies a change in mind-set from just looking at one's own risk capital. We are beginning to sense that risk and opportunity in crises depend on *ex-ante differences in risk capital.* Consequently, it becomes a matter of interest to find out how well stocked up our competitors are in terms of capital. If we find that they appear to have a rather weak balance sheet and are low on liquidity, we may have spotted *a conditional strategic opportunity.* This is a latent opportunity to invest counter-cyclically that is granted to us because of a weakness in our competitor. Had they been stronger and accumulated more risk capital, the opportunity would not be there. For whatever reason, they did not, and we have to evaluate whether their lack of risk capital means anything for our strategy. Our focus shifts from our own resilience to the question of whether we are going to be able to execute any opportunity that may arise in a crisis scenario. We may find that we have enough risk capital to get us through a worst-case scenario largely unharmed (i.e. Taming the Swan), but that we are unlikely to be able to muster the strength to acquire assets in such a situation (i.e. Catching the Swan).

To go on the offensive we need something more than the risk capital that keeps us safe. I will refer to this as *opportunity capital*. It consists of the same kind of financial resources that make up risk capital. The purpose, though, is different. Whereas risk capital absorbs losses, *opportunity capital absorbs the losses of our competitors* and allows us to act as providers of liquidity in the worst-case scenario. From this perspective, there is yet another sense in which a cash balance may be 'working'. Before we said that cash might be working as part of ongoing operations (taking care of incoming payments and assorted surprises), to which we added that cash might be working in the sense of absorbing potential cash flow shortfalls. We now take it a step further and claim that cash might be working by providing financing for countercyclical investment opportunities.

The idea of opportunity capital is perfectly consistent with managers' well-documented preference for 'financial flexibility', which is usually defined in terms of having the financial muscle to grab value-creating opportunities when they arise. By nature opportunistic, managers like the idea of being financially unconstrained so that they can act at short notice (and without having to go to the markets and ask for the money). Financial flexibility thus defined is not necessarily a countercyclical concept, even though that possibility is absolutely in the cards.

To an outsider, it can be hard to tell if the cash is working from the point of view of targeting the assets of less fortunate competitors because there is an element of stealth going on. A company would not normally make an open declaration about such intentions, because it might alert the target firm that somebody is preying on them. As discussed, keeping opportunity capital in the form of an outsize cash balance becomes a matter of trust between the firm's management team and the investors and analysts who take an interest in the firm. Arranging stand-by credit facilities can be a way to prepare for counter-cyclical opportunities that attracts less scorn from investors than large cash balances. Either way, it provides a lens through which to look at apparently over-capitalized firms. Before rushing to the judgement that a firm is overcapi-talized, we should at least hold the thought that a large cash position is working in other senses than being around for immediate liquidity needs. Figure 6.1 sums up this perspective, illustrating how a cash position could in principle consists of three parts – all working in some sense (but with question marks around two of them). We have to look at the firm's competitive landscape and the health of balance sheets in that industry to be able to tell – and the scope for some wild uncertainty.

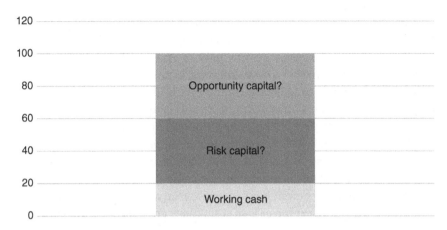

**FIGURE 6.1** Strategic cash

Since countercyclical investment opportunities are buried deep in the tail of the distribution, it is generally more efficient if opportunity capital – just like risk capital – is made conditional rather than sitting on the balance sheet at all times. What we would like, ideally, is a source of financing that is conditional on the same events that trigger the investment opportunity. That is, if tail risk event X leads to assets being put up for sale at attractive discounts, the financial contract we hold should be such that the capital becomes available if X happens, but not otherwise. In that way, cash is not sitting idly on the balance sheet across all scenarios. Instead, we specifically engineer a solution that provides us with the capital we need in those scenarios where the opportunities arise. Financial contracts could be written with countercyclical investment opportunities in mind. For this to work, we need a trigger point that as closely as possible reflects the circumstances under which competitors would near financial distress and where it can be assumed that asset sales would be part of the response to that distress.

Writing contracts of this sort is, as we have seen, possible in principle. The tyre maker Michelin, for example, in the year 2000, structured a five-year bank credit facility that included an option to draw down on an insurance facility. The trigger event for the option was a decline in GDP growth in the US and Europe, such that the facility would be activated if this growth rate fell below 1.5% (in the first three years) or 2% (in the last two years). The logic behind this structure was that Michelin's revenue was deemed to be highly correlated with the growth of the overall economy. The facility thus had a risk-dampening function: the funds would be released, on reasonable and pre-negotiated terms, if business activity fell far enough and reduced Michelin's ability to generate cash flows internally. To see how this kind of contract could support counter-cyclical acquisition strategies, we only have to imagine that, instead of GDP growth, the contract refers to some indicator of the industry's performance. Even gutsier would be to write the contract such that it releases the funds if the performance of a group of select peers falls below a certain level (where it can be assumed they would be going through hardship and the possibility of fire sales is very real). This represents a more targeted form of financing of counter-cyclical opportunities. First of all, it improves the odds that sufficient financing can be obtained should that day come. In theory, it also saves on costs because the trigger event has a low probability, so the fee or interest paid to the bank is less than in the case of a standard credit facility, which can be drawn down anytime.

To further illustrate the idea of a more precise and conditional form of opportunity capital, consider commodity-producing industries. For these products, there are often derivative markets allowing you to write financial contracts of various kinds, like forwards, swaps and options. The strike price in a put option contract can, in principle, be set to coincide with the financial distress of important peers. It should be possible to approximate the price at which they will run out of liquidity, at which point some extra financial muscle would make a lot of sense for a relatively stronger firm. Therefore, if an oil firm, for example, senses that an oil price of $45 would spell trouble for some of its competitors, it may find it opportune to buy put options with $45 as a strike price. That would release a cash flow in precisely the scenario in which the marginal value of liquidity is likely to be high, and thus boost the scope for offensive strategies.

While very elegant in theory, it may not strike you as realistic to make the financing of countercyclical acquisitions available conditional on the opportunity presenting itself. True, it is probably not something that can be applied very frequently. Given the advances of financial engineering, however, more of these types of contracts have become possible. So why not give the idea some thought when you develop your next financial strategy. Perhaps you have spotted that a handful of peers with interesting assets have been growing aggressively lately using lots of debt, which has brought their resilience to dangerously low levels. If your conclusion is that they would clearly be in trouble if something major happened, well, perhaps you should make certain preparations by adding a clause to the facility so that suitable financing would be available *in the event*. The extra basis points that you would pay for this conditional credit line would be made up for, we may presume, by the possibility of being able to grab the opportunity of a lifetime.

Some astute and forward-looking financial strategies may in fact be necessary because of an inherent feature of the market for corporate assets. An interesting theory on this topic was published in 1992.[8] The authors of the study, Professors Andre Shleifer and Robert Vishny, argued that there is something called 'the equilibrium aspect of asset sales'. By this, they meant that all firms in an industry tend to be impacted negatively by the same forces that drive some of them to make asset sales to survive. Because of this feature, there might not be enough buyers within the industry to pick up the distressed assets. In their place, financial investors, whose salient feature is deep pockets, step in. Because they do not have the specialized skills to realize synergies, they cannot make as high a bid for the assets as industry buyers. Therefore, the selling firm loses out even more, because they are at the mercy of money-men who want to exploit their weakness and who see no synergies they are willing to pay extra for. This aspect of their theory was borne out by the aforementioned study by Pulvino. His data shows that the overall market conditions, and who is on the buying side of the tranactions, matters as expected. The fire-sale discount is at its largest when the industry is in a recession and few industry players have the ability to bid. When financial institutions step in to act as providers of liquidity, the discount reaches its peak at 30% to fundamental value!

The equilibrium aspect of asset sales is a point that should be absorbed by any would-be countercyclical acquirer. It is most likely that they too will be affected negatively by the circumstances that bring their peers to desperate measures like selling assets. The cash flows of any company in that sector will take a hit. Therefore, what may seem like a suave move based on today's outlook may be a very different, and much riskier, proposition once things have started to go sideways for the industry. While the would-be acquirer may be able to pull it off anyway, luck favours the prepared. This observation strengthens the case for making a countercyclical move part of your strategy and something whose execution should be actively planned for. Some preparations could make the difference and give us both the speed and financial muscle to act. To underscore this point, we can come back to Norsk Hydro's countercyclical acquisition of Saga and ponder the fact that Statoil, the other major player in the Norwegian oil and gas industry, did not buy Saga despite having eyed it for years. Statoil was also hurting from the low oil prices and, much as it would have liked to, it could not raise the equity capital it would have needed swiftly enough because of the ownership by the Norwegian state. It was thus experiencing some binding financial constraints at the time the opportunity

---

[8]Shleifer, A. and R. Vishny, 1992. Liquidation values and debt capacity: A market equilibrium approach. *Journal of Finance*, 47, pp. 1343–1366.

presented itself and thus had to cede it to Norsk Hydro. The fact that Saga had overleveraged its balance sheet and was struggling with its strategy were signals that an opportunity may be about to present itself. That should have enacted creative financial strategies whose purpose would have been to capitalize on it, such as buying out-of-the money put options. To the eternal delight of Norsk Hydro, this never happened.

## FLIGHT TO SAFETY

Catching the Swan through buying assets on the cheap, we have seen, is conditional on a difference in access to risk capital that buffers the shock that arises. Those with the biggest cushion of capital are most likely to be in a position to take advantage, so we have to start thinking about the state of our balance sheet relative to those of our competitors. There is another factor at work here, one that tends to amplify any pre-existing differences in vulnerability – in favour of those who are already relatively stronger.

What I have in mind is the fickle mood of financial markets, or what is sometimes referred to as its 'risk appetite'. The market's willingness to accept risk, history teaches us, can change in the blink of an eye. Risk appetite, as it were, is 'time-varying'. Financial markets oscillate between conditions of excess and despair. At times, they are almost oblivious to risk and happily take on any risky prospect without asking much in the way of critical questions. At other times, the mood is almost the exact opposite – the market wants safety above all and shuns risk almost completely.

To see how this time-changing risk appetite comes about, consider that in good times optimism flourishes, capital is abundant and, as a direct consequence, asset prices rise. During an expansionary phase, any difficulties in obtaining funding are temporarily suspended – what the treasurer asks for he or she has a very good chance of getting. Actually, we may start to see what we never expected: poor businesses, strategies that should never have been launched, getting funded on easy terms. This happens with a minimum of due diligence on the part of the financiers. Everyone is primarily worried about arriving late to the party. Standards fall and more and more lenient terms are offered as financial intermediaries climb up the risk scale. Banks no longer insist on covenants to the same extent that they did previously and prospectuses get ever lighter and vague on potential risks. Private debt accumulates rapidly and bad investments are made in the process. This is the story of countless booms.

Booms can go on for years, until some news arrives that causes the process to go into reverse. The booms carry with them the seeds of their own eventual reversal because they misallocate resources. When the folly is finally exposed, the bad investments are revealed for what they are: a waste of somebody's money. Scores of investments have to be written down. For financial intermediaries, these asset impairments can spell trouble because they deplete their equity base, possibly to the point where banks' survival is called into question. Predictably, their willingness and ability to perform their main function – channelling funds from savers to productive projects – largely disappear.

At this turning point, there is a sudden shift in the overall appetite for risk. The boom becomes a bust and everyone rushes for the exit. Risk is no longer wanted. On the contrary, investors now put a premium on safety and stability. A mad dash in the other direction ensues: a so-called 'flight to safety'. Such runs lead to an increase in the price of any asset bestowed with that epithet (so far in its history, the US dollar has been a reliable safe haven, as has gold). Outside those few assets that manage to convey an air of safety, everyone else in need of funding is likely to find that capital becomes scarcer and more expensive. The historical pattern is that access to capital becomes more of a deciding factor for corporate strategies during times of crises. The uncertainty and general confusion about where the company (and the world, for that matter) is headed increases.

Interestingly, the flight-to-safety logic opens up for some new creative financial strategies for arranging opportunity capital, i.e. for having the means to act on any opportunities that may open up during times of extreme uncertainty. If you believe something is likely to increase in value during such turmoil in the economy, you may want to have some of those assets on your balance sheet. The fact that their value appreciates when the rest of the economy is melting down could provide you with the countercyclical financing you need. According to this rationale, having excess cash in US dollars makes sense given that the currency's tendency (so far) is to appreciate countercyclically. Somewhat more controversially, investing in gold may actually make sense – even if you are a manufacturing firm! While this strategy is hardly about to go mainstream, US firm Palantir Technologies Inc. did in fact begin to stockpile gold during 2021, citing the desire to hedge against future Black Swan events.[9] That is quite apart from their day job of making software. The company did not explicitly state a goal of capitalizing on opportunities during future crises, but that is wholly understood.

---

[9]Palantir buys gold bars as hedge against 'Black Swan Event', Bloomberg.

At the same time that the flow of external capital dries up, another dynamic is likely to play out that also aggravates the misfortunes of vulnerable firms – to the benefit of their stronger peers. In this case, the issue revolves around access to internal liquidity. Recall the observation that in 2009, in the midst of the financial crisis, Volvo Car's cash position increased by 13 billion kronor. The biggest single explanation for this increase was a substantial reduction in working capital. As the company watched its order book shrink by the week, it decided to reduce its costs. There is nothing surprising about this. We know from before that flexibility means less risk, and they were exercising the option to discontinue some of their purchases, which translated into large decreases in investment in inventory. Producing out of existing stock explains the increase in cash flow that Volvo experienced. Therefore, at a potentially dangerous time, this mechanism generated a helpful influx of internal liquidity. While beneficial to Volvo, it did not mean that the risk went away. It was just pushed further down the supply chain, to Volvo's suppliers and their suppliers. The drying up of orders from a behemoth like Volvo created instant problems in this ecosystem of firms, many of whom are small and rely heavily on the car producer for their income. In a system, the risk from an external shock has to land somewhere and it tends to be in the lap of the most vulnerable.

The flight-to-safety logic, and the working capital mechanism, are important mechanisms for our story on Catching the Swan. They are very consistent with a general pattern of *risk falling disproportionally on the weak*. When a crisis occurs, any disparity in wealth is more likely to widen than not. Many of the financially weaker segments of society have incomes that are more fragile and dependent on businesses that are highly cyclical. This was on full display during the C-19 pandemic, as the so-called 'gig-economy', i.e. flexible and often short-term jobs in the hospitality business, suffered badly from the restrictions that were put in place. The gig-economy consists of many low net worth individuals living paycheck to paycheck, so the lockdowns very quickly spelled pain. In contrast, the already wealthy enjoyed a windfall from a booming stock market fuelled by the generous fiscal and monetary policies. Many subsequent reports showed that the pandemic greatly boosted wealth inequality, which reinforced pre-existing differences along many lines – gender, ethnicity, age and geography. Gabriela Bucher, Executive Director of Oxfam International, noting that billionaires had quickly recouped their losses and that, for them, the recession was already over, commented that:

> 'We stand to witness the greatest rise in inequality since records began. The deep divide between the rich and poor is proving as deadly

as the virus . . . women and marginal racial and ethnic groups are bearing the brunt of this crisis. They are more likely to be pushed into poverty, to go hungry, and to be excluded from healthcare.'[10]

That the weakest bear the brunt of a crisis is an important principle that seems to be built into the structure of things. Taleb notes as much, confessing at one point that he, as a humanist, hates the Black Swans because of the unfairness that they tend to bring (Taleb, 2007, p. 272). Since the wealthy do not do warfare anymore, as the nobility once did, the only time risk falls disproportionally on the rich is when there is a revolution.[11] While overall the 'risk-falling-on-the-weak' phenomenon is a deplorable feature of episodes of drastic change, we have taken an interest in one particular aspect of it, namely that it catches out players in business whose own polices have left them vulnerable. At least as businesses, we need to be thinking about whether or not this predictable mechanism might lead to opportunities.

To sum up, following a crisis, the frail see incomes and margins disappear at a quicker rate than their stronger peers. They are to a larger extent shunned by capital providers who prioritize safety. They end up bearing the consequences of risk-reducing measures at the hands of the stronger players (such as inventory reductions). They struggle to invest enough and therefore fall behind in the competitive landscape. They resort to liquidating some of their assets as a means to survive, which presents buying opportunities for stronger players. These are built-in patterns that repeat themselves, which is why they should be internalized by a management team that wishes to create strategies for a world of wild uncertainty.

Before moving on, we can reflect on the fact that during the C-19 pandemic, despite the initial panic and draconian responses, the capital markets did not start to dysfunction. We did not see a flight to safety with the force that might have been expected. Partly this was because banks were better capitalized compared to The Great Recession and did not switch into panic mode. However, more than anything, it was the generous policies of governments and central banks, who decided to flood the markets with liquidity, that made the difference. In recent times, this has become the go-to response when a systemic crisis hits. Policy-makers have learnt from the mistakes made during the

---

[10]Mega-rich recoup COVID-losses in record-time yet billions will live in poverty for at least a decade, Oxfam International.

[11]Or perhaps not only then. Security is becoming a massive issue for the wealthy, as they are obvious targets for hits. Investing in more security always seems to be the answer, rather than trying to eradicate the inequalities that gave rise to the precarious situation in the first place.

The Great Depression in the 1930s when the policy response was contractionary rather than expansionary. Now the need to maintain the public's confidence in the system is well understood. We do not want animal spirits to spiral out of control, because a vicious downward spiral quickly becomes self-fulfilling. Hence the Obama administration's TARP programme aimed at saving troubled financial institutions during the Great Recession. Hence the thunderous declaration by Mario Draghi during the euro crisis in the early 2010s that the ECB would do 'whatever it takes'. Hence Alan Greenspan, the then-Chairman of the Federal Reserve, had the famous inclination to lower interest rates at the first sign of trouble, thus 'bailing out' the markets (this behaviour was so consistent that it even got a name, 'the Greenspan put').

Since policy-makers have learnt their lesson so well, have we managed to do away with the worst aspects of the flight-to-safety phenomenon? Certainly, they have managed to stave off some of the worst consequences. Which is good, because it is a very dangerous thing when confidence in the future is broken. However, there is something called moral hazard, which is when market participants take note of this generous underwriting of previous excesses and take new risks knowing full well that there is a floor for how bad things can get. The benefits of risk-taking are private whereas the consequences are socialized (observe how the executives of Lehman Brothers made off like bandits despite the collapse of their firm). Reckless risk-taking is, in a way, encouraged by the system, which sets us on a path to the next crisis. There may also come a time when the system cannot be saved, because the bubbles get ever bigger and the governments' ability to counter them is ever more taxed. Every time the officials step in, their capacity to do so yet one more time is impaired. Public debt grows and the printing of money undermines the currency.

It is not just preppers who worry that these perverse incentives could herald a future financial collapse. In their book *The Rise of Carry* from 2020, Lee, Lee and Caldiron argue that the world economy has been in a powerful 'carry regime' since at least the early 1990s, by which they mean that volatility has consistently been suppressed by policymakers.[12] The interest rate policy has been subjected to the immediate goal of bailing out previous excesses and supporting asset prices rather than long-term stability. In a carry regime, the system generates lots of leverage and liquidity, which supports the markets but simultaneously makes the system fragile. If the support is withdrawn through an unexpected increase in interest rates, markets could topple with the result

---

[12]Lee, T., J. Lee and K. Coldiron, 2020, *The rise of carry: The dangerous consequences of volatility suppression*. McGraw Hill: New York.

that leverage unwinds and the provision of liquidity contracts. There may be a 'tipping point', the authors speculate, when the ability to bail out the system has been exhausted. Because of how the carry regime is intrinsically linked to the system of central banking and fiat monies, its ultimate collapse could mean the end of the current system itself. At some point, amidst runaway inflation, the central bank itself becomes insolvent and unable to exercise control over interest rates (i.e. push the rates low enough to protect asset prices). This 'inconceivable' event would be a Black Swan for the ages.

##  RISK AS STRATEGY

Catching the Swan is about acting on opportunities that would not have presented themselves were it not for a highly consequential event that did not announce that it was about to occur, i.e. a Black Swan. If you are stronger than your peers by a sufficient margin, chances are that you are not only resilient but also antifragile. The meaning of antifragility in this context is that you have a reasonable shot at benefitting from the current disorder, at least on the level of doing noticeably better than most of the competition and advancing your position (at their expense).

The idea that has been introduced is that relative strength is a strategic variable that should be viewed as such by management teams. We should not prepare for wild uncertainty from an exclusively firm-centric perspective but rather consider the impact the shock would have on the system of which we are a part. In a world where periods of calm are regularly punctured by massive shocks, we must make a habit of applying this perspective as part of the corporate strategy process.

Of course, the first priority is to verify that our buffers and flexibility are such that we can reasonably withstand a shock. Getting our own house in order, or Taming the Swan, is number one on the agenda. However, after that we should look out of the window and ask some further questions. What system are we a part of and how will it be likely to adjust to the same shock? How will different players in the system fare in such an event? Who are the most vulnerable? What is their resilience likely to be compared to ours? If it hits the fan, who is likely to be shut out of the capital markets? Do we sense any opportunities here that could arise from differences in relative strength?

The strategy we are talking about is not unlike a contrarian investment strategy in that we stand to gain from someone else's financial distress in order to benefit from their presumed panicky actions when the day comes.

We touched earlier on the curse of the contrarian investor, however, which is the fact that, while you are occasionally right, most of the time you are not, and losing money while at it. Legendary stories exist out there of contrarians hitting it big, but considered as a whole it is not a well-performing strategy financially. It is important to see, though, that from a corporate perspective, it is not *the* strategy. The 'real' business strategy is in place and doing its job in all scenarios: the firm enters new markets, develops new products, and so on. Catching the Swan by acting on countercyclical investment opportunities is an *add-on* to that business strategy.

To mitigate the contrarian curse and make sure the strategy is worthwhile we should first verify that there is a realistic chance of defensive action by certain competitors that we can capitalize on in the next downturn. An analysis of their financial condition should be carried out, and only if it points convincingly to an undeniable vulnerability do we proceed. There has to be discipline amidst the opportunism. We are not just looking to add any odd asset that might come along. Rather, it should be about targeting assets that make for a good strategic fit, ones that we have some advantage in operating and managing. These are things that we would like to add to our portfolio regardless, but find to be either unavailable or too pricey in normal circumstances. Without these two conditions being present – a clear possibility of defensive action by peers and the assets in question being a good fit – the value of opportunity capital quickly fades to zero. We should not be swayed by nice-sounding memes about 'buying when others are weak' and so on and take its inherent appeal as an excuse for not doing the diligence. The approach needs to be analytical.

What we are looking for are cues that some players are clearly more vulnerable than us to the same shock. Highly leveraged and cash strapped entities are of particular interest, especially if they have been growing rapidly in recent times. If you have developed a high-calibre decision-support tool of the type discussed in the previous chapter, why not take an afternoon and run some of the competitors' numbers through it? Apply a stress test and see how they come out.

When a difference in resilience has been confirmed, the strategic implications of this can be explored. To turn it into an opportunity, we also need to be able to identify a plausible mechanism. Are we talking about acquiring a competitor or some of their assets in a partial liquidation? Is the idea to grab market share by expanding in a way that they cannot match? Or is it to drive them out of a market by lowering prices in a way that they, because of their thin margins, cannot match? Whenever possibilities like these are found to be realistic, we may want to incorporate them into our strategic plan and start making some preparations, so that, if and when the shock occurs, we are well placed to act. If the analysis points in this direction, we can justify adding opportunity capital to our buffers to make sure we are in a position to capitalize.

The upshot of this strategic analysis of liquidity is that the weaker we find our competitors to be, the more cash *we* should stock up on. If we spot a competitor that is close to their pain thresholds, and therefore vulnerable to a shock, the marginal value of liquidity, from our perspective, goes up! Again, recall that any countercyclical move is going to require investment. This is obvious for asset acquisitions, as we need money to execute the deal. However, the same is true for any expansion aimed at grabbing market share. Expansion always takes investment.

A more subtle point is that by making such a move, we are going out on a limb and increasing our risk profile substantially. This goes back to the earlier distinction between risk capital and transaction capital. To make a strategic move, you need both. In the midst of a crisis, we are already presumably burning through our risk capital, which is there precisely to absorb such a blow. Opportunity capital needs to provide not only transactional capital for our countercyclical expansion, but also some risk capital to support it. Without it, our own wipeout risk and the risk of strategy disruption could quickly become constraining factors. The reason is that, obviously, things could get even worse. Getting the timing right is the overarching difficulty with contrarian strategies. When things bottom out is only clear with hindsight, and as long as things keep deteriorating, it will look as if they will go on doing so for a lot longer. We are essentially betting on the view that things will return to normal and we stretch our resources thinner at a time when such a reversal is by no means ensured. As noted, many took the view that the C-19 pandemic was a temporary shock that was superimposed on the world and that it would revert back to its normal self once it passed. If this was your belief, it indeed must have looked like a buying opportunity and a good time to go on the offensive. However, anyone who took actions based on such a view ran the risk that new variants of the virus would emerge to defeat the vaccines. Only when the history books are written much later does it crystallize into one of those 'self-evident' buying opportunities.

It follows that countercyclical investing should be seen as a case of conscious risk-taking with its own risk-return trade-off: the chance of making a killing, but at the cost of increasing the risk of a subsequent distress-induced strategy disruption. As long as opportunity capital is not spent, it works as risk capital in the sense of buffering against further shortfalls. Commit the money to capitalize on what seems to be an opportunity and you will be at a greater risk of a subsequent liquidity squeeze if the hard times continue. In other words, be careful out there and, more importantly, do not push through a countercyclical move just because you have fallen in love with the idea and want the bragging rights it brings. In a world of wild uncertainty, ideologies and pet ideas should never drive policy, as that tends to become the seeds of our own undoing.

In the tail of things, the boundaries between risk and opportunity blur. There are massive redistributions of wealth on the line. Some strategies are broken, to the benefit of others. Some of these redistributions may, to a degree, be possible to anticipate, meaning that we should start looking at them as contingent investment opportunities. By taking some proactive measures, we can increase the odds that we do well should such a scenario unfold. We are prepared, ready to act, and know what to look for. Given the nature of Black Swans, there is no way of knowing what will be the driving forces next time around. The specifics of the mayhem always look different. However, the patterns we have discussed in this chapter are quite general. Ultimately, shocks are translated into impacts on revenue, costs and asset/liability values, and from that point on risk capital is likely to shape the competitive dynamics in any given peer group in rather predictable ways. The weaker ones underinvest, cut back and sell assets, whereas the stronger ones can expand, buy assets and generally look for opportunities.

Catching the Swan is a quintessentially strategic perspective because it is about competitive dynamics during times of disorder. We are trying to manoeuvre to get the upper hand, to be part of the winning side, even when the industry goes through a dark moment. As we do, turning risk into opportunity becomes a conscious part of corporate strategy. However, throughout this book, the strategic role of risk management, even without bringing any competitors into the picture, should be clear. One of the key arguments have been that Black Swans have the potential to create significant collateral damage – to disrupt the strategy. We have also concluded that they have the potential to end the strategy altogether – the wipeout scenario. A more typical format of risk management is to take the identified risks and evaluate various risk mitigation actions for each of them on a risk-by-risk basis. This 'identify and assess' approach, while potentially very useful, is not 'strategic' in the conventional sense of the word. When instead we start by analysing the scope for variability in the top line – revenue – and ask how the cost structure and various liabilities respond to that, the setting is much more strongly related to the fulfilment of important corporate objectives. It is in this context that we are able to say something meaningful about whether the firm is resilient to tail risk and whether it is likely to survive and thrive across a large number of scenarios. When we extend that kind of analysis to cover competitors and other constituents of the ecosystem we operate within, the 'strategicness' of risk should be clear.

Viewing relative risk as a strategic variable takes a certain mind-set. It is a dynamic and forward-looking attitude. We earlier met software maker Palantir, which has engaged in 'artistic' financial strategies such as investing in gold. Palantir styles itself as a group of free-thinkers, unconstrained by conventional wisdom. They certainly seem to have internalized the fact that wild uncertainty is the name of the game. Perhaps this is one of the main assets in such a world: being able to think ahead in creative ways, taking in the bigger picture, and not caring so much whether your strategy follows the established patterns of the past. Just administering a firm as if it were an island, referring to the proven textbook practices, might not prime you for success when uncertainty is wild.

Furthermore, a manager in a world of wild uncertainty needs to be attuned to the role of contingencies and anticipate their importance for corporate strategy. When there is substantial variability in performance, mechanisms that hitherto are hidden from view are activated. Covenants may be breached, margin calls may be triggered, key employees may leave, and so on. Similarly, competitive dynamics are set in motion that would never take place under normal conditions. Risk managers should be experts in understanding such contingencies and mapping them out. The firm with the keenest understanding of future contingencies is at an advantage. They can make the necessary preparations and therefore act with more resolve. Looking ahead, the future is always opaque, pure uncertainty. However, we know enough about broad patterns – demand destruction, flight to safety, fire sales, and so on – to have an idea of along which lines things are likely to play out, and corporate strategy should be informed accordingly. The baseline strategy, i.e. the concept of how the firm is to make money, should therefore come with an add-on that is designed to perform in the event of wholesale disorder – designed, that is, for the purpose of Catching the Swan.

7

# Riding the Swan

W E HAVE SEEN THAT with risk comes opportunity and that something objectively bad can be turned into an outcome that is, at least in some respects, beneficial. Firms that manage to do so meet the criteria for being considered antifragile, because they stand to gain from disorder. A firm that is antifragile can be said to be risk-loving, a term that describes a preference for more volatility rather than less. This is a departure from the more normal state of risk aversion, which indicates a preference for certainty and stability.

We will now explore another logic by which firms should positively love risk and the upside that comes with it. The change in perspective is that, this time, we do not wait for a crisis to happen before we strike. Instead, with a respectful nod to the Black Swans, we launch ourselves headlong into an adventure, guns blazing. Even our usual foe, the wipeout, may be a fully accepted possibility in these cases. The goal now is to maximize upside potential, come (almost) what may. This is the strategy of Riding the Swan, of holding on to its neck and following it up towards the sky.[1]

This chapter will explain how such a risk-loving attitude may come about. Before setting out to do that, I remind the reader that there is nothing in the Black Swan framework that rules out massive *positive* consequences. Perhaps it is telling of our mental wiring that the concept has come to be so closely

---

[1] Yes, swans can fly. What is more, they fly at a high altitude, which is fortunate for this metaphor.

associated with low probability events with catastrophic consequences. However, Taleb makes it clear that part of our approach should be to gain exposure to positive Black Swans and try to have a good run with them. The strategy, he encourages, is to tinker as much as possible and try to collect as many Black Swan opportunities as we can (Taleb, 2007, Prologue, xxi). Riding the Swan is very much in this spirit, with the difference that it becomes our strategy mainly when the tinkering has already yielded an opportunity that looks set to take off.

 ## RISK SHIFTING

Riding the Swan is going to put a spotlight on the potential for differences in attitude to risk, for which there is abundant evidence. Some people like the quiet life and gardening, others free climb steep cliffs in Mexico. A host of complicated factors contribute to these differences. There are physiological factors that determine how our brain processes fear. A specific part of our brain called the amygdala, for example, has a key role in the neural system that detects and responds to threats. Men are generally considered more willing to take risks, suggesting that testosterone levels matter. Socio-economic factors, such as wealth and income, are also known to impact risk tolerance. Situational variables do as well, such as whether our most recent experience was a gain or loss. The list of variables that determine our attitude to risk becomes very long.

Individual differences aside, risk aversion is our normal state. In most situations, we prefer less risk to more, and go to some lengths to avoid it. The opposite to risk aversion, pure risk-loving behaviour, is a comparatively rare thing. Adrenaline junkies do exist, but as a proportion of the population, the number appears to be relatively small.

Risk management is a good thing if you are a risk-averse individual. If you place a premium on certainty and safety, it makes sense to narrow the range of possible outcomes. Such individuals would typically place a large portion of their savings in low-risk interest-bearing instruments, knowing full well that the stock market promises higher returns. You might even be willing to pay actual money for risk management, because the added certainty might provide you with enough peace of mind to make up for the cost. Risk lovers, in contrast, make a very different assessment. Given their inclination, they would likely gravitate towards the risky end of the investment spectrum, like IPOs and derivatives. They may choose the riskier alternative even when they expect to lose on average (i.e. when the expected value of the transaction, in monetary terms, is negative). The thrill of 'winning big' outweighs the fact that the deal is not favourable in statistical, average terms, which is the principle that creates a market for lottery tickets.

Are firms risk-averse or risk-loving? That is an interesting question. We should not answer that they are risk-loving simply because running a business is clearly risky. Accepting high levels of risk is not what is meant by the term 'risk-loving' in its academic sense. Most firms believe in what they do and *expect* to gain from their ventures, so the risk is worth taking. The counter-intuitive answer is that firms should be neither. They are supposed to be, in theory at least, risk-neutral. At least this would be the conclusion if we posit that firms are on a mission to maximize long-term value.[2] To do that, firms should maximize the expected value of cash flow (which is to say the mathematical expectation) regardless of the distribution of gains and losses. They are not supposed to care about that distribution of payoffs across different scenarios: the decision rule is always to go for the alternative that has the highest expected value. While risk neutrality is hardly descriptive of the firm's managers as persons, this is actually how they are called on to behave in economic models of the firm that assume value maximization.

Once we introduce the prospect of collateral damage in the form of wipe-outs and strategy disruption, the calculus changes. It is when the expected value of this collateral damage is added that risk management has a case. Risk aversion, remember, is a precondition for risk management to be considered a good idea. With the addition of the expected costs of collateral damage occurring in the tail of the distribution, it is *as if* the firm were risk-averse. Everything is still about maximizing expected value, though, so it has nothing to do with managers actually being risk-averse. They just respond rationally to information about the negative consequences that would occur in the tail of the distribution, factor that into the future expected cash flows and the result is what appears to be risk-averse behaviour. This collateral damage logic, which we have already met in Chapter 3, is what underpins theories of risk management in the corporate finance literature.

Are there circumstances where it would make sense for firms to act as if they were risk-loving? Actually, there is, and the theory making this argument is called *risk shifting*. To understand what this theory is about, we have to begin

---

[2]This premise is by no means widely accepted. Many emphasize corporate social responsibility and argue in favour of a more balanced scorecard than just firm value. I refer the reader to my book *Empowered enterprise risk management* for an extended discussion on this topic.

by brushing up on why lenders and shareholders think differently with respect to risk-taking. Lenders only care about getting their principal back and collecting the interest for as long as the loan is still outstanding. This outlook makes them naturally conservative and cautious rather than risk-seeking. (I know, it can be hard to believe when you read about lending sprees leading up to financial crises, but bear with me. This is, for the time being, a textbook description.) Banks prefer higher profits in the firm they lend to only insofar as it makes their loan safer and because it might lead to repeat business. What they definitely do not want is for managers to make reckless bets, because that increases the risk of ending up with a non-performing loan.

Shareholders make a very different calculation. They realize that once debtholders are fully repaid, any surplus wealth belongs to them. From that point on, it is pure upside potential. There is thus a clear potential for windfalls. As far as the downside is concerned, they actually have something working for them 'for free'. It is that remarkable feature of corporate law called *limited liability*. The essence of limited liability is that shareholders are not personally responsible for the firm's debts. The firm is a separate legal entity. This entity is a counterparty to any loan agreements and assumes all responsibilities in relation to them. In the event of default, debtholders can only collect assets held in possession by the firm itself and not those of anyone who has invested in its equity. The bank cannot reach through limited liability to have investors cover any negative gap between the value of those assets and the amount claimed by the bank.[3]

Limited liability has far-reaching implications. The first is that *shareholders can only lose their original investment*. This is already a significant risk management device because they can just walk away from a firm that is collapsing, i.e. one where the value of the debt exceeds the liquidation value of the assets. The lenders, in these cases, are left picking up the bill. The second and highly related point is that shareholders may, thanks to the protection afforded by limited liability, become risk-loving in the extreme. When we follow through on the idea, we reach the startling conclusion that incentives to reduce risk in a company can be suspended entirely. In fact, a risk manager, according to the logic of risk shifting, is called on not to reduce risk but to engineer more of it!

---

[3]In sole proprietorships and general partnerships there is unlimited liability, meaning that the partners (investors) are personally liable for the debt incurred by the firm. Also, banks may require the firm's directors, even in a limited liability company (a corporation), to sign an agreement that makes them personally responsible. However, that is a separate agreement between the bank and the directors, and the directors can refuse it if they do not want that risk.

How does this happen? The theory on risk shifting, introduced by Professors Jensen and Meckling,[4] asks us to see that shareholders actually have what can be described as a call option on the firm's assets. In this case, the strike price, the value at which the option holder would choose to exercise his or her option, is the face value of the debt. Because of limited liability, the payoff for shareholders can never go below what they paid to acquire the option (their equity investment at origination). This payoff structure is exactly the same as for any option traded in the marketplace: one pays an upfront option premium but can never lose more than that amount. However, the sky remains the limit, because when the value of assets exceeds the notional value of the loan, shareholders collect that windfall. This is why limited liability *by itself* can induce a risk-loving attitude, regardless of whether shareholders behave in a risk-loving way in other domains of life.

In a world of wild uncertainty, limited liability indeed looks like a gift from the gods. It is a seemingly perfect device: if an extreme negative event occurs, we will just walk away from the mess. On the other hand, if a positive Black Swan occurs, we will reap all the gains. We should look at shareholders as facing similar incentives as option holders, or at least realize that it is a perspective that may sometimes apply. Options, as we know, love volatility.

If you feel this turns everything we have said up to now on its head, you are just about right. We have discussed risk and all the disruption costs that occur as a firm's strategy starts to dysfunction, and concluded that these are outcomes best avoided. The presence of potential collateral damage motivates a risk-averse attitude and, by extension, risk management. The logic of risk shifting indeed contradicts this basic stance. If both can be true, it means that the managers of a firm simultaneously face incentives to reduce risk and to maximize it. With two opposing forces at work, the life of a risk manager is apparently more complicated than we first thought.

Which side dominates? The answer is that, most of the time, it ought to be risk management. Shareholders and their managers, in all likelihood, want to keep the firm going rather than relying on the crude risk management tool of limited liability. Wipeout risk and strategy disruption impose the larger costs. For a firm that is either profitable or expects to be, it usually makes little sense to bet everything in one single act of risk-maximization that relies on limited liability to bail them out. Instead, the value lies in executing the strategy and investing in good projects on a continuing basis, which promises to yield

---

[4]Jensen, M. C. and W. H. Meckling, 1976. Theory of the Firm: Managerial behavior, agency costs and ownership structure. *Journal of Financial Economics*, 3, pp. 305–360.

benefits over an indefinite time horizon. This is the key difference compared to financial options, because the latter have a finite life. You win or you lose, but either way the dust is settled. When they expire, we have to start anew. This is why holders of such options are reliably anti-fragile and risk-loving. They want mayhem and chaos every day of the week. Shareholders and managers, in contrast, are interested in continuity, because much of the value lies in realizing new projects down the road that make use of the firm's comparative advantages.

To these purely economic arguments, we can add the emotional attachment that many owners feel for the business they have created. Most owners care about their employees and the legacy they leave behind. Therefore, they would refute the notion of doubling down on some adventurous project, despite the lure of impressive windfalls if it were to pay off. Further working against risk shifting is the fact that bankers are not blind to the possibility that equity investors might sometimes favour aggressive risk taking. When such actions on their part is a real concern, bankers will raise the interest charged as a form of compensation for the added risk. The mere suspicion that something like that could go down is enough to motivate a higher premium. In those cases, shareholders end up bearing the costs for latent mischief in the form of higher interest expenses or even credit rationing. If they want a lower interest rate, they have to convince the bank that they are going to implement the agreed-on business plan, plain and simple. This promise effectively puts their reputation at stake. If managers say they are all about the business plan and then proceed to do much riskier stuff, that will not go down well in banking circles. Reputation effects, therefore, put another lid on risk shifting, unless we are talking about outright fraudsters who are about to leave the country.

Rather than relying on managers' incentives for preserving their reputation to protect their interests, banks can also demand that the loan agreement come with one or more covenants. The purpose of these covenants is partly to limit management's ability to take actions later on what would be unfavourable to debtholders from a risk point of view. The covenants might stipulate, for example, that if performance falls below a certain threshold, the firm is obliged to take actions like issuing more equity or halting capital expenditures. The covenants could also be about restricting certain actions that would be negative from the bank's perspective, such as paying a dividend or issuing a new loan whose claim would have higher seniority in a legal process. Covenants are very common in practice and can be seen as a concrete mechanism for dealing with the problem of post-deal changes in the firm's risk profile.

The risk-shifting logic, though a favourite among academics, is a highly stylized model. Essentially, it takes place in a one-off kind of setting, where you have a chance to make a bet and either it pays off or it does not. This is not descriptive of most real-world decision-making situations. In fact, it takes a very specific – and rare – situation for the real world to resemble the theoretical model. This occurs when firms are getting precipitously close to bankruptcy. At this point, there may not be much hope of success or even viability on the current trajectory. Because of poor performance, the value of the firm's assets has already fallen close to the value of debt, and insolvency looms. Then reality starts to look a lot more like the risk-shifting model. If all is lost anyway, why not go for broke and make strategic use of limited liability? For these reasons, severe financial distress is the context in which we might actually observe firms behave in accordance with the risk-shifting hypothesis.

Except that the data does not bear the risk-shifting story out, even in these situations. Professor Erik Gilje investigated a large sample of US firms, several of whose financial performance was in decline.[5] As they edged closer to the point of distress, there were no visible indications that they were ramping up new and risky investment projects. Instead, and contrary to the risk-shifting hypothesis, the more distressed firms invested less, and in less risky projects, than their healthier peers. The reasons are twofold. First, loan covenants are effective in restricting overly risky behaviour. Second, money is quickly getting scarce in firms approaching distress, so there may simply be a lack of funds to carry out risky bets. In that sense, the whole thing is self-regulating. Even if you wanted to bet the house, you may struggle to come up with the down payment for making that move. Being distressed usually means being financially constrained as well, i.e. there is a general lack of resources. Even more fundamentally, what is there to say that there would be, for most firms, some attractive high-risk project just waiting to be executed? How could a Mid-western manufacturing company, let us say, suddenly risk-shift? Would they decide to jump on a shipping venture in the Indian Ocean that they heard about from a friend? The truth is probably that options recede quickly as performance takes a turn for the worse and that the existence of a suitable high-risk project on stand-by is a fidget of the academic imagination.

What do we make of limited liability and risk-shifting? Well, the conclusion is that risk-shifting, understood as a massive and partly devious bet on a

[5]Gilje, E. P., 2016. Do firms engage in risk-shifting? Empirical evidence. *Review of Financial Studies*, 29 (11), pp. 2925–2954.

speculative venture is probably not the way to approach things. Covenants, reputation effects and a lack of money for executing the bet all get in the way, as does the fact that the right kind of high-risk projects are in short supply.[6] Risk-shifting in the purest sense of the term is not the main road to unlocking great potentials, and Riding the Swan has to be done differently. Limited liability, however, will still be an important part of the story.

## A BEAUTIFUL STRATEGY

There is another, more straightforward, way that firms can 'love risk' – by seeking exposures to positive Black Swans and making a conscious decision to make wild uncertainty work for them. It is not 'going for broke' so much as simply 'going for it'. When we spot opportunities that are of a once-in-a-century or once-in-a-decade nature, we are not supposed to hold back and exercise general caution. Instead, we maximize our exposure to this thing by *pulling all the levers at our disposal*. This is the essence of Riding the Swan. Limited liability is part of the picture, but not in the sneaky way assumed by risk-shifting theorists (saying you are going to do A and then doing the risky B instead). Rather, it is risk loving in plain sight, for all the world to see. I will propose that Riding the Swan is opportune when you have a beautiful strategy that is scalable. Beautiful in this context means that the strategy is right for its times. It is tapping into a momentum that has started to stir, yet which has not been fully exploited.

Talking about a massively outperforming strategy brings us into the field of corporate strategy. Theorists in this field are forever trying to find the magical essence of a strategy that is sure to lead to success, be it dynamic capabilities, organizational culture, being customer-centric, or something else. All those things are surely important and deserve attention, but most of the time when we observe a successful strategy it seems that something just went very right at the right moment. An outperforming strategy, in this view, is a result of a bet that paid off – the world changed and somebody was perfectly positioned for that transition. Out of luck, foresight, or some combination thereof, they

---

[6]This does not mean that banks can congratulate themselves for a job well done on controlling corporate mischief. The risk profile can be shifted in other ways. Firms may pay out a dividend, depleting risk capital that might well be needed in the firm. It is especially harmful to debtholders if combined with a practice called 'asset stripping' whereby the firm first sells a cash flow-generating asset and then pays itself a dividend with the proceeds. The firm that emerges has a reduced ability to generate cash flows to support the debt (because of the unit divested) and a reduced equity base (because of the extra dividend). Banks can of course write covenants against this as well, but banks sometimes seem to forget to insist on covenants, especially during boom times.

got it right. They managed to put themselves in a spot where they could give the world what it wanted. For a while, Nokia was hailed as an inspiration as they produced some of the finest mobile phones the world had seen. Looking back, it just seemed they got things right. There was something about the company and the times that clicked, and, for a while, it worked like a charm.[7] A beautiful strategy can thus be thought of as a concept whose time has arrived and can be monetized – in a big way.[8] If you suspect that your idea qualifies as such, you want to scale it up for maximum exposure. The growth gas-pedal must be slammed on to the floor, pushing it beyond risk-neutral and well into risk-loving mode.

Hitting the gas pedal means forgetting all the words of warning against uninhibited growth put forward earlier in this book. The advice of going for growth also runs contrary to some important empirical findings showing that it is difficult to grow one's way into profitability on some vague hope that, down the road, when volumes build up, there will be enough demand and economies of scale. One of the leading textbooks on valuation, by Professor Tim Koller and co-authors, suggests that it is generally better to first fix the business model and then grow.[9] If you are profitable, according to these findings, it is a fine idea to add growth. The notion is to take what is good and scale it up, whereas businesses that are sub-par are not fixed by growing them. It is important to keep in mind, however, that these are average effects, as in true most of the time. For a representative firm, the advice offered by Koller and co-authors is probably worth heeding. Forcing growth, hoping that it will lead to profitability, is fraught with high failure rates. Parallel to this, however, another logic exists, the Black Swan logic. If there is some chance that your strategy could take off in a big way, you might want to go for maximum growth fully aware of the average effects (which would seem to advise you against it). The difference lies

---

[7] Of course, some beautiful strategies stick and continue to generate superior returns seemingly indefinitely. When Coca Cola arrived, it brought not only an exciting flavour, but a look, feel and attitude that was different from other soft drinks. The success it drew allowed it to create lock-in effects: its brand became entrenched in the culture and it built massive distribution networks on a global scale. For some lesser beverage makers at the time, Coca Cola was effectively a Strategy Swan. Because of this quasi-monopoly, Coca Cola's good run seems to extend permanently into the future. Being able to lock in a monopoly or quasi-monopoly is the only strategy that seems to reliably work over extended periods of time.

[8] The monetization aspect is an important caveat. A wonderful product is not the same thing as a wonderful investment, especially in these times when large parts of the population believe that things should be free and immediately available online. Those of you who were too cheap to pay and instead downloaded this book illegally know what I am talking about.

[9] Koller, T., M. Goedhart and D. Wessels, 2020. *Measuring and managing the value of companies*, 7th edition. John Wiley & Sons: Hoboken, New Jersey.

in the context. The representative firm does not offer the potential for massive upside, whereas a beautiful strategy could be your one shot at being part of a Black Swan-like take-off towards the skies.

It is often pointed out that the world is increasingly turning into a place where there are a few spectacular winners against a backdrop of a large number of people and companies that perform in a more mediocre way. Think of the Amazons and the Facebooks, the winners who grabbed all or nearly all. A system that generates a handful of winners, or hits, and lots of mediocrity, produces distributions characterized by a long tail. These are the frequency distributions that are heavily skewed to the right, the power law distributions. What they have in common is that the great mass of outcomes is concentrated in the range slightly above the minimum value. That is, these units perform okay at best. Beyond that, there are the winners, causing the tail of the distribution to be much longer and thicker than implied by the normal distribution. This is where the famous 80–20 rule comes into the picture. Originally, it was framed in terms of the relation between inputs and outputs, as in 20% of the efforts (the crucial ones) generate 80% of the results. Applied to management, for example, the rule suggests that 20% of customers generate about 80% of the firm's sales. Tweaked somewhat for our purposes here, it suggests that in situations governed by power laws, some 80% of the spoils are captured by 20% of the players. Many important real-world phenomena follow this kind of distribution rather than being approximately normal. The distributions for book sales and followers on Instagram, for example, look like some version of a power law distribution.

Some business models are entirely predicated on the idea that they can capture enough of the winners, while showing admirable tolerance for the duds. The movie business, for example, operates on a hit-logic. Many films do not resonate with the audience and therefore fail to generate revenue that exceeds production costs. The blockbusters, however, make up for all that. Venture capitalists (VCs) and other early stage investors also have a business model that relies on a few winners to deliver returns that compensate for all the projects that fail to make it. They are acutely aware of this, as evidenced by the very high hurdle rate they use for discounting the future cash flows on their investments. It can be as high as 30–40%, which is a return that far outstrips anything we should reasonably ask for according to conventional models of asset pricing. It means that venture capitalists require projects to show a potential for a return on investment of about 500–1000%, with an exit expected to occur within, say, 3–5 years. Going by the hurdle rates found in conventional finance, VCs are saying no to good projects by setting the bar so high. If you ask them about this, they will tell you why it makes sense. The reason they use it is to make sure that the project at least *has the potential* to be a smashing hit. If that potential is not even there, they are not interested. Why? Because they know that, out of 10 ventures, something like 9 are either total losses or just manage to break even. That remaining winner must produce returns that truly take off, else the VC will lose money. This is why they insist on seeing some serious upside potential in any business proposal that they are presented with, the kind of thing that can really take off.

Firms and investors seeking 'hockey stick' growth potential are typically drawn to certain industries, such as those based on the internet, telecommunication, IT, life science, biotechnology and clean/green technology (cleantech). This is of course no coincidence, because these industries offer projects of the kind they look for, which is to say high impact–high risk. For simplicity, let us refer to these industries as 'tech'. Why is tech producing a disproportionate number of positive Black Swans? Well, tech is at the forefront of innovation itself. Digitalization has taken over large parts of our existence and most innovations that have implications for the way we live come from tech applications these days. When money and talent combine, as they do in places like Silicon Valley, we get extraordinary innovation, which is heavily slanted towards tech.

There is also something even more fundamental about how tech works that makes it Black Swan prone. The distribution costs, at least for certain kinds of content, is much lower than in the physical world, and the reach is on a different level. Because the internet is worldwide, you can instantly make your product or service available in any corner of the globe that is connected (and not too harshly controlled by its government). This is the scalability issue. In the digital arena, almost any business idea is 'born global' if it has general appeal. There are also network effects doing their part. Network economics refers to situations in which the value of a good or service increases the more users there are. Games like Fortnite, for example, benefit from such effects, as more players make it even more attractive for others to join. This happens for a variety of reasons. There are more opportunities to play, there is a buzz around the product, the makers of it generate profits they can reinvest to make the game even more fun to play, and so on. Success very much feeds on itself when network economics are operating. Many a YouTuber has found that once you reach a certain number of views, the algorithms that dictate search results start sending more and more users your way. You become wildly successful just because you first managed to become moderately successful. Once the buzz is on and the sharing starts, everything escalates from there.

Beautiful strategies in the sense the term is used here are, for the above reasons, likely to be found in the digital domain. Such business models are free of some of the constraints and costs of physical structures and can therefore take off in a way that can be hard to match for firms with a heavier presence in the so-called real world. However, the latter is by no means ruled out. Scalable strategies with global appeal exist in many other domains as well. One may consider, for example, the kind of disruptive strategy favoured by Sir Richard Branson. His formula is: find a staid, uninventive industry where the incumbents have long since stopped caring about customers. Present an upgraded and customer-friendly version of the core offering without the legacy costs. Then proceed to take the incumbents down. This too could make for a business concept whose time has come and is in for a good run. Beautiful strategies capitalize on an untapped longing for meaningful change and, to some extent, in this disruptor role they *are* the (Strategy) Swans to the extent that incumbents, who, numb from their taken-for-granted success in the past, never figured something like that would happen.

Whether a strategy is truly beautiful or not cannot be known with certainty before the fact. As far as making decisions is concerned, it comes down to what evidence is gathering to suggest that it is. When the case is getting more compelling by the week that we are on to something, that this may be it, then we should start to ponder the possibility that we have one and act accordingly. That is when you go for it. A beautiful strategy calls for stupendous growth, so the question is how this can be engineered. What exactly does hitting the gas pedal mean for firms looking to grow? In the sections that follow, we will look at different ways to lever up. We want to apply maximum leverage across several domains to get the most exposure possible to what promises to be a positive Black Swan. Leverage, we shall see, can be applied not only in the financial sense but also in the human domain. Contrary to normal advice, we now want speed and leverage – all sorts of it – to the hilt. Even wipeout risk or strategy failure do not scare us anymore, because accepting that is the admission to the Black Swan exposure we seek.

 ## FUEL FOR GROWTH

Going for growth and scaling up sounds simple, but, of course, there will be many challenges in executing a growth strategy. It will tax the organization in many ways as it struggles to find the right employees, trustworthy suppliers, attractive outlets for its products, and so on. There is also that other catch with growth that we have already touched upon several times: it must be funded. Somebody has to put up the money, because the benefits from investing in additional growth will accrue later. Revenue lags expenses. It may not be until many years from now that the venture yields cash flows that are large enough to fund a meaningful portion of its ongoing investment needs. So how should growth be financed to support the rolling out of an ambitious strategy? Well, according to textbooks in corporate finance, somebody sits down and figures out the optimal mix of debt and equity by looking at the pros and cons of each, as if both were just nicely available in any quantity, and we can just take our pick. Maybe in a mature and stable company with dispersed ownership, managers can sit down like that and think about the financing mix while assuming they have complete discretion over the proportions. For such a company, however, growth is hardly the main issue.

When we talk about scaling up a beautiful strategy, the appropriate perspective is that of the original equity investors, by which I mean those that commit the equity that gets the company started. They want to go about the whole thing in such a way that it maximizes their upside potential and exposes them to positive Black Swans. Upside preservation is a first-order goal here. We are talking about a strategy that is not just attractive but quite possibly a world beater. Given the scarcity of positive Swans, such *upside potential is precious*. This being so, you do not want to let in lots of other equity investors because it dilutes your stake.

Something else that is very precious is also at stake here – control. Control is something we cherish, almost for the sake of it. It brings benefits over and above the added purchasing power we get from financial gains. For one thing, we get to decide. Being the chieftain has value in and of itself. In that capacity, we get to enjoy the respect of the organization and its outside stakeholders and can pose as pillars of society. Giving back as philanthropists once we have done well enough for ourselves must be one of the sweeter moments in life. Consistent with the view that control is worth paying for, the financial markets evidently place a substantial premium on it. Whenever a transaction takes place that implies a change in control, the buying party has to pay up in excess of the market value that prevailed before the deal was negotiated. This control premium partly explains why acquisitions are so expensive – the owners who currently enjoy control must be given a sweet enough deal to let go. Whenever there is a battle for control in a company, the share prices of stocks with higher voting rights tend to increase in value relative to those with fewer. Control is clearly dear to us.

The basic premise when scaling a beautiful strategy should be that we are *equity constrained*. What this term means is that we do not view constantly

**TABLE 7.1** Leverage and growth

|  | Equity ($) | Debt ($) | Assets ($) | Return on Assets | Return on Equity |
|---|---|---|---|---|---|
|  | 100 | 0 | 100 | 10% | 10% |
|  | 100 | 100 | 200 | 10% | 20% |
|  | 100 | 200 | 300 | 10% | 30% |
|  | 100 | 300 | 400 | 10% | 40% |
| Growth | 100 | 400 | 500 | 10% | 50% |
| Scaling up | 100 | 500 | 600 | 10% | 60% |
| Expansion | 100 | 600 | 700 | 10% | 70% |
|  | 100 | 700 | 800 | 10% | 80% |
|  | 100 | 800 | 900 | 10% | 90% |
|  | 100 | 900 | 1000 | 10% | 100% |

tapping into the equity market as a realistic option, or at least not a desirable one. The real goals are to preserve control and to avoid diluting our Black Swan exposure. All of which points to that other source of financing – debt – being the most appropriate way to scale up a beautiful strategy. It is not risk shifting in the sense of trading an expected loss for a small chance of hitting it big. Because the strategy is beautiful (we believe) the eventual strong performance will ensure that the cash flows generated will not only be sufficient to service the debt but also to generate a monstrous return on equity.

Compare the above pro-leverage argument to the way the benefits of debt are presented in textbooks. There, you will learn about something called the 'trade-off theory', according to which the firm trades off the tax benefit of debt versus the cost of financial distress. Essentially, interest payments are tax deductible, but introduce the risk of running into financial trouble.

Being tax deductible is all well and good, but that is not where the true benefits of debt lie. *Since it allows scaling up without dilution or loss of control, the most valuable benefit of debt is leverage itself*. Leverage, here understood as the proportion of assets that is financed by debt, amplifies the return on equity. It can take a decent return and send it through the roof. This amplification of returns is illustrated in Table 7.1. The perspective is that of starting out with 100 in equity capital. We assume that the expected return on assets is 10%. If we just invest those 100, the return will thus be 110, implying a gain of 10 that we can put in our pockets. As more debt is added, the return on equity grows with it in a linear way. If we go for maximum leverage, the expected return on equity is 100%. We now pocket 100 – a doubling of our initial investment![10] All the while, we keep control and get to enjoy the stardom of being a successful investor/entrepreneur. This is the real reason why leverage is so tempting to so many people.

Let us stop and think about what Table 7.1 really means. One thing that we have assumed is that the investment opportunity *can* be scaled up. That is, when we commit our first 100 of funds, we get a 10% return on that investment. As we repeatedly decide to commit more funds, that 10% return is still available, all the way to when we are at 900 in overall investment and decide to go for 100 more. Is this realistic? Should not the marginal return on investment decrease? That would tend to be the case if we go for the juiciest parts first and then exploit those that are still good, just not quite as good as the first, all the way down to the ones that are only just profitable but still worthwhile. This is an assumption that certainly has to be checked in any real-world venture before making any decisions. However, with a beautiful strategy, in a world of wild uncertainty and winner-takes-all effects, it is plausible that the marginal return actually *increases* the more you scale it. As discussed, this happens because initial success attracts even more success as network effects and word-of-mouth do their thing.

There is no question that levering up comes with a catch. That catch is higher risk – wipeout risk even. The equity we have committed is very much on the line here – all of it. A total loss of capital is on the table. The acceptance of this risk is the key shift in perspective. If we lose all of it, so be it. It is worth the risk because of the exposure we get to a positive Black Swan, a rare thing that it would be a mistake not to pursue with force and conviction. Thanks to limited liability, it cannot get any worse than losing our investment. This is what changes the conclusion compared to the situation of a more established firm, in which case losing out on control and long-term value-creation because of short-term turmoil is considered a distinctly negative outcome. However, with a massive upside potential beckoning, our tolerance of wipeout risk increases markedly.

Riding the Swan, and the heroic tolerance of risk it implies, does not imply having a cavalier attitude to it, as the Silicon Valley ethos of 'move fast and break things' might seem to suggest. On the contrary, risk, or short-term variability in performance, should be tightly controlled to the extent possible. We can do without all the risk that is not directly related to the very success of the

---

[10]For ease of exposition, I have not considered the interest expense when calculating Return on Equity. This expense should really be subtracted from Net Income, the numerator in the formula.

strategy itself. VC firms, for all their tinkering in search of Black Swans, have a very disciplined approach to risk taking. The diligence is extensive (most proposals are rejected). They monitor the business development in a very hands-on way through active involvement. They understand reasons for failure well.[11] And so on. Execution is tightly controlled.

As noted, travelling at a higher speed inherently increases risk. When leverage is added to the mix, everything gets amplified, risk as well as return. It is often remarked that, in a way, time and uncertainty are synonymous – extend the time horizon and you will have more uncertainty. The same thing can be said about the relationship between speed and risk. When we start pushing down the gas pedal by ramping up leverage and growth, there will be more things that can go wrong. We can look at Tesla, whose early years of growth at break-neck speed is a horror story of one thing after the other going wrong. This, given leverage, can be an issue, because margins for errors will be lower. Getting tripped up and having to tangle with creditors because of an avoidable mishap is not something we want, as it could make the ride much too short. This makes risk management more crucial, not less. By risk management, I mean the kind of process for identifying, assessing and responding to threats that could derail the performance of the venture discussed earlier. As risk expert John Fraser (cited earlier) has argued, this process enables the right prioritization to be made. That is, resources and managerial attention can be directed to where they are most needed to ensure successful strategy execution. His point is that the faster the rate of change, the more you need a risk management process.

Riding the Swan, while predicated on the idea of maximum leverage, thus comes with close attention to risk. With any venture comes a host of activities and risk exposures that we have to accept just to execute the business idea. Annoyances like currency risk and IT crashes start becoming issues. One of the things a risk management process is hoped to do is to remove as many of those distractions as possible, allowing us to focus on the core of the business and – in some cases – to even take more of that kind of risk. The commercial success of the venture is the exposure we are seeking, or the 'good' risk if you will. A concept in the literature called 'comparative advantage in risk taking' holds that, because of some combination of skills, experience and resources, we are uniquely positioned to excel in a certain area and to deal with any risks that arise within that field of expertise. Therefore, the fewer unrelated

---

[11]Shortcomings on the part of the management teams involved is actually number one on this list. A product or technology that does not work as originally envisioned is not in the top three.

risks that remain, the better, because the venture becomes a pure play on the core strategy. We want, as cleanly as possible, to isolate the commercial success of the strategy *and then leverage that.*

 **NARCISSISM REDEEMED**

Leverage allows for faster growth and holds the key to spectacular returns when combined with a strategy that delivers. If we want to accelerate even faster, we may consider trying to align the culture of the organization with the mission of Riding the Swan. Somewhat uncomfortably, all the things that were said to be problematic from a Taming the Swan point of view, even to the point of generating Swans, now start to look like interesting options. For one thing, you want to get people to outperform themselves and give everything they have for the cause. Perhaps a supremely optimistic attitude will do that for you, even if it means zero serious discussions about tail risk. Failure is not an option anyway, so why even talk about it? Alternatively, if you are a believer in instilling fear in people as a way to maximize performance, maybe now is the time to really give that a go and paint a dark picture of the consequences that would ensue if important objectives are not met. When it comes to Riding the Swan, the end justifies the means.

On top of the financial leverage, we can add the kind of leadership personality and incentive structure that really get people to execute like mad. That way, all cylinders are firing, and if we have some luck, we will be Riding the Swan. I hesitate to call what I am talking about as 'human leverage' because it is not a pretty term, but it gives you an idea. The point is that the Herculean challenge involved in Riding the Swan might call for a certain kind of individual at the helm. Somebody with a sufficient appetite for success to make the necessary sacrifices. Somebody who can handle the pressure and make tough decisions without being held back by doubts. Somebody so attracted by the monetary gains and the elevated status that comes with it that they will do whatever it takes.

Is this description of our ideal candidate beginning to sound like a narcissist? As a matter of fact, it should. The lack of sensibilities that we lambasted earlier for creating Swans from within now becomes an asset. When Taming the Swan by building resilience is the goal, narcissistic CEOs liable to engage in attention-grabbing ploys can be a problem. When Riding the Swan is the goal, those same qualities start to work for us! What you do not want to do is put a narcissist in charge of a stable, low-growth company. The lack of exciting opportunities means that their craving for glory must find other outlets. This a potential source of problems, because to close the gap between ambitions and reality they may decide to tamper with financial accounts, make acquisitions or engage in speculative derivative strategies. These are all tactics that generate attention, excitement and the possibility of self-affirming success, but they all bring higher risk where it serves no purpose from any other stakeholders' point of view.

Therefore, we again face the risk-return trade-off that comes with leverage, except this time in the arena of human capital. We may be prepared to increase our liabilities (by hiring near-sociopathic managers who easily could create trouble for themselves and the company) in return for the boost that their forcefulness can give to the value of the assets and, by extension, the return on equity. When we contemplate Riding the Swan, the upside potential is much higher, and therefore also our risk tolerance. We might do well to put up with otherwise obnoxious narcissists simply because they can deliver the goods. Professor Kets de Vries explains the trade-off involved as follows:[12]

> '. . . having a narcissistic disposition – grandiose, self-promoting, larger than life – is a prerequisite for reaching the higher organizational echelons [. . .] But *although their drive and ambitions can be effective in moving organizations forward, excessive narcissistic behavior can create havoc and lead to organizational breakdown.*' (Emphasis added.)

Take Elon Musk, for example. I am not going to speculate whether he would be clinically diagnosed as a narcissist, but his extreme drive and ambition are plain for everyone to see. At least by the academics' standard method for classifying people as such, he easily qualifies. Witness the following statement and take note of the way he uses the pronouns 'I' and 'me' in places where he clearly speaks for the company:[13]

> 'Earlier today, **I** announced that **I'm** considering taking Tesla private at a price of $420/share. **I** wanted to let you know **my** rationale for this, and why **I** think this is the best path forward. [. . .] **I** fundamentally believe that we are at our best when everyone is focused on executing, when we can remain focused on our long-term mission, and when there are not perverse incentives for people to try to harm what

---

[12]How to manage a narcissist (hbr.org).

[13]This quote is taken from a letter to Tesla's shareholders, 'Taking Tesla Private', published 7 August 2018.

we're all trying to achieve. [. . .] Here's what **I** envision being private would mean for all shareholders, including all of our employees. [. . .] Basically, **I'm** trying to accomplish an outcome where Tesla can operate at its best. . ..'

'Impossible' hardly seems to be part of Elon's vocabulary. He even touts the idea that humans populate a distant planet that lacks an atmosphere and many of the critical life-sustaining resources on which we rely. He is said to tolerate failures and believe in psychological safety, but accounts by people who have worked with him make it clear that his presence can be very intimidating and extremely inspiring at the same time. In the eyes of his employees, his praise is worth having. The result is a strong desire to meet expectations and put in maximum effort. In other words, we get people willing to do whatever it takes to realize the wild ambitions of their front man. Which is exactly what we wanted for the purpose of Riding the Swan. Unfortunately, you may not be able to simply give Elon a ring and have him take charge of your venture. The point here is rather that some of the traits that are so evident in him are what you should look for in the individuals you consider hiring for the job when the strategy is beginning to look beautiful. A safe pair of hands is for another time.

Apart from dosing up on ambition, as well as inspiring and intimidating leadership, we can notch things up even further by stretching performance goals. The incentives we give the company's leadership is another lever for increasing speed. True to this idea, Musk's compensation packages have been the stuff of legend. In 2018, Tesla's board approved a plan with staggered targets that would, if met, give Musk very handsome paydays. In 2020, the first tranche was secured as the market capitalization of Tesla came in at well over the $100bn requirement on a 6-month average basis. Tesla at this point was the world's most highly valued carmaker – despite not breaking a profit on its car business. For his part in this feat, Musk was handed options valued at approximately $600mn, propelling him to fifth place on the Forbes billionaire list. For anyone with a narcissistic streak, that validation may carry as much value as the monetary reward itself.

If we grant that Tesla's strategy had world-conquering potential at the time the bonus plan was devised, it made sense. Once more, we reach a different conclusion than in Chapter 2, where we said that overstretched targets are a source of negative Black Swans, as they induce desperate behaviours. The setting determines the approach. Hand powerful option programmes to executives in mature businesses and you will get 'pump-and-dump': various sketchy practices aimed at bolstering the short-term share price just around the time the options can be exercised. However, having a beautiful strategy makes the difference, especially if it is perceived to be an all-or-nothing deal, a largely binary situation. The implicit logic is, let us get rich together or fail utterly together. Stretching the incentives is part of pressing down the gas pedal, allowing us to climb even further up the risk and return scale.

The future will tell if Tesla takes over the world, as implied by valuations at the time of writing this book. It could also become the Black Swan that takes the world down with it. If the market realizes that profits have no chance of materializing to the extent believed, its valuation could collapse, causing a reassessment of valuations more broadly. The stock market crash that follows suit could trigger a recession in the real economy, a loop that would drive sales of Tesla cars even lower. Increasingly desperate executives might then resort to fudging sales number and the scandal that this inevitably unleashes would seal the fate of Tesla for good. If this scenario happens, anyone involved will be castigated for their lack of judgement and the misery they brought on everyone. However, the original investors, whose perspective we should take, have already cashed in. Because Tesla did have the tell-tale signs of a beautiful strategy, they were right to go for Riding the Swan.

##  A TAIL OF TWO COMPANIES

Another company that developed a beautiful strategy and took it for a run was Netflix. It was founded in 1997 and dabbled for a while in renting DVDs, but eventually streaming caught the attention of its founders. It was a nascent technology looking for applications. As far as corporate strategies were concerned, it was largely unexplored. Spotify, for example, was launched in 2006, about the same time as Netflix got serious about the idea. Again, there was no magic strategy bullet at work. It was just an idea whose time had come, and a handful of people, through a combination of skills, vision and luck, got it right. One of Netflix's founders, Marc Randolph, confesses that there is no such thing as a good idea that, when executed, simply turns out to work.[14] The approach taken is instead to tinker with several ideas, learn why they do *not* work and then modify them in an iterative process until at least one of them clearly does.

In the case of Netflix, the strategy would in due time evolve from streaming licensed content to producing it in-house. This move into in-house content is a fine example of strategic risk-taking. They were prepared to make a big bet that

---

[14]How success happened for Netflix, Co-Founder Marc Randolph (entrepreneur.com).

this is where the future lay. Whereas early on there had been many detractors ('that will never work' was heard so often that it eventually became the title of Randoph's book), it must have become increasingly obvious at some point that they were on to something and that Netflix could be the next big thing – if they played their cards right. There was only one problem with regards to the new strategy: producing content in-house is very expensive and Netflix would have to invest significant amounts to deliver it. Now how would you finance such a large-scale expansion? In Netflix's case, the answer was debt. The company went on a borrowing spree. Between 2006 and 2020, the company added some $16 *billion* in new debt. As for equity, they did in fact issue some $1.2 billion in that time span, but they also retired stock worth over $1 billion, so the net is a tiny number in comparison. Consequently, Netflix's leverage shot up. At several points in the company's history, its liabilities-to-assets ratio has stood at over 80%.

True to the ethos of Riding the Swan, what Netflix's story amounts to is a beautiful strategy that was executed at full throttle, fuelled by debt. And then they came, the Black Swans that took the strategy to even higher altitudes. First, the world developed a serious addiction to streaming and to devouring series in particular. 'Binge-watching' became the thing. In a way, the world changed and does not seem intent on going back any time soon. Another Black Swan swooped in and reinforced this fundamental change in our ways: the C-19 pandemic. Holed up in homes and immersed in gloom, streaming services offered a way to stay entertained. We could indulge even more in our addiction, this time without even feeling bad about it. Netflix was one of the winners, not least because of the fact that their bet on in-house content had turned out well and given it a leg-up on its competitors. The world veered on to a new path, and, as always, some will have positioned themselves to reap a windfall from that change. Netflix was certainly one of those. Its market cap in late 2020 was well over $200 billion. Those who got in on it early and rode the Swan made fortunes.

Now, on to another company that was starting to awake to its potential around the same time as Netflix. The company in question was Norwegian Air Shuttle, or Norwegian for short, an Oslo-based airline. It is perfectly understandable if a reader questions how an airliner could ever be mentioned in the context of beautiful strategies, but Norwegian had a few things going for it. It went for a fuel-efficient fleet and a lean cost base, and had a gorgeous brand that capitalized on the image of healthy and salmon-eating Norwegians trekking around their fjords and mountains. They also had the benefit of an upstart's attitude, the liberators that challenged the price monopolies of stale and predatory incumbents. They managed to avoid the rough vibe of some of the hard-core low-cost airlines, yet had a cost base that was significantly below that of the legacy carriers. To many onlookers at the time, it seemed like the right way to do an airline. So, if you are in a generous mood, the strategy was kind of beautiful, and a potentially scalable one at that. In fact, economies of scale are quite important in this business as airplanes, super-expensive things as they are, must be kept busy. Norwegian had to take it to the world.

Consequently, Norwegian pushed the gas pedal as far down as it went. Again, we find a concern about losing control and diluting upside potential limiting the inclination to issue equity. Lenders, however, made themselves very available and Norwegian was extended generous terms by the airline manufacturers and leasing companies. In early 2006, Norwegian had a some-what higher leverage than Netflix (60% vs 40%), was briefly surpassed by them in 2012 (79% vs 81%), but ended up clearly in the lead by 2019. By that time, Norwegian's leverage had reached a stunning 95%, whereas Netflix's had started to trend down towards the low 70s. The tolerance of risk in Norwegian was remarkable, perhaps explained by the fact that its founder, Björn Kjos, was a former fighter pilot attuned to brinkmanship. They also had a vast appe-tite for success. Anyone who reads Kjos's autobiography comes away with an appreciation of exactly how indignant he and others in the company felt about the practices of their ruthless competitor, Scandinavian Airlines. Because of this company's monopolistic bent, the common man in Norway was, the way they saw it, grossly overpaying for airline tickets.

For all these reasons, Norwegian was going to tolerate a lot of risk – and boy did they get it. Its history is full of accidents and missteps, reminiscent of Tesla's chaotic upstart. For example, they were caught up when air traffic came to a halt following the volcanic eruption in Iceland in 2010. A large number of travellers were left stranded in faraway places over Christmas in 2014 due to technical problems. Boeing's 737 MAX, in which the company had made significant investment, was grounded. A currency hedge created massive losses and nearly killed the company off. They were, for a lengthy period, spied on by Scandinavian Airlines in a blatant case of industrial espionage. As you begin to sense, their experience during these years is a nice illustration of how stepping up growth simultaneously creates risk, and how speed and risk go together. Things were often slipping out of control because the volume of activities was expanding quicker than the organizational ability to administer and govern.

Throughout all this, the company seemed intent to overcome it all and just march on. The world could still be theirs. Until the C-19 pandemic hit them. All airlines saw massive revenue drops due to the restrictions on movement

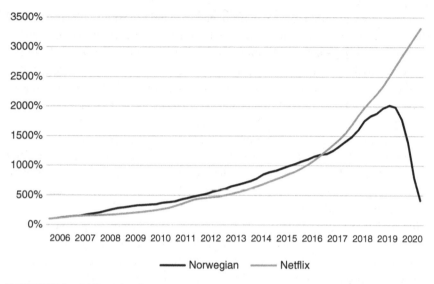

**FIGURE 7.1**  Riding the Swans

that ensued, typically around 65% year-on-year between 2019 and 2020. For Norwegian, with all its leverage, the consequences were savage. Its year-on-year decline was close to 80%, and measured between Q4 2019 and the same quarter the following year, it was even worse, coming in at an astonishing 93%. Figure 7.1 contrasts its accumulated growth since 2006 with that of Neflix's (calculated as a rolling sum of revenue in four consecutive quarters normalized by revenue in 2006). It illustrates the scaling up of their strategies as they began Riding the Swan. It also makes it clear how the C-19 pandemic made Norwegian's ride come to a screeching halt, whereas it sent Netflix's performance even higher.

The company's strategy was decimated, as it struggled to fund its ongoing operations. At one point during 2020, a group of employees were even denied a hotel room because of a fear that the company would not be able to pay on checkout. That is about as close as you can get to a complete breakdown of a strategy.

 **END OF THE RIDE**

Was Norwegian wrong to do what it did? Was it, as some of its critics claimed, a vulgar use of debt that should never have been permitted? Well, as always, it comes down to your perspective. I would like to encourage the reader to look at this from the vantage point of the original equity investors, those that boarded during the first couple of years. From that perspective, things look a lot different. By Riding the Swan, and going for debt-fuelled growth, they scaled up their strategy in a way that would otherwise not have been possible. Whether the strategy was beautiful or not, enough people seemed to think so at the time. Its market cap was a few hundred million kroner in the early 2000s, only to surge to close to 14 billion during the 2010s.[15]

It bears repeating that Norwegian was not a case of risk shifting – promising to behave and then risking up. It was risk-loving in plain sight. The vision, ambitions, and risk tolerance of the company should have been obvious to anyone. This leaves the argument that Norwegian should have 'cared more' for its stakeholders – employees, suppliers, customers, debtholders, etc. – looking unconvincing. If employees were uncomfortable with what their company was doing, they could take a job elsewhere. Customers who feared Norwegian might not be around to honour their obligations could have booked with another company. Lenders, with no exposure to Black Swan induced upside potential, supported the venture throughout two decades. There is nothing in Kjos's autobiography to suggest that he would consciously bet the firm in full awareness of the implications of limited liability (as the risk shifting hypothesis would have him do).[16] Instead, what comes across is a man who loved his company dearly.

What is interesting to note, however, is that Kjos gradually divested himself of his shares in the company, both in the lead-up to the C-19 pandemic and as it began to unfold. The investment company owned by Kjos and a long-time ally, Bjorn Kise, held 26.8% of the shares in the company at the start of 2018. In 2019, that number had been reduced to around 17% and it kept coming down. On March 31, 2020, it fell all the way to 4.6% as the divesting continued. What Kjos did was to exercise his exit option. Exit, as we have touched on earlier, is an important risk management tool. It means getting out of a position that has become less attractive, either to cut losses before too much pain is incurred or to secure some of the gains that have been accumulating up to then. Any investment strategy should come with an exit plan and it becomes especially pertinent when Riding the Swan. If the strategy is beautiful and scalable it will be well received, because it gives the stock market both a

---

[15]Interestingly, one of the peaks occurred just before the pandemic. In the fourth quarter of 2019, Norwegian's market capitalization again rose above 13 billion krone.

[16]Kjos, B., 2015. *Hoyt og Lavt*. H. Aschehoug & Co: Oslo.

story to fall in love with as well as rapid growth. The valuation windfall can therefore be the stuff of dreams even if the strategy ultimately fails to reach the point where the profits finally materialize. For the original investors, this counts for a lot, because they can get fabulously wealthy just from being part of the ride. For that purpose, it is enough if the strategy *appears* beautiful for long enough and that the exit option is exercised while there is still time.

The ultimate success of the strategy is therefore another matter. Sure, Kjos and his team would have preferred it to play out according to the script and reach an end-state where Norwegian was a confirmed winner and delivering not only promises but also profits. If denied that, the next best thing is to tap into the wealth created by the strategy before it is disrupted. That is where the exit plan enters the picture and it is why it is an integral part of Riding the Swan. Early on in the venture, there may have been an understanding, and acceptance even, of the possibility of losing all the invested money. That is part of the gamble involved as it takes some risk-taking to get the ball rolling. However, there is no reason to accept the same total loss of capital once the strategy has begun to generate significant value. It makes perfect sense to break away with some of the bounty.

Where does all of this leave the notion of stoic owners stepping up in the hour of need to save the firm? That notion may be a bit too romantic in this world of ours, but heroes do exist. Richard Branson was on a different mission during 2020 – that of saving as many jobs in the Virgin Group as possible. As his airlines burned through cash, Branson even put Necker Island, his beloved Caribbean island cum holiday resort, up as collateral to secure loans that would keep them going. We should also give Kjos his due. In the early days, he put up his own house as collateral when Norwegian went through one of its periodic flirts with disaster. The bottomless pit that was C-19 was just too much to handle, so exit was necessary to salvage some of the gains.

 ## SWANS TO THE RESCUE?

Does the strategy really have to be beautiful for Riding the Swan? Above we hinted that massive value can be generated just by the mere perception that it is. One could, in fact, go even further and make the case that a non-beautiful strategy could also be useful for hitching a ride as long as the perception is one of beauty or, put differently, that enough people act as if it were beautiful. Some may decide to go down this road perfectly aware that the strategy is decidedly not a good one fundamentally.

What I am getting at is the 'greater fool' approach to asset pricing. Taking this approach, one does not care about fundamental factors like cash flow or risk. Instead, what drives a willingness to invest is the very expectation that prices will continue to rise – that there is a greater fool who will be willing to pay even more later on. This is at the core of asset bubbles – a detachment between fundamentals and observed prices. 'A crisis occurs when people forget about valuation principles,' states Professor Koller and co-authors.

Now, paying more for an asset than it justifiably could be worth based on the information at hand would normally make you a sucker. In a world of wild uncertainty, we have to let go also of this as an absolute notion. It may actually make good sense to join in on a bubble, even if it has all the markings of a Ponzi scheme. Why? Because they are, after all, few and far between, and they can make you economically independent. They are Black Swan material. This would seemingly encompass instances of willingly joining the ranks of suckers – or at least behaving like one for the time being – a non-sucker consciously acting like a sucker, essentially. When we buy for keeps, we certainly need to pay close attention to the fundamentals. However, if your goal is to win the lottery by exposing yourself to some interesting wild uncertainty, the greater fool approach starts to look pretty good. You may well realize that the asset is a sham and that what we are seeing is mispricing and misallocation of capital on a broad scale – yet still invest. John Maynard Keynes, one of the greatest thinkers of the twentieth century, got around to this view after some early misadventures as an investor. His way of putting it was that we might do better by 'aping unreason'. Having realized as much, he subsequently went on to rebuild his fortunes.

Consider, as an example, Bitcoin and all the other digital coins, whose ascendance during the 2010s and early 2020s was phenomenal. To many of us, these coins have all the usual appearances of market madness: origins in an underground, anti-establishment movement, very limited to no practical use, touted by snake-oil sellers left and right and cheered on by the masses of day traders. So how should we proceed? One way to create Black Swan exposure is of course to call out the suckers. If feasible, one can create short positions that effectively are big bets that the bubble is about to burst.[17] Investors like Steve Eisman did precisely this just before the financial crisis in the late 2000s,

---

[17]I am less sure now that the digicoins are useless devices whose very existence is due to speculation. If the dollar and central banking go out the window, the digicoins may become an integral part of the new system that emerges from the ashes of the current one. In that case, the rise of these coins could be seen as our collective subconscious telling us that the breaking point is getting near. Perhaps it is not too late to get in after all.

thereby providing the inspiration for the Hollywood film 'The Big Short'. Their call was that the markets for collateralized debt obligations were built on foundations of sand (house mortgages that could never be repaid). This small clique of investors got their contrarian analysis right, but, more importantly, also the timing.

The other way to get exposure to a positive Black Swan is to join the party on the view that the music could be playing for a long time still. We concede the lack of a case based on fundamentals, but instead of shorting the position, *we go along with it on account of the Black Swan nature of the possibility it brings.* It might take having to swallow one's pride, but who cares if we are richly rewarded for it. If it does not end well, you do not have to let anyone know that you lost money in what was obviously (with hindsight) a Ponzi scheme. The hard part is of course getting in early. The longer the price keeps going up, the greater that nagging suspicion that we are nearing the end of the run, the inevitable collapse.

The rational underpinning for this dance-to-the-music approach is the well-known love affair between stock markets and technologies with a story. In the markets, nothing can get the juices flowing like the promise of a technology-led revolution. This was widely on display in the lead-up to the 2001 stock market crash, as anything that smacked of the internet (easily obtained by appending .com to your venture) got a warm welcome. Everybody wanted in. The stock-market bull run in the 15 years leading up to the collapse in 2001 was marvellous.

What does all this mean for corporate leaders? Well, such extended runs offer an opportunity to tap into the wealth and gullibility of investors, as so many coins have done in the wake of Bitcoin's unlikely ascendancy. In bubble environments, you do not really have to be a real entrepreneur – just sell your tech story coated with lots of sugar (i.e. promises of growth), get one of the influencers in the day-traders' chat rooms in on it and watch things take off. No matter how much we love positive Black Swans, that sort of thing we will consider below our dignity. So, it is back to tinkering, eyeing for those opportunities where there is no clear cap on the upside. These are Swanmakers, except that now we scan the environment for positive exposures.

For a bit of old-fashioned tinkering, consider Norsk Hydro's decision in 1965 to join a consortium drilling for oil in the North Sea. This was pure opportunism, as Hydro had up until then been a producer of fertilizers and light metals (the world was more forgiving toward diversification by operating companies back then). Striking it big was exceedingly unlikely, as scientists had for decades been saying that there was no oil to be found on the Norwegian continental shelf. In 1958, the Geological Survey of Norway even urged the Ministry of Foreign Affairs to discount the possibility of finding oil off the Norwegian coast. Yet strike oil they did, which was the beginning of Norway's journey to become one of the richest nations, per-capita, in the world.[18] It also catapulted Norsk Hydro on to the world scene as a major player in three industries.

Contrast that with the same industry in the early 2020s. As increasing outside pressure forces them towards green energy, they are discovering that this is a landscape devoid of positive Black Swans. Everywhere they look, there is nothing but low-margin projects. Times used to be better. Resource exploitation as a source of Swans may increasingly be a thing of the past (though there is talk of mining asteroids). The most recent wave of Black Swans has been the tech giants – Amazon, Google, Facebook, and so on – but also in the tech industry, there is a sense that some of the lowest-hanging fruits have been picked. In a paper from 2020, Professor Nicholas Bloom and co-authors set out to investigate the relation between the amount of research being done, research productivity and economic growth.[19] While the amounts of resources that pour into innovation grows, there is a steady decline in its productivity. They summarize their findings as follows:

'We present evidence from various industries, products, and firms showing that research effort is rising substantially while research productivity is declining sharply. A good example is Moore's Law. The number of researchers required today to achieve the famous doubling of computer chip density is more than 18 times larger than the number required in the early 1970s. More generally, everywhere we look we find that *ideas, and the exponential growth they imply, are getting harder to find*.' (Emphasis added)

If the first round of positive Swans (from a commercial point of view) was about exploiting the Earth and the second about technologies that kept us blissfully distracted while it was being destroyed, perhaps the third round will be about inventions that help us get out of this hole that we have created for ourselves. It is beginning to look like a long shot though. Only the Black Swans can save us now.

---

[18]The industry itself refers to large productive fields as 'elephants', not Black Swans. What I am suggesting is that these initial elephants were also Swans, given their massive consequences and the low probability assigned to them by the scientific community.

[19]Bloom, N., C. I. Jones, J. Van Reenen and M. Webb, 2020. Are ideas getting harder to find? *American Economic Review*, 110.

# Epilogue

S O WHAT HAS THE Black Swan framework taught us? Well, I can only speak for myself. It has had a profound effect on my world-view. I have become much more sensitive to the distorting effect that rigid ideologies and (about to be outdated) scientific paradigms can have on our decision-making. I have become very good at sensing, in myself and others, the crucial mechanism of creating an attractive story and then nourishing it by selectively interpreting the incoming evidence. This pattern is all over the place. In our increasingly polarized society, people find purpose in opting into ideological tribes that feed them a sense of righteousness and belonging. However, these communities frequently end up being echo chambers that relish, more than anything it seems, harshly clamping down on dissenting views. Whatever common sense would have you think, be damned. The party line is not negotiable. It seems that the narrative and confirmation biases have gone into overdrive. They are having a field day in the post-truth era we find ourselves in. It is a dangerous path, because if the core mechanism is on steroids, that might be true for the Black Swans that follow as well.

Amidst this, Taleb's approach is very refreshing. It is an altogether different frame of mind. It is an empirically grounded way of looking at the world, free of prejudice and ideologies (well, almost). It has us trying to figure out what really works – what has proven robust under real and possibly harsh conditions. It respects skills rooted in practice that transfer across situations, like street fighting, seduction, and off-map hiking. It encourages us to be open to unexpected turns of events and to have a dynamic sense of the opportunities that this presents. It tells us to be wary, on the other hand, of convoluted and stylized constructs that can only exist in highly protected and unnatural environments (like academia). Take note of those trying to impose 'Platonic' beauty where none can exist, and, if you can, utilize it to your advantage. Unlike them, we get over ourselves, and just smile when we catch ourselves in the act of going along with one of the tricks that our mind likes to play on us, like believing that we have it all figured out, that the model really works. It all makes perfect sense to me.

What I have tried to do in this book is to overlay various theories of the firm on the Black Swan framework. For all its majesty, the framework does not specifically look at wild uncertainty from the angle of value-maximization, which is how companies must approach things. Sure, we would like to ensure survival and become super-robust, but it cannot come at any expense. Resources are scarce and we cannot distract too many of them from the goal of thriving in the here and now. We want to pour our energies into creating new and exciting ventures, not into preparing for disasters. I have used preppers as an illustration of what it means to tilt too far in one direction. They may well be robust in the extreme and time may undoubtedly prove them right one day. Yet it is not the way to go for most of us. We want to make the most of ourselves and engage with this still-wondrous world of ours – to have a good time pursuing opportunities and expand our vistas, rather than narrowing them towards that singular objective of surviving the next disaster.

The lesson I think we should heed from our exploration is that we need to make a small provision for the possibility that something out of the ordinary will happen. We look for ways to shore up our vulnerabilities in whatever ways we can. The trick is to do this without being weighed down by it. There is no fuss. It is just standard protocol – no big deal. At all times, we remain functional, effective and confident, always pushing forward to fulfil the dream, always tinkering and looking for opportunities for fun and profit.

I have long since stopped believing that I am special or will be spared. It is up to me to try to keep the probability of a wipeout as close to zero as I can. Therefore, when I go for a drive I do not take overtaking other cars lightly, which I once was only too happy to do. Especially when my children are in the car, it takes an exceptionally straight road and unimpeded view for me to go for it. By sticking to this rule, there is a tangible reduction in the probability of a wipeout. It does not cost me anything, because I have fully absorbed the truth that a more aggressive style of driving only reduces my total travel time by a few minutes. There is no inner conflict about the whole thing or tedious negotiations with myself. It is just protocol. It also helps that I have realized, finally, that the driver going too slow is actually not doing it to annoy me – me specifically. In essence, I have managed to find a way to manage tail risk that does not interfere with my quality of life. When I am looking at the green arrow, I never forget to throw a glance to the other side. That is my small provision for tail risk in a world of wild uncertainty. My instructor from back in the day, who knew about Black Swans, would have been pleased.

Writing this book also made me take the final steps towards acquiring a respectable survival kit. You know those encouragements that the authorities in your country send out on occasion, hoping to coax you into taking some measures? Well, stocking up to deal with a three-day interruption of the basic functions in society is actually a rather sensible thing to do for most individuals. It does not cost a great deal of money: some dried food, a water purifier, a portable stove, a battery-driven radio and a few other items along the same lines. Those things will make quite a difference if and when that crisis comes. Imagine everything going dark and shops closing down, and your children looking at you thinking that this is scary but daddy surely has everything covered. How would it feel to have to tell them that, sorry children, we have absolutely nothing to eat, drink or use for warmth? That thought alone should be enough to get us to pull ourselves together.

Despite the obviousness of it, we never seem to get around to creating even a basic continuity plan. For years, I wholeheartedly agreed that it was a good thing to do, but could just never bring myself to do it. What got in the way was not the money – the overall expense is not even a third of that of buying a new TV. The real problem was that it was just too boring. We much prefer to remain in the vegetative, pathetic state induced by our mobile phones. It also takes time that we often feel we do not have. Harried as we are by work, child-rearing and other perceived musts, we prefer not to use what little time we have left over on preparing for unknown disasters.

But I finally did it. And when I did, I got a sense of what the preppers mean when they say that, in preparing, you find solace. It was quite satisfying and fun. If you have children, make an afternoon out of it. Go shopping for the gear with them. Bring out the sense of adventure and discuss what you can do together to cope. So again, we can manage tail risk while imposing no burden on our present. It is about attitude.

I actually went for a 14-day supply of dry food rather than the recommended three. I have never experienced one in my life, but I have no problem visualizing a breakdown of international trade, one of modern society's key vulnerabilities. And I believe the preppers when they say that we are, when deprived of our supplies, only 72 hours away from turning into animals. If people can pull knives over toilet paper, imagine what would happen if trade really broke down. I drew the line at 14, because two weeks into it, I figure either the powers that be have managed some kind of response that gets basic supplies in working order again or they are out of the picture altogether. In that case, we are headed for a world without rule of law and I have no intention of preparing for that. We will just have to improvise at that point, although I accept that I am likely not going to make it for very long. Note that I do not care much about *what* could cause the interruption in trade. Many Black Swans could bring about such an interruption – it does not matter greatly which. This is the 'level' at which Swans really start to make themselves felt, so that is what I build my scenario around.

All in all, I have made a small provision for wild uncertainty, feel much better for it and can get on with things. It has made me more resilient at a cost that was entirely negligible. Or so I like to believe, because I also avoid thinking that the plan is fool-proof, that I am completely insulated now. Some modesty regarding the limitations of our ability to know how things will go down is in order, as always. Maybe the nice elderly lady next door will shoot me dead one day into the ordeal to grab my supplies. That would be a Black Swan relative to my contingency plan. As tends to be the case, risk does not go away by our response to it, it merely shapeshifts. But at least my preparations are something rather than nothing, an altogether proportionate Black Swan response. At least I have given it a think through and got myself to act on the conclusions from that thinking. In my view, those are risk management victories no matter what.

Firms walk a similar line. They also need to make some provisions for tail risk to protect the value-creation process in that event, but in a way that does not overly distract from ongoing *current* efforts to pursue business opportunities. A host of factors pull corporate leaders away from preparing for highly consequential but hard-to-conceive events. To mobilize action, they too need to articulate the problem, get the conversations going, and then draw the line.

Throughout the book, I have emphasized that there are economic arguments for making provisions because it makes wipeout and strategy disruption less likely, but there are also other values that should be respected. In a way, drawing the line is a character test. For me, it was the thought of my children in that situation that nudged me into action. Corporate leaders should also realize that a great number of people depend on the policies they implement – employees, small suppliers and committed customers all stand to suffer if the company falls into distress. While executives surely filled up their pockets a long time ago and are set for life, the same is not true for many of the other stakeholders. The burden of failure is bound to fall on them. So do you care enough? Will you go ahead with that debt-financed acquisition even if it clearly shortens the distance to wipeout? Will you leverage up 30:1 so that you can cash in on some earnings-per-share related bonus? Will you push costs rock bottom despite the long-term vulnerabilities that this introduces for somebody else to deal with? What are your true motivations?

Laird Hamilton, the legendary surfer who knows more about balancing wipeout and reward than most people, has the following to say on excellence:

> 'There's a depth of character that underlies all great performances, and it all comes down to this question: Who are you? Are you someone who cares about others, who'll notice someone struggling and stop what you're doing to go over and help. Are you a person of principle – or a creature of opportunity? . . . If you cut corners in your integrity, it doesn't matter how many trophies you've got stuffed in your case.'[1]

---

[1] Hamilton, L., 2008. *Force of nature: Mind, body, soul, and, of course, surfing.* Rodale Books: New York.

# Index